HANDFULS ON PURPOSE

SERIES V

BY

Pastor JAMES SMITH

**Author of "A Survey of the Wondrous Cross,"
"Spiritual Patterns," etc.**

WM. B. EERDMANS PUBLISHING COMPANY

Grand Rapids   1955   Michigan

American Edition

———

Published in 1947, by

WM. B. EERDMANS PUBLISHING CO.
by
Special Arrangement with

PICKERING & INGLIS, LTD.
14 Paternoster Row, London, E.C.4
229 Bothwell St., Glasgow, C.2
Manchester—Newcastle—Liverpool—Edinburgh

Guide to Series 1 to 12

SERIES 1 to 10 .. By Pastor JAMES SMITH
SERIES 11 and 12, .. By ROBERT LEE
SERIES 13, COMPLETE INDEX TO SERIES

PREFACE

IT is with deep thankfulness to the Giver of every good gift that we send forth this FIFTH Series of "Handfuls on Purpose." It is very gratifying to us that the interest taken in them has been steadily growing since the first; and as they have been the means of leading many Christian workers into a closer study of the Word for themselves, we rejoice, as this was one of the chief objects of their publication. We were much cheered lately on receiving a note from a Pastor abroad who has evidently been greatly blessed and helped by them. Some of the Press notices have been a little amusing. In one review of Volume Four, the writer says, "This is another *compilation* of sermon outlines." In the sense of being gathered out of other books, they are *not* compiled. **As far as the Author knows, only one Outline in these five Volumes has been copied,** and the Author's name is given. Not that we would in the least disparage others, but that is outside of our present purpose. Our aim has been to examine those portions of Scripture in the light of the teaching of the whole Bible, and where opportunity offers to emphasise those deeper truths which have been blessed to so many at Keswick and other Conventions. Another reviewer has termed these notes *"Skeletons."* We almost shudder at the name. Whatever they are, we trust they are not fleshless, bloodless, breathless, lifeless skeletons. They are sent out as "living creatures," on a ministry of love and mercy to needy souls. We fondly hope that they may be what the Editor of *Joyful·News* says they are, "Handfuls of the kind of wheat which makes bread for hungry souls."

JAMES SMITH

INDEX OF SUBJECTS

INDEX OF TEXTS

INDEX OF TEXTS.—Continued.

Handfuls on Purpose

Expository Outlines.   Old Testament

THE STORY OF RUTH

RUTH, THE DECIDED PILGRIM.

CHAPTER 1.—"Choose ye this day. "

THE BOOK OF RUTH, like the Song of Solomon, is full of grace and truth. It evidently belongs to the times of the Judges, perhaps to the early days of Gideon, when the Midianites prevailed and "destroyed the increase of the earth, " thereby causing a "famine in the land" (Judges 6. 1-6), which constrained this "certain man" to sojourn in Moab (v. 1).

Verse 2, "And they came into the country of Moab, and continued there. " Famine *drove* them there, and Moabitish connection *kept* them there. "In the days of adversity consider"—for adversity will either drive a Christian nearer his God or nearer the world. If faith does not cling to Him the flesh will drag from Him. Did ever any believer make anything of going to Egypt for help? What did Lot make? or the Prodigal, or Elimelech? Naomi lost both her husband and sons through her journey to Moab. It was all right to go to Egypt for help when Joseph was there, because there was corn in Egypt; but now the true Joseph has been exalted to Heaven, and woe

must come upon them that seek help apart from Him.
Those who go to the world for help instead of to Him are
likely to come back like Naomi a weeping widow bereft of
all, or like the Prodigal, repentant in shameful rags.

"Then she arose" (v. 6). The Prodigal also remembered his father's house in the far country, and said,
"I will arise." "Naomi *heard* that the Lord had visited
His people, and given them bread," and this was gospel
to the afflicted wanderer. She believed the tidings, and
her faith brought her back. She *heard*, she *believed*, she
acted. "Faith cometh by hearing." The Gospel of God
is good news from a far country. Man has wandered far
from God. The good news has reached the world, that
God has visited the people in the person of His Son, and
given them bread—"The Bread of Life." Oh! that the
weary, famished, broken-hearted wanderers who have
heard the good tidings would, like Naomi, "Arise."
Many have heard this blessed Gospel in the far country of
alienation, but how few have believed the report; the
majority seem content to dwell in Moab, and feed on the
husks that the swine do eat.

"She went forth OUT of the place" (v. 7). There
cannot be a *returning* without a *separation*. "Come out
from among them, and be ye separate" (2 Cor. 6. 17). If
Heaven would be gained the world must be shunned; if you
would eat at the Father's table the swine-troughs must be
forsaken. "Ye cannot serve God and mammon" (Luke
16. 13). Choose whom ye will serve. "If any man love the
world, the love of the Father is not in Him" (1 John 2. 15).

"Surely we will return with thee unto thy people"
(v. 10). This is the language of Ruth and Orpah, and
seemingly both alike earnest. But those who would follow
the religion of Jesus Christ must endure trial, and to
stand must be decided. There are many Orpahs who,

through adversity or excitement, run well for a time, but by and by they forsake, like Demas, because they love the world, and not unfrequently do such sever themselves, like Orpah, with the kiss of pretended friendship. Rest, in the Moab of this present evil world, is what rebel man would like; but Matthew 11. 28 is God's way.

"**And Naomi said, Why will ye go with me?**" (v. 11). The motives of every professed disciple must be tested. No earthly inducement is offered. No worldly preferment can be gained. "*I am too old to have an husband.*" Undying love alone to the Person of Jesus will spurn every worldly temptation and go forward.

"**Behold thy sister has gone back**" (v. 15). Why? Was not Bethlehem in her eye? Ah, yes! but Moab was in her heart. "Remember Lot's wife." There is no neutral standing; it must be either back to your people and your gods, or "thy people shall be my people, and thy God my God." It becomes those who name the Name of Jesus to depart from all iniquity. There may be mouth profession where there is heart division, and to trust in profession is to lean on a shadow.

In verse 7 Orpah **went out**; in verse 15 we see her **gone back**. The going back of one will always prove an additional trial to another; but see how Ruth overcomes the temptation. She said: "**Entreat me not to leave thee.**" What decision there is in the words and tone of her reply, and why *so* decided, and why did Naomi cease to try her? Because she was "**steadfastly-minded**" (v. 18). The double-minded are unstable. Her heart was fixed. Would that all the disciples of Jesus were like-minded. She could truly say: "One thing I do, forgetting the things that are behind, I press toward the mark for the prize of the high calling" (Phil. 3. 14). And did she not gain the prize of the high calling when she was made the wife of the wealthy Boaz? "Let no man take thy crown" (Rev. 3. 11).

Every true believer in Jesus can use the language of Ruth in a deeper spiritual sense. They can say: "Whither Thou goest I will go, where Thou lodgest I will lodge; Thy people shall be my people, Thy God my God." They can also add: "Where Thou diest I have died, and there have I been buried (but now risen again, and nothing shall part Thee and me. Neither life nor death, nor any other creature shall be able." Every Gospel hearer makes their choice either to go "out" or "to go back." What is your choice? "Wilt thou go with this man?" was asked of Rebekah. Her reply was, "I will go." In Luke 14 they began to make excuse; in 2 Chronicles 30. 10, "they laughed them to scorn."

"**So they two went until they came to Bethlehem**" (v. 19). . Can two walk together except they be agreed? Here we are reminded of the two on their way to Emmaus. Naomi and Ruth walking together is a beautiful picture of our fellowship one with another on our way to the heavenly Bethlehem (house of bread) with the mutual understanding that naught but death can part us; but our walk with the Lord Jesus death cannot even interrupt. "Because I live, ye shall live also" (John 14. 19).

Bethlehem may represent the Church; so we read, when they came to Bethlehem all the city was *moved* about them. There was joy in the house when the Prodigal came back: there is joy among the angels when one sinner repenteth. This joy is real, because the Church is a family in *nature* as well as in name.

But they say in astonishment: "Is this Naomi?" (v. 19). What a change, few perhaps can recognise her. Ah! the far country experience is generally a sad one, the pleasant is turned into bitterness, plenty transformed into poverty, fullness gives place to emptiness. She has to confess, "I went out full, and the Lord hath brought me home again empty" (v. 21). So with the Prodigal. He gathered all *together*, but he came home empty, and if the servants did not know him, the father did, and that too a long way off. You remember how the man came back that went down to Jericho and fell among thieves.

When a Christian backslides down into the world, how can he escape being robbed of all he possesses, robbed of his peace, his joy, and his testimony, and when the Lord brings him back (for the Lord will bring him back), it will be in sorrow, shame, and in bitterness of soul, but yet Ruth may be with him, a child of the far country, an experience that will be a blessing to him in the future.

Now, Naomi in reviewing her wilful wanderings, has to acknowledge that "the Lord hath testified against me" (v. 21). He testifies against every backslider. Are you as near the Lord as you used to be? Is He testifying against you? Return, O wanderer, to thy home!"

OUTLINE OF CHAPTER I.

I. **A God-Dishonouring Choice** (vv. 1, 2). Elimelech means, "My God is King." Why, then, should *he* go to Moab, and come under Chemosh, the fire-god of the heathen? When we fail to trust the true God we come under the power of the god of this world.

II. **A Miserable Experience** (vv. 3-5). Naomi lost her husband and two sons in the far country. Forsaking God for worldly advantages and material prosperity will surely bring *soul* misery.

III. **A Soul-Moving Story** (v. 6). "The Lord had visited, and given them bread." Such is the Gospel, the story of Divine supply for the needy.

IV. **A Testing Time** (vv. 7-13). "She went forth."

Faith leads to definite action. Her action powerfully influences others. Ruth and Orpah are both deeply moved. "They, seeing your good works" (Matt. 5. 16).

V. A Final Decision (vv. 14-18). The one *follows* no more, the other clings as for very life. The *unstable* kiss and go back. The *steadfastly minded* leave all and press on.

VI. A Humbling Confession (v. 21). "I went out full, but come back empty." Yes, we need to be *emptied* that we might be restored to faith in God. But, thank God, the way back is still open.

VII. A Hearty Welcome (v. 19). "All the city was moved." To come back to a life of simple trust in God is to come into the warmth of a home. Such a backcoming is always *seasonable* (v. 22)—the *beginning of harvest*.

RUTH, THE HUMBLE SEEKER.
CHAPTER 2. 1-12.—"Seek and ye shall find."

"**Naomi had a kinsman, a mighty man of wealth**" (v. 1). Then why did she go to Moab instead of coming to her wealthy kinsman? Why do many in the time of trial forsake the Fountain of living water and go to broken cisterns? Boaz means strength. What foolishness it is then in the hour of weakness to forget the *friend* that is strong. Our kinsman Redeemer is a mighty man of wealth, and if I speak of strength, lo! He is strong.

Perhaps the spirit of independence and self-will restrained Elimelech and his wife from asking help from Boaz. They would shift for themselves rather than bow to beg; but what disappointment it brought, what a sorrowful failure it proved. It is always so if we are too proud to let our requests be made known unto God. He may allow us to follow our own stubborn way until we have spent all the strength and energy we had. Then shall we be glad to come back in our emptiness, and be thankful for the gleanings from the fields of our rich kinsman. "Ye have not, because ye ask not" (James 4. 2).

Ruth said to Naomi, **"Let me go to the field and glean"** (v. 2). Ruth may here represent an anxious soul in search of the truth. She has forsaken her old companions and her gods. "Left all," but she has not yet found rest to her soul; but like an earnest seeker, she is not ashamed to gird herself with the gleaner's apron. Those who are ashamed of the truth of God's Word are those who don't know its sacred worth. Many would be glad to get the corn of the heavenly Bethlehem for their souls, but they are ashamed to confess their anxiety by appearing as a gleaner or a seeker. Rather than seek they starve. They deem it prudent that no one should *know* their need. Ruth did not need to be driven to it, or even persuaded; she went because she *desired* to go. When any one is really anxious about their souls they will not need to be compelled to search the Scriptures.

Notice also that Ruth knew *where* to go to glean. **"Among the reapers"** (v. 3). This is the most likely place to find. Where is a troubled honest seeker most likely to find the needed blessing? Is it not by following after the ministry of those who are "reapers," those who know what to bring *in*, and what to leave *out*. As in Leviticus 19. 19 some, heedless of this command, gather in all, they don't rightly divide the Word.

"Her hap was to light on a part of the field belonging to Boaz; ... and behold Boaz came" (v. 3, 4). "The steps of a good man are ordered of the Lord" (Psa. 37. 23). Many a seeker has been constrained to use language like this. "They happened just to light on a part of Scripture that talked about Jesus, and as they went on, wondrous revelations were made." Behold the Master comes and talks with them. While Ruth was gleaning Boaz appeared, and after saluting his servants (for there is mutual love and confidence between Boaz and his workers; he comes with grace in his heart and a blessing on his lips, and his servants bless him; so is it with the willing servants of Jesus, mutual confidence and mutual blessing) he inquires, "Whose damsel is this?" (v. 5) "The Master is come and calleth for thee" (John 11. 28). His compassionate eye rests kindly on the anxious stranger. He draws near, he speaks, "Hearest thou not, my daughter" (v. 8). It is quite possible for one to be so busy *seeking* that they do not at first hear the voice of the Master. His words to the seeker are full of grace. "Go not to glean in another field, but abide here."

The law allowed her to glean (Lev. 19. 9), but only grace would say, ."Abide here." Here the Master has found the seeking one. The Good Shepherd seeks till He finds. When a seeking sinner is earnestly following the "reapers" and searching the field of revelation the Master is sure to meet him, and bless him with that grace that fills His heart, and constantly flows from His lips. *His* grace is good news to the weary gleaner. Grace came to Ruth by Boaz. He knows how to speak a word to the weary.

"Go not to glean in another field" (v. 8). The field of carnal reason will offer you only chaff and stubble. If ye *abide* in Me, ye shall ask what ye will, and it shall be done unto you. Grace brought to Ruth far above what she could ask or think. Not only "liberty," but "protection." "He charged them not to touch her" (v. 9). Such is the privilege of all those who share this grace "wherein we stand."

Now, what effect had this manifestation of grace upon Ruth, did it make her self-confident and boastful? Oh, no!

"She fell on her face, and bowed herself to the

ground" (v. 10). When a weary, heavy laden soul sees the exceeding riches of *His grace* self is bowed to the ground. When Saul met the Lord he fell to the earth. It is not the wrath of God that leads us to repentance, but His *goodness*. The hammer of the law may break the icy heart in pieces, only grace can melt it, but it is easiest melted when broken.

After being bowed down with a mighty sense of unworthiness, she asks, "Why have I found grace in thine eye, *I* a poor stranger, *thou* a mighty man of wealth" (v. 10). "Grace," and oh, such grace! "Why?" Just because *He* is gracious. It is a sure sign that grace is received and enjoyed when this question is so spontaneously asked, "Why have I?" There is astonishment that such unworthiness should be so highly favoured. These are the first feelings of the new born soul. "Herein is love" (1 John 3. 1).

And Boaz said, "It hath been fully showed me all that thou hast done unto thy mother" (v. 11). "I know thy works" (Rev. 2. 2). It hath been fully showed Him (Jesus) all we have done, whether good or bad. "Inasmuch as ye did it unto these, ye did it unto Me" (Matt. 25. 40). Naomi was the friend of Boaz. Is it not comforting to remember that He knows all the little deeds of kindness we do, no matter how much the blinded world may misjudge our acts?

> "Where He may lead I'll follow,
> My trust in Him repose;
> And every hour in perfect peace,
> I'll sing He knows, He knows."

OUTLINE OF CHAPTER 2. 1-12.

I. Her Great Humility (v. 2). In desiring to become a *gleaner* she shows her willingness to take the place of a *poor one*. But she would rather do that than go back to

Moab. Her separation from her old life was complete. She is not ashamed to take the place of a *seeker*.

II. Her Good Fortune. "Her hap was" (v. 3). She may have gone out trembling, but the guiding Spirit of God was with her, as He is ever with those who have turned their backs upon the far country and its gods. It was while she was *seeking* that she met the mighty man of wealth.

III. Her Character Searched Out (vv. 5-7). The master *considers* her case. Nothing is hid from him. "It has been fully showed me," he said. "I know thy works, and labour of love."

IV. Her Path Made Plain (v. 8). "Go not, abide here." All fear is now dispelled by the assurance of his grace. Truth-seekers in the field of His Word will find grace upon grace.

V. Her Grateful Acknowledgment. "She fell, and bowed, and said," etc. (v. 10) "Why have I?" Just because he is gracious. She could not plead that she *deserved* such grace, but she thankfully acknowledged it.

VI. Her Heart Comforted. (1) Comforted with the assurance that *he knows all about her* (v. 11). (2) Comforted with the assurance that *he is in full sympathy with her* (v. 12). He desired for her *refuge* and *rest* under the wings of Jehovah. All this our heavenly Boaz (Jesus) gives to them that *trust* Him (Matt. 23. 37).

RUTH, THE SUCCESSFUL GLEANER.
CHAPTER 2. 13-23.—"Grace reigns."

IT now becomes the subject of grace to acknowledge the blessing received. Ruth said, "**Thou hast comforted me, Thou hast spoken friendly** (to the heart—*margin*) **unto thine handmaid**" (v. 13). When the Master speaks He speaks home to the heart. He well knows the trouble is there; He came to bind up the broken-hearted. Ruth's confession of grace received just opened the channel wider for the outflow of grace, for Boaz said unto her, "At meal-time come thou hither, and eat of the bread" (v. 14), the bread provided by Him for His servants. She now enjoys the privilege of the servant sitting at the Master's table, eating the Master's bread in fellowship with the Master's servants.

"She sat beside the reapers" (v. 14). No doubt these were seasons of rest and times of refreshing (Isa. 28. 12) to this weary labourer; and, moreover, "He reached her parched corn, and she did eat, and was sufficed" (v. 14) How sweet to get the bread fresh from the Master's hand. This is, indeed, soul-satisfying grace. Many get their bread at second-hand, and are rarely satisfied. Ruth's was a hand-to-mouth existence, but it was from *His* hand to her mouth, the hand of the mighty man of wealth.

What a lovely little picture is here of those memorable times of blessing wherein our Lord and Master refreshes the hearts of His servants while they are bearing the burden and heat of the day. When He invites them to "Come and dine" (John 21. 12), and they sit down with Him, and receive from His own hand those things which He hath provided for them, "My God shall supply all your need" (Phil. 4. 19). Yet although Ruth had experienced *great grace*, there is still more to follow, for it is all of grace from beginning to end. Salvation by grace, and the life of faith, are beautifully manifested in this touching story. Ruth offers no excuse, but thankfully receives all He gives. She does not dishonour Him by thinking *He* is giving too much. Many Christians dishonour the mighty Son of God by living more like paupers than princes.

"All things work together for good" (Rom. 8. 28). While Ruth is busy gleaning, Boaz is busy planning for her com-

fort and success. "He goeth before" (Matt. 28. 7).
Boaz commanded the young men, saying, "Let her glean
even among the sheaves, and let fall also handfuls on
purpose for her. " What words of grace are these. Gleaning
among *the sheaves* is the privilege of those who have found
favour in the sight of the Master; and what rich sheaves of
promise we have in the field of His Word! But only believers have the liberty to glean here (Eph. 2. 12), and
according to your faith be it unto you. Those also who have
found grace in His sight find many an unexpected handful
that has been dropped on purpose for them. And notice,
these handfuls did not fall by chance, they were each a
gift of his grace. So our blessed Master does not leave His
servants to the caprice of blind chance, or to pick up what
joy and comfort they may; but many a rich handful He
drops on purpose to comfort and cheer them in their work.
Gleaning among the greedy and the selfish is most
arduous, miserable work, and such is the worldling, seeking
satisfaction in other fields. But how different in the field
where grace reigns! *There* the handfuls are dropped on
purpose. If you go to glean on other fields be sure the
handfuls will cease. Jesus says, "Follow Me. "

Now we read that she "beat out that she had gleaned,
and took it up" (v. 17). While gleaning in the field of
Revelation, among the thoughts of God, how apt we are to
gather also the chaff and straw of the foolish thoughts of
our own evil hearts. The chaff and straw may increase the
bulk, but they will not increase the value of what we may
have gleaned. The wheat is precious in proportion as it is
pure. So there is much need for the beating *out*, and this
can be best done where Ruth did it—in the field. If, like
her, we are more anxious for quality than quantity, then
by comparing Scripture with Scripture the truth of God
will be clearly beaten out. This is the fine wheat, take
it up, and let the chaff go to the wind and the straw to the

fire. Preach the Word; if you can't eat the chaff yourself, don't give it to another.

It is also worthy of notice that "she brought forth, and gave her mother" (v. 18) not only what she had gleaned, but also the prepared corn which she had received direct from the hand of Boaz (v. 14). She had received it all through grace, and she kept nothing back. If Naomi represents "pure religion," why does it lack so much? Is it not because many of the gleaners keep back part of the price, laying up for themselves while the kindred of Jesus are in need?

Then Naomi said, "Where hast thou gleaned to-day?" (v. 19). Ah! she had been with the "mighty man of wealth," and in the fat pastures where the handfuls are dropped on purpose. Ruth answered, "The man's name is Boaz." (v. 19). That was enough. When servants come out from the presence of Jesus to speak of His Name they come as those bearing much precious seed; there is a heavenly beauty and freshness about them, so that some may be constrained to ask: Where hast thou gleaned to-day? But the answer immediately follows: We have been with Jesus, the mighty God, the Prince of Peace.

Ruth went home and told her friend what great things Boaz had done *for* her and promised *to* her. Those who value the grace and fellowship of Jesus will also value the privilege of telling others what His grace has done for them. "Come and hear, all ye that fear God, and I will declare what He hath done for my soul" (Psa. 66. 16).

OUTLINE OF CHAPTER 2. 13-23.

RUTH went out empty, but she came back laden with blessing and beaming with joy. So much so that Naomi was constrained to say, "Where hast thou gleaned to-day?" (v. 19). The secret of her success lay in this—

I. **She had been with a mighty man of wealth** (vv. 1-19). Like Christ, Boaz had (1) a wealth of *possessions*; (2) a wealth of *influence*; (3) a wealth of *grace*.

II. **She had been with a near kinsman** (v. 20). She knew not of the near relationship, but he did. The kinsman had the right to *avenge* or *redeem*. Our Kinsman Redeemer came not to condemn, but to give His life a ransom for us.

III. **She had been with one who understood her need.** He spoke to her heart (v. 13, *margin*). This is always the manner of our Redeemer, for He knows what is in man.

IV. **She had been with one who was not ashamed to acknowledge her publicly** (v. 14). "She sat beside his reapers: and he reached her parched corn." He gave her a time of refreshing from his own presence. Ruth never says "No" to the gifts of his grace.

V. **She had been with one who planned for her good.** His eye was over all the field, and all were ready to do his bidding. So handfuls were dropped on purpose for her, "according to His will" (Rom. 8. 28). They are blessed indeed who come into touch with the unsearchable riches of Christ.

RUTH, THE RESTFUL BELIEVER.

CHAPTER 3.—"Rest in the Lord."

THEN Naomi said, **"My daughter, shall I not seek rest for thee?"** (v. 1). Ruth had found favour in the sight of Boaz, and had tasted the exceeding riches of his grace, but she had not yet found the rest of *unbroken* fellowship. She was not yet in the yoke with Boaz by the marriage tie. "Take my yoke upon you, and ye shall *find* rest unto your souls" (Matt. 11. 29). This was the rest that now remained for Ruth. Union to the mighty man of wealth is the almighty remedy for her poverty. Are there not many timid believers who have rejoiced in the grace of Jesus but cannot yet call Him *My* Lord, *My* Shepherd?

The only way to abiding communion and uninterrupted fellowship is Ruth's way, "faith and obedience." She believed all that Boaz told her, and did all he bade her (v. 5).

"Behold he winnoweth barley to-night" (v. 2). This is not the reapers' work, they have gone to their rest. Now He comes whose fan is in His hand, He will thoroughly purge His floor. Every day's work has to be winnowed by the Master, and to the servants of Christ this is a source of comfort, for with the barley, if much labour, there is also much chaff. So they are glad to have this work purged ere it reaches the garner, knowing that they are rewarded for the wheat, and not for the chaff, whose end is the fire because there is no *life* in it.

And Naomi said, "Wash thyself" (v. 3), and get thee down to the floor. This advice given to Ruth was practical and common sense, for although she had experienced great grace at the hand of Boaz, yet in approaching him for higher favours still she must use every means possible to secure the blessing desired. And so should we in making our requests known unto Him. If we regard iniquity in our heart the Lord will not hear. First, be reconciled to thy brother, "wash *thyself*," put away and incline your heart (Joshua. 24. 23).

Naomi also said, "Mark the place where he shall lie" (v. 4), and lay thee down at his feet, and he will tell thee what thou shalt do. If we want to learn the will of our Master toward us we too must be willing to lie at His feet. Mark the promise He has given, for this is where the Master lies, and lay thyself down there and pull the skirt of His Word over thee, and wait patiently for Him, for He *will* tell thee what thou shalt do. Notice the three steps of Ruth to the feet of Boaz: (1) WASHING. (2) WATCHING. (3) WAITING.

"When Boaz had eaten and drunk, and his heart was merry, he went to lie down" (v. 7). The master had sown the seed and carefully watched it from the blade to the earing. Now the harvest is past, the winnowing is over. His soul is satisfied, and he rests. Shall not our Divine Master also see of the travail of his soul, and be satisfied when He shall with the fan of judgment winnow the mixed mass on the floor of the world? Shall there not be enough to satisfy His longing soul and make glad the heart of Him who went out from the home of His glory, bearing precious seed, and who sowed in tears? (Luke 19. 41). Shall He be sorry that the chaff has been blown away? He shall rejoice over His people with singing (Zeph. 3. 17).

"And it came to pass that at midnight he said, Who art thou?" (v. 8). Though He tarry, wait for Him. His voice is often heard at *midnight* by the waiting one, while others, it may be, are all insensible to His presence. The special blessing is often received through special waiting.

OUTLINE OF CHAPTER 3.

NAOMI had great faith in their Kinsman Redeemer. Now that Ruth had put her case into his hands, she is told to "Sit still, for the man will not be in rest till he have *finished* the thing" (v. 18). See how Ruth entered into that blessed rest.

I. **She casts herself at his feet** (vv. 4-6). She had offered a *request* before (chap. 2. 7), but now she offers *herself*. It was in the darkest hour of the night that his voice was heard.

II. **She claimed him as her kinsman** (v. 9). She

claims the fulfilment of his office as redeemer in her behalf. It was a great demand for a poor stranger to make, but the mighty man of grace looked upon it as an act of kindness showed Him (v. 10).

III. **She received his promise** (v. 10-13). There was no reluctance in Boaz to perform the part of a kinsman redeemer. She asks, and at once the promise is given. He is faithful who hath promised. Ruth does not make him a liar by guilty doubt.

IV. **She rests in his work.** She sits still now, leaving him to do the redeeming work. What else could she do? The *work* was not hers, but his. She had his promise that he would finish the thing. So she *rests in faith*. Rest in the Lord. Trust also in Him, and He will bring it to pass. (Lev. 16. 30, 31).

RUTH, REDEEMED AND CLAIMED.
CHAPTER 4.

"**Then went Boaz up to the gate, and sat down there**" (v. 1). What to do? To *intercede* for Ruth. And success is sure with such an intercessor, being "a mighty man of wealth." He is a man of mighty influence, and must prevail. Are we not reminded here of Him who has ascended up on high, and is set down at the Father's right hand to make intercession for us who have been found of Him? He that delighteth in mercy, and who is able to save to the uttermost (to the end) all that come unto God through Him, seeing He ever liveth to make intercession for them.

And Boaz said to his kinsman, "**Redeem, for there is none to redeem beside thee; and I am after thee**" (v. 4). This kinsman, like the law, had the first claim, but not the ability to *redeem*. The law is our *kinsman condemner*; but Jesus, like Boaz, is our *Kinsman Redeemer*.

By the law is the *knowledge* of sin, not the *forgiveness* of sin. This we can have through the precious Blood alone, the great redemption price. By the deeds of the law shall no flesh be justified. The answer *this* kinsman gave was, "I *cannot* redeem. " But Boaz, the mighty man of wealth, is well able to redeem, therefore what the law could not do "in that it was weak" (Rom. 8. 3), abounding *grace* hath accomplished, for "He hath redeemed" (Gal. 3. 13).

Boaz said, "**What day thou buyest the field, buy (it) also of Ruth**" (v. 5). Ruth, as emblematic of the Church, is the real treasure in the *field*. The field is the world; the treasure is the Church, as in Matthew 13. 44. And our heavenly Boaz, who was rich, for our sakes became poor, because He sold *all* that He had and bought the field, that He might secure the hidden treasure.

"And Boaz said unto the elders and all the people, Ye are my witnesses that **Ruth, the Moabitess, have I purchased to be my wife**" (v. 10). A few points are worthy of notice in connection with

This Redemption.

I. **He only could redeem.** He had the *right* as kinsman; he had the *power* as a mighty man of wealth; he was also in the right *condition* to redeem, being alone; and now the redemption itself brings joy and satisfaction to his own soul. And shall not the redeemed Church be to the heart of her Redeemer a *new* source of eternal joy and satisfaction? He shall be satisfied. Christ only can redeem. His incarnation made Him our Kinsman, and gave Him the *right* to redeem. His divinity made Him mighty, and gave Him the power to redeem. We have redemption through His Blood (1 Peter 1. 18, 19).

II. **This was a Willing Redemption.** Boaz did not grudge the redemption money. How could he when his *heart* was set on the purchase of Ruth? He willingly offered the full price, although that price included the **gift** of *himself*. So was it with Jesus, our princely Kinsman, who loved us and gave Himself *for* us, that He might give Himself *to* us. Nor did He hesitate to pay the awful price of sorrow, suffering, and blood, that He might redeem **us** from the curse of the law, being made a curse for us.

III. This was a Gracious Redemption. Boaz was not ashamed to redeem Ruth, the poor stranger. The prince of wealth stoops to lift the poor helpless one, who cannot redeem herself. He hath regarded the low estate of his handmaiden; he hath shown strength with his arm; he hath exalted them of low degree, he hath filled the hungry soul with good things, and now the soul of Ruth shall magnify her lord.

The wealthy Prince of Heaven is ashamed of none who look to Him for redemption. He says, "Look unto Me, and be ye saved." He *invites* the wretched, the miserable, the poor, the blind, and the naked to look to Him and trust in Him. Yea; He stoops in His redemption work to lift the helpless from the horrible pit on to the Rock of Strength, to lift the poor and the polluted from the dunghill, to rank among princes, and to be co-heirs with Himself. He is not ashamed to call them brethren. So the gleaner, through grace, becomes an heir of His glory.

IV. This was a Public Redemption. There were many witnesses to the fact that the price was paid; this thing was not done in a corner, but in the presence of the elders of *all* the people. When Moses smote the rock, it was in the presence of the elders. The Rock Christ was also publicly smitten, they put Him to an *open* shame. He suffered *without* the gate. As Boaz went up to the gate to finish the work in behalf of Ruth, in the sight of many witnesses, so Jesus went up to Calvary and finished the work the Father gave Him to do in behalf of His people,

Afterwards, when the price was paid, He rose from the dead; and as Boaz, when the bargain was settled, "plucked off his shoe," Jesus plucked off the grave-clothes as a token that the covenant was sealed and the inheritance redeemed; and the apostles say, "We are witnesses." He was *seen* of many.

V. The Purpose of this Redemption. "That the name of the *dead* be not cut off" (v. 10). In Adam all have *died* unto God; but in Christ, through His redemption, all that believe are made *alive* unto God. Thus spiritual seed is raised, according to the gracious purpose of God. "Boaz did not redeem Ruth to be his slave." He says, "Ruth have I purchased to be *my wife*," to be part of himself. What more could he do for her than that he had done? Communion has now culminated in union. Her service henceforth shall be that loving, ready service which is the glad outflow from unity of heart, and purpose, and interest, and in the self-sacrificing spirit of those who abide in the Master's presence, and who know that He hates putting away. Ye are not your own, ye are bought with a price; therefore glorify God in your bodies and spirits, which are His. It was the grace alone of Boaz that transformed the life and relationship of Ruth, and by faith she got access into this grace wherein she now stands and rejoices in hope.

VI. This was a Perfect Redemption. "Boaz took Ruth, and she became his wife" (v. 13). The prophecy of Naomi has now been fulfilled. "The man will not be at rest until he hath finished the thing" (chap. 3. 18). Our Kinsman Redeemer shall likewise come and finish the thing by taking His purchased Bride home to be with Himself, for where He is there shall we be also. The day that Boaz redeemed Ruth that same day he took her. The present dispensation is the day of salvation (redemption) to the

Gentiles. At the close of this same day our Divine Kinsman shall appear, and take His redeemed Church to Himself. So shall she be for ever with her Lord and Saviour.

When Ruth knew that Boaz had purchased her to be his wife, would she not be anxiously looking for him every moment to come and take her to be with himself? Is not this the present position of the Church? Working, waiting, watching, till He come who hath redeemed us by His own Blood, for the Lord Himself shall descend, and when He shall appear we shall be like Him, we shall see Him as He is, and dwell in the house of the Lord for ever.

May the Lord direct *your* heart into the love of God, and into the patient waiting for Christ!

HANNAH; OR, THE TRIUMPH OF A SORROWFUL SPIRIT.

1 Samuel 1.

"Why comes temptation, but for man to meet
And master, and make crouch beneath his feet,
And so be pedestall'd in triumph."
—BROWNING.

IT is refreshing to find such a gracious spirit as Hannah in the midst of the moral ruin that followed the priestly rule of the kind-hearted but *weak-willed* Eli. The man who is more concerned about the honour of his sons than the honour of God is sure to bring the holy cause into ridicule (chap. 2. 29). Hannah means *grace*, and she is true to her name; so the grace of God is made sufficient for her. There is much we might learn from her.

I. **She was Sorrowful.** "A woman of a sorrowful spirit" (v. 15).

1. BECAUSE SHE WAS CHILDLESS (v. 5). Believing that "Children are a heritage of the Lord" (Psa. 127. 3), it

vexed her soul that this heritage was not hers. She counted it a shame to be fruitless. Has your fruitlessness for God ever vexed your soul? It is a shame for any Christian to be barren in the work of God (2 Peter 1. 8).

2. BECAUSE SHE WAS MOCKED. "Peninnah, her adversary, provoked her sore, to make her fret" (v. 6). Her childless condition brought upon her the sneer of the ungodly. It is a heart-searching and deeply humbling experience for any child of grace, as Hannah was, to have the finger of derision and ridicule pointed at them by one who loves not the Lord and yet seems to enjoy more of His favour than the other. Is God ungracious? No; but those fiery shafts of the enemy may be permitted by God to convict us deeply of the barrenness of our lives, that we may cast ourselves the more unreservedly upon the Divine all-sufficiency.

3. BECAUSE SHE HAD A VERY SENSITIVE NATURE. If she had had more brass in her heart she would have had fewer tears in her eyes (v. 7). There is great hope for any Christian worker who can weep over the fruitlessness of their lives. It is good that we should feel this "bitterness of soul before the Lord" (v. 10). Woe unto them that are at ease in Zion.

II. She was Prayerful.

1. SHE PRAYED. "She prayed unto the Lord, and wept sore" (v. 10). She did not return railing for railing; being reviled, she threatened not. We may thank God for the trials that send us into His presence, to plead, with full purpose of heart. The scourges of the enemy only serve to drive her into the place of blessing.

2. SHE VOWED. "O Lord, if Thou wilt give unto Thine handmaid a man child, then I will give him unto the Lord." (v. 11). She purposes in her heart that if the Lord will, in mercy, roll away her reproach, she will consecrate His

gift entirely to His service. This is a mighty argument with God. What will He withhold from those who seek not great things for themselves, but who desire to honour Him with His every gift.

3. SHE BELIEVED. "So the woman went her way, and her countenance was no more sad" (v. 18). The Lord had spoken to her heart, as Boaz did to Ruth (Ruth 2. 13, *margin*). She brought her burden to the Lord, and she went away *without it*. It is one thing to *tell* the Lord about our burdens; it is quite another thing to *cast them* on the Lord (1 Peter 4. 7). The countenance is sure to be changed when the heart has found rest in the will of God.

III. She was Joyful (chap. 2. 1).

1. HER PRAYER WAS ANSWERED. "She called his name Samuel, saying, Because I asked Him of the Lord" (v. 20). She asked a *son*, and the Lord did not give her a daughter. Whatsoever ye ask, believe that ye receive, and ye shall have. He who can make the barren woman to be a joyful mother of children (Psa. 113. 9) can also make the fruitless Christian worker a happy winner of souls.

2. HER TESTIMONY WAS GIVEN. "I am the woman that stood by thee here, praying; and the Lord hath given me my petition" (vv. 26, 27). What a simple, yet powerful, testimony this is. She knew that He heard her, now she has the petition that she desired of Him (1 John 5. 15). "Ye ask, and receive not, because ye ask amiss" (Jas. 4. 3).

3. HER VOW WAS PERFORMED. "As long as he liveth he shall be lent to the Lord" (v. 28). She paid her vow unto the Lord (Psa. 116. 18). In the giving back of Samuel she was forming a powerful link of connection between herself and the Lord that must have enriched her whole life with blessing. Every sacrifice we make for the honour of our Lord will certainly increase our interest in Him.

Be not like the wicked and slothful servant who hid his lord's money (Luke 19. 22), but use for His glory every gift received, and every victory won, through the prayer of faith.

THE CALL OF SAMUEL.
1 Samuel 3.

"Often through my heart is pealing
Many another voice than Thine;
Many an unwilling echo stealing
From the walls of this Thy shrine.
Let Thy longed-for accents fall:
MASTER, speak, and silence all."

—F. R. HAVERGAL.

"THE Word of the Lord was precious (rare) in those days; there was no open vision." Why? The spiritual heavens were shut up, because of the unbelief and unrighteousness of God's professing people (chap. 2. 12-17). In these degenerate days God takes the child Samuel and sets him in the midst, that out of the mouth of this babe He might ordain strength (Psa. 8. 2). God hath chosen the weak things to confound the mighty (1 Cor. 1. 27). Samuel was "lent unto the Lord" (chap. 1. 28). Now the Lord takes the loan of him that He might through him speak to all Israel. We may learn here—

I. That the Call of God may Come very Early in Life. Samuel must have been quite a child when the Lord spoke to him, perhaps about six years of age. Is it not wonderful that the Almighty, the "Ancient of Days," can make His will known to a child? "They that seek Me early shall find Me" (Prov. 8. 17). "The High and Lofty One that inhabiteth eternity" dwells with the humble spirit (Isa. 57. 15).

II. That the Call of God may come, although we may have had no Personal Experience of God. "Now Samuel did not yet know the Lord" (v. 7). He believed in

Him, but as yet he had had no personal dealings with Him. The existence of God was known to him,' but the *Word of the Lord* had not yet been revealed unto him. He earnestly worshipped the Lord, according to the traditional faith (chap. 1. 28), but as yet he had received no definite message from Him. What a difference it makes in one's religious life when His Word has been heard, and His will concerning us as individuals has been clearly revealed. This is eternal life, to know Him and Jesus Christ whom He hath sent. Those who honestly seek like Samuel shall surely find.

III. **That the Call of God Comes at an Opportune Time.** "Ere the lamp of God went out" (v. 3). There is something melancholy in the very idea of the lamp of God *going out.* Had He not expressly commanded that the light of the holy lamp-stand was to *burn continually* (Lev. 24. 2). Does it not reveal the backslidden condition of the priesthood, that the *lamp of God* was allowed to go out? It is suggestive of the watchful grace of God that He spoke to Samuel ere the sacred light had died away into midnight darkness. How fares it with the lamp of God in our own hearts? Is our testimony dying down for the lack of fresh oil?

IV. **That the Call of God may Come in a very Natural Way.** "The Lord called Samuel, and he ran unto Eli" (vv. 4, 5). The voice was so humanlike that he thought it was the voice of Eli. Let us take care that those calls or rebukes that come to us in familiar forms may not be the very voice of God to our own souls. The Lord had a purpose in speaking to Samuel as He did. He wished Eli, the priest, to know at the lips of the child that the Lord had spoken. Samuel's instantaneous *obedience* to the call reveals what manner of spirit he was of.

V. **That the Call of God Demands an Answer to God** "Speak, Lord, for Thy servant heareth" (v. 10). Eli

could give Samuel no answer to the *call of God*. Those
called of Him must respond to Him for themselves. It is
so in the matter of salvation. Every one who has gone
astray from God must turn back to Him, and with a
willing ear hear what God the Lord will speak. It is so
in the matter of consecration and service. No man can
do this for us. We must *yield ourselves* unto God (Rom. 6.
13). It is with Him we have to do. The mighty God, the
Lord hath spoken. Hear Him.

VI. **That the Call of God may Involve Painful Testimony.** "Samuel feared to show Eli the vision" (v. 15).
It was a solemn and humiliating message that he had
received for Eli. He and his house were to be set aside
as unworthy of the priesthood. But the truth must be
told, and let it be said to the credit of the old weak-kneed
priest that he was prepared to hear *all that God had spoken*,
and to acquiesce in His will (vv. 17, 18). There be many
who say, "Prophesy unto us smooth things," and who
would be sorely offended if the whole counsel of God was
told out in their ears. But the Lord will fulfil all His
purposes, whether men will bear or forbear. When the
learned and honoured Eli prove unfaithful, then the Lord
will speak to some consecrated boy and make him a preacher
of righteousness.

VII. **That the Call of God Insures Fellowship and
Victory.** "The Lord was *with him*, and did let none of
his words fall to the ground" (v. 19). He never sends
us a warfare on our own charges. When the Word of God
is brought home to our hearts by the power of the Holy
Spirit it is that it might be fulfilled in our own experience.
His presence with us, in the preaching of His Word, is the
guarantee that He will bring it to pass. "If the thing
follow not, nor come to pass, that is the thing which the
Lord hath not spoken" (Deut. 18. 22). The word was

not Samuel's, but the Lord's, so it will not return unto
Him void. The secret of success in the Lord's work always
lies in the doing of His will. "Whatsoever He saith unto
you, do it" (John 2. 5). "Take My yoke upon you, and
learn of Me, and ye shall find rest unto your souls. "

THE LOSS OF THE ARK OF GOD.
1 Samuel 4. 1-11.

> "Yet the Power appears to-morrow
> That to-day seems wholly lost,
> And the reproductive sorrow
> Is a treasure worth the cost.''—HOUGHTON.

THE capture of the Ark of God by the Philistines was the
sorest blow that had ever fallen upon the nation of Israel.
The corrupt state of the priesthood was to blame for this
national failure and disgrace. There is a closer connection
between holy living and national prosperity than many in
these days seem to think. The Philistines, as the enemies
of the Lord's people, are always aggressive when Israel is in
a backsliding condition. The lusts of the flesh are sure to
prevail when the soul gets out of communion with God.

I. **What the Ark signifies.** It was the symbol of the
presence of God. It was the throne on which the Lord sat,
and from which He ruled and taught His people (Exod. 25.
22). It was also the mercy-seat, the medium through
which He communed with Israel. What the Ark was to
them Christ is to us, the resting-place, the medium of
communion, and the channel of revelation and blessing.

II. **When the Ark was brought out.** After they had
been smitten before their enemies they said, "Let us fetch
the Ark of the Covenant of the Lord out: it may save us"
(v. 3). It is good to fall back on God in the day of defeat,
but is the favour and help of God only to be sought after
we have done our best to succeed without Him? "Man's

extremity may be God s opportunity," but why should
God's opportunity only come after we have persistently
ignored Him till we are dead beat?

III. **The Dread of the Philistines at the Ark.** "When
they understood that the Ark of the Lord was come into
the camp they were afraid" (vv. 6-8). So well they might,
if that Ark represents the presence of that Almighty God
who smote the Egyptians with plagues, and wrought such
miracles in the wilderness on their behalf (v. 8). If this
is so, then in battling against the people of God they will
be found fighting against God Himself. Alas! how often
we Christians forget what the men of the world remember,
that if Christ is *with us* mighty works should show themselves, and that the more closely we are identified with Him
in our work and warfare the more difficult and desperate
does their own condition appear. The ungodly still dread
a man full of the Holy Ghost. Well do they know that to
oppose such they need to screw up their courage and "quit
themselves *like* men" (v. 9; Luke 16. 8).

IV. **The Faith of Israel in the Ark.** "It *may* save
us out of the hands of our enemies" (v. 3). It is quite clear
that their faith in the invisible God had withered up into a
superstitious reverence for the material Ark. They
worshipped the form, but denied the power. The God-
deserted Ark (Psa. 78. 60) was everything, while He who
inhabiteth eternity had no place in their hearts. Instead
of saying, " Let us fetch the Ark, " had they said, "Let us
confess our sins and return to the Lord, " He would doubtless have saved them. Multiplying forms in religious
services will afford no security against the inroads of the
enemy. The Gospel that is not in the power of the Spirit of
God is only the Ark with the glory departed. The Philistines of to-day are in great force against the people of God.
Let us fetch out the Gospel of God, but let us see that our

faith is not in the mere form of words, but in the God of the Gospel. "The kingdom of God is not in *word*, but in *power*" (1 Cor. 4. 20).

V. The Capture of the Ark. "The Ark of God was taken" (v. 11). The object of their confidence was taken from them, that their faith might be in God only. Let us learn from this—

1. THÁT UNGODLY MEN CANNOT PRESERVE THE POWER OF RELIGION. The dissolute and licentious sons of Eli had charge of the Ark of the Covenant (v. 4). What a God-dishonouring association. Is it any wonder that the cause of God is turned into ridicule when self-seeking and un-principled men have charge of the holy things? They must be clean that bare the vessels of the Lord.

2. THAT THE LORD WILL NOT PROTECT FORMS WHEN THE SPIRIT IS GONE. There is nothing in an empty dish to satisfy either God or man. The Pharisaic spirit is always ready to contend for the outward and the formal, because it is blind to the spiritual and the eternal.

3. THAT SIN ALWAYS BRINGS DEFEAT. If we regard iniquity in our heart the Lord will not hear. The secret sin of Achan brought open shame in Israel. The dis-obedience of Saul led to the departure of God from Him. "The wages of sin is death" (Rom. 6. 23).

THE ARK OF GOD IN THE HANDS OF THE PHILISTINES.

1 Samuel 5. 6.

"Blind unbelief is sure to err,
    And scan His work in vain;
God is His own interpreter,
    And He will make it plain."—COWPER.

WHILE the jubilant Philistines were bearing away the Ark as a trophy, little did they think that they were bringing the judgment of God down among themselves. The Ark, like the Bible, may be a dead letter to some, but in the hands of the Holy Spirit it is a two-edged sword. It is always a solemn and critical thing to be brought into contact with that *presence* and *power* of which the Ark was the visible symbol, that power which killeth and maketh alive, that bringeth low and lifteth up (chap. 2. 6-8). The experiences of the Philistines, with the Ark of the Covenant, are very much the same as those of the ungodly now under the power of the Gospel of Christ.

I. Their Religion was Completely Upset. "Dagon fell upon his face before the Ark of the Lord, and his head and his hands were cut off" (vv. 3, 4). They put the Ark in the temple of their god, thinking to keep both. But God and Dagon cannot both rule in the same house. "Ye cannot serve God and mammon." When Christ comes in the false theories and opinions of men must fall. The Dagon of self may stand erect, and claim all the homage and worship till the Ark of the Truth of God comes into the temple of the heart, then he must fall on his face before the Lord, and part with both his *head* and his *hands*. Until self is completely broken he will be *set up* again and again. Men still think that they have to do many and great things to merit the salvation of God; but when they come into the presence of Christ the Ark, their lofty thoughts and imaginations must fall down before Him.

II. They were Severely Smitten. "The hand of the Lord was heavy upon them, and destroyed and smote them" (vv. 6, 12). Not only was their god destroyed, but they themselves afflicted with painful tumours. The Ark of His presence brings no *comfort* or encouragement to those who are *His enemies*, nothing but the wounding and bruising of conviction and humiliation. "When He, the Spirit of Truth, is come, He will reprove the world of sin, because they believe not in Me" (John 16. 8, 9). The Gospel will be the savour of death where it is not the savour of life. The Ark of the Lord is a dreadful possession to the unsaved.

III. They were Utterly Perplexed. "What shall we do to the Ark of the Lord?" (chap. 6. 2). They had sent it from city to city, seeking to get it peacefully disposed of, but this only increased their suffering and alarm. We are solemnly reminded here of how others, in after years, sought to get quit of Jesus Christ, the true Ark of God, until Pilate, almost in the exact words of the Philistines, said, "What shall I then do with Jesus?" Paul was playing the part of these troubled enemies of God when he kicked against the goadings of the Word of Truth (Acts 9. 5). There is a tremendously important question that still presses with perplexing urgency upon ungodly men to whom the Gospel has come. How are you going to dispose of the claims of God and of His Christ? Submission or rejection?

IV. They Sent it Away. They made a new cart, put the Ark on it, and with a trespass offering they sent it away (vv. 7, 8). Suppose we read it thus: "They made a new cross, put Him on it, and as a trespass offering they sent Him away!" The Philistines would not have this Ark to rule over them. Away with it. Christ, like the Ark, was delivered up at the instigation of the chief priests (chap. 6. 2). The presence of the holy Ark of God's covenant testified against them, but there was no repentance of sin, no pleading for mercy, but a growing desire to get back to their former Arkless condition. They felt that they could not keep it and continue as they were. They must either send IT away, or be reconciled to God. How shall we escape if we neglect so great salvation?

V. They had Clear Evidence of its Divine Character.

"See if it goeth up by the way of His own coast, then the Lord hath done this: if not, then it was a chance that happened to us. And the kine took the straight way to Beth-shemesh" (vv. 9-12). Thus they had another proof, in the *manner of its home-coming*, that the Lord God of Israel was with it, and had been dealing with them through it. Well might they have said, as the centurion did, when he saw the *manner* of the home-going of the rejected Saviour of men, "Truly this was the Son (Ark) of God" (Mark 15. 39). The Gospel of God is still as the "Ark of the Covenant" among men. Mighty deeds are still being wrought through it, false systems of religion fall down before it, and the enemies of the Lord are smitten with terror in its presence. By its works it asserts its own divinity. Yet many, though fully convinced that it is of God, treat it as the Philistines did the Ark, they refuse to *yield* to its claims, and politely send it away with an offering, and'remain the enemies of God.

EBENEZER.

1 Samuel 7.

IF in the past we have been faithful, we will now have much cause to be thankful. Before Ebenezer comes—

1. *Contrition*—"Israel lamented after the Lord" (v. 2).

2. *Confession*—"We have sinned against the Lord" (v. 6). After this there had to be—

3. *Conversion*—"Return unto the Lord" (v. 3).

4. *Separation*—"Put away the strange gods" (v. 3).

5. *Consecration*—"Prepare your heart unto the Lord, and serve Him only" (v. 3). These steps are always sure to lead up to Ebenezer: "Hitherto hath the Lord helped us." This "Stone of help" has many tongues.

I. **Ebenezer Speaks** of Redemption. *"Hitherto."*

This points us back to the bondage of Egypt—to the slavery of sin—to the hole of the pit whence we have been dug (Exod. 12. 12, 13; Eph. 2. 12, 13).

II. **Ebenezer Speaks of Preservation.** "Hitherto *hath.*" The Lord thee keeps. He kept them by His mighty power, and guided them by the skilfulness of His hands (Psa. 78. 72). While walking through the dark shadows in the valley of life we need fear no evil (Psa. 23. 4). He keepeth the *feet* of His saints, and their *way* too (Prov. 2. 8). May the prayer of Paul in 1 Thessalonians 5. 23 be fulfilled in us!

III. **Ebenezer Speaks of Answered Prayer.** "Hitherto hath the Lord *helped.*" "Samuel cried unto the Lord, and the Lord heard him" (v. 9). The rain *comes* down according to the vapour that *ascends* (Job 36. 27). The incense was put upon *burning* coals. Prayer must ascend from a burning heart. "Whatsoever ye ask *believing.*" Every believing prayer will yet have its store of testimony.

IV. **Ebenezer Speaks of Victory.** While Samuel offered the Lamb, the Lord discomfited the enemy (v. 10). This was indeed victory through the Lamb. We, too, must overcome through the Blood of the Lamb (Rev. 12. 11). It is when the Lamb of God is lifted up in presence of the ungodly that the Lord thunders with the voice of conviction.

V. **Ebenezer Speaks of Divine Faithfulness.** "Hitherto hath the Lord helped us"—helped us *all the way.* Not one good thing hath failed (Joshua 13. 14). He is faithful that hath promised. His promises, like the barrel of meal, waste not (1 Kings 17. 16). He that hath begun the good work will perform it (Phil. 1. 6).

VI. **Ebenezer Speaks of Testimony.** "Hitherto hath *the Lord* helped us." This is a noble, God-honouring confession. They give *Him* all the praise. What have we that we have not received? Yet not I, but Christ in me (Gal. 2. 20). What have we done worth doing that He hath not wrought in us? (Phil. 2. 13). "To God be the glory, great things He hath done."

VII. Ebenezer Speaks of Encouragement for the Future. The Lord who hath blessed us "hitherto" will also bless us *henceforth* and for ever. He who *hath* delivered, and *doth* deliver, WILL YET deliver (2 Cor. 1. 10). "Be of good cheer" and "have faith in God."

SAUL, THE CHOICE YOUNG MAN.
1 Samuel 9.

"Life is the day of grace,
Up! Strive to win the race;
Lo! Grace and Truth have come;
Turn, listen, be not dumb."—GROSART.

THE morning of Saul's life was calm and bright, and full of promise; the midday was cloudy and threatening; the afternoon was cold, and dark, and stormy; the evening was terrific with the thunderstorm of despair, and suicidal blackness. His life began with a day of grace, and ended with the "wages of sin." In this chapter we have Saul brought before us as a *"choice young man,* and goodly." Let us take a look at him. He was so in his—

I. Personal Appearance. "There was not among the children of Israel a goodlier person than he" (v. 2). He had what almost every young man covets to have— an attractive and commanding *persona.* God had richly blessed him with a finely-formed and superior physical body. This is an inheritance that is not to be lightly esteemed, although many, both young men and young women, use this gift of God only for their own selfish ends. A healthy and well-formed body makes a beautiful temple for the Holy Spirit, and may be a mighty weapon in His hands to the pulling down of the strongholds of Satan.

II. Child-like Obedience. He went at once at his father's bidding to "seek the asses" (vv. 3, 4). Although Saul was "head and shoulders higher than any of the people," he was not too big to obey his father. This is a lovely trait in the character of a handsome young man. When the disciples strove about who should be greatest in the kingdom of God, Jesus took a little child and set him in the midst as an example of the true spirit of greatness, and said, "He that will be chiefest among you, let him be the servant of all" (Mark 10. 44). He loved us, and gave Himself for us.

III. Filial Thoughtfulness. "Come, let us return, lest my father leave caring for the asses, and take thought for us" (v. 5). He was not so anxious about the objects of his pursuit as to forget the anxious thoughts of a loving father. There be many young men who leave home in the pursuit of business who, in their new surroundings, forget the yearnings of a father's heart, so that their letters home are long in coming. They are wise fathers who are more concerned about the *safety* of their sons than the success of their worldly business.

IV. Generous Disposition. When his servant suggested that they should consult the prophet about the lost asses, he at once reminded him that he had "not a present to bring to the man of God" (vv. 6, 7). This is quite an incidental revelation of the kindliness of his nature. He could not think of asking a favour, even from "the man of God," without recompensing him in some way (Judges 6. 18). It is said that "generous natures go most readily astray." The very depth and force of their generous affections may be their greatest temptation. But the shallow inconsiderate and selfish young man is already far astray. Look not every man on his own things (interests), but on the things (interests) of others (1 John 2. 15).

V. Relationship to God. "When Samuel saw Saul, the Lord said unto Him, Behold the man! . . . this same man shall reign over My people" (v. 17). Not only was he "a choice young man" in the sight of men, but he was "a choice young man" in the sight of God. The highest honour any young man can have on earth is to be a *chosen* one of God; it is worth sacrificing all the world for such a favour. And this honour have all the saints in Christ Jesus. A young man may have many lovely features in his character, many rich moral qualities, yet if this link of *Divine approbation* is awanting he is like a beautiful ship laden with valuable goods, but *drifting* aimlessly on the ocean of life. He is out of harmony with the purpose of God. Saul did not find the asses, but he found a kingdom. His disappointment was God's appointment. The Gospel of Christ is God's call to every man to inherit the kingdom of Heaven. Ho! weary seekers in the world of business or pleasure, turn aside and seek the Prophet of Nazareth, He will give you a kingdom.

SAUL, THE ANOINTED.
1 Samuel 10.

"Take my life and let it be,
Consecrated, Lord, to Thee;
Take my moments and my days,
Let them flow in ceaseless praise."—HAVERGAL.

ARNOLD has said, "While life is good to give, I give." This is beautiful. Why should we wait till our youthful strength and vigour are shrivelled up before we yield ourselves to God? Samuel, Saul, and David were all chosen of God while they were young. Surely the best of masters deserves the best of servants. We have seen Saul as "a choice young man." Let us look at him now as the "chosen of God." See how he was—

I. Separated by Anointing. "Samuel took a vial

of oil, and poured it upon his head" (v. 1), as a sign that the Lord had anointed him. Priests and kings were usually called out in this fashion (Exod. 29. 7; 2 Kings 9. 3). All God's chosen ones still are to be separated unto Himself by an holy anointing (1 John 2. 27). There was but a very short interval between the revelation of the Divine purpose to Saul and the outpouring of the oil of consecration upon his head. As soon as we know the will of God we should be separated unto Him. "After that ye believed, ye were sealed with the Holy Ghost" (Eph. 1. 13).

II. **Encouraged by Promises.** The prophet gave him a threefold word of assurance. There was a promise—

1. CONCERNING HIS BUSINESS. "Two men shall say unto thee, The asses are found" (v. 2).

2. CONCERNING HIS BODILY WANTS. Three men would give him two loaves of bread (vv. 3, 4).

3. CONCERNING HIS SPIRITUAL NEED. "The Spirit of the Lord will come upon thee" (v. 6). Thus he was assured that as the chosen of God all things would work together for his good, and that God would make all grace abound toward him. This threefold assurance have all those who have received the anointing of the Holy Spirit (Rom. 8. 32). The Lord never sends any one a warfare on his own charges.

III. **Changed by Grace.** "God gave him another heart" (v. 9). We may not reckon this change as equal to *regeneration*, but by the grace of God new motives and desires were begotten in the bosom of Saul. This sudden and unexpected revelation of the purpose of God concerning him had, morally, made him another man than what he was before he knew this great transforming truth. When "the grace of God that bringeth salvation" is revealed to us and received by us, it will certainly make new creatures of us. No man can be the same after receiving the kingdom of God.   If the Gospel has not brought to us *another heart* we surely have not believed it.

IV. Assured by Circumstances.   "All those signs came to pass" (v. 9).   It is a blessed experience to find that our outward circumstances are made to conform and confirm the thoughts and intents of the inner life. When the purpose of God has been revealed, and our hearts and lives willingly yielded to the fulfilment of that purpose, we shall certainly see, in the providence of God, many confirming tokens.   The outer wheels of our circumstances never move contrary to the inner workings of the Spirit of God.   There may be wheels within wheels, but they are "full of eyes," and so cannot err (Ezek. 1. 18).

V. Moved by the Spirit.   "The Spirit of God came upon him, and he prophesied" (vv. 10, 11).   When the Spirit of God comes upon any one there are sure to be signs following.   It *is* but natural for Saul to join in the song of the prophetic band when he was possessed by the same Spirit.   Thus the word of Samuel was fulfilled (v. 6).   Man at his best, apart from the power of the Holy Ghost, is but a poor weakling in the service of God; but the gift of the Spirit is the assurance of God to us, that all the resources of His grace and wisdom are within our reach for the honour of His Name (John 16. 13, 14). This was a priceless privilege conferred upon Saul, an *astonishing* favour.   "Is Saul also among the prophets?"

VI. Humbled by the Prospect.   "Saul was taken, and when they sought him he could not be found.   Behold, he hath hid himself among the stuff" (vv. 21, 22). While he was little in his own eyes, all things kept working together for his good.   It is not the grace of God that puffs up, but the wind of self-conceit.   The kingdom had come to him, not because he had sought it, or wrought for it. It was to him the gift of God.   He was deeply conscious of the insignificance of the tribe to which he belonged, and the smallness and poverty of his family (chap. 9. 21). But grace delights to lavish its wealth and honour upon the weak and unworthy (2 Cor. 12. 9, 10). They that be whole need not a physician.

VII. **Despised by the Worthless.** "The children of Belial said, How shall this man save us? And they despised him," etc (v. 27). These sons of *worthless* men had perhaps known Saul from his boyhood, and like the modern sons of Belial they make no allowance whatever for the *call of God* and the *anointing* of His Spirit. It is no new thing to be despised and sneered at because we have had a new and soul-uplifting revelation of the goodness of God. The more God honours us the more will the lewd and self-deceived despise us in their hearts. But in this we are made partakers of the fellowship of the *sufferings of Christ*. The carnal mind is enmity against God. But here Saul, like our Lord and Master, was patient in suffering. "He held his peace." It is an unmistakable proof of a young man's moral strength when he can treat his enemies with magnanimous silence.

SAUL, THE COURAGEOUS.
1 Samuel 11.

"Blessed are those who die for God,
And earn the martyr's crown of light;
Yet he who lives for God may be
A greater conqueror in His sight."—PROCTOR.

ALTHOUGH Saul had been already declared king (chap. 10. 24), he had seemingly gone back to his old occupation, and was tending the herd (v. 5). This in itself was a notable proof of the dignity and strength of Saul's moral character. Had he been a small, shallow, fussy soul he would have reckoned that his promotion to the kingdom had lifted him above the menial task of a herdman. Those who are conscious that God is with them can well afford to wait. "He that believeth shall not make haste." In this chapter we have brought before us a—

I. Sorrowful Message. Messengers came to Gibeah, and told how the city of Jabesh was besieged, and that Nahash the Ammonite would make a covenant with them, only on condition that he may thrust out all their right eyes for a reproach upon all Israel (vv. 1-4). No wonder the people wept at such humility and barbarous tidings. But will ever the people of God be able to make a covenant of peace with the enemies of God without suffering loss? Such compromising was contrary to the Word of the Lord (Exod. 23. 32). The enemy of our souls, the world, is still ready to make a covenant with us if we are willing to part with our spiritual eyesight.

II. Divine Call. "The Spirit of God came upon Saul when he heard those tidings, and his *anger* was kindled greatly" (vv. 5, 6). A man may be as much under the power of the Holy Spirit when his soul is hot with burning indignation as when it is melted with tender compassion. There are different manifestations, but the same spirit. The source of his anger was doubtless the reproach threatened to all Israel (v. 2). Does the call of God not frequently come by the awakening in the soul of some overmastering desire? Look at the case of Gideon (Judges 6. 34), of Jephthah (Judges 11. 29), and of Samson (Judges 14. 6). If the Holy Spirit has kindled in the heart any burning desire, we may take it as the call of God to go in and possess that thing so desired.

III. Fearless Challenge. The hewing of the yoke of oxen, and the sending of the gory pieces throughout all Israel (v. 7) was like the blast of a trumpet from Heaven to a drowsy nation. "The fear of the Lord fell on the people." When a man is acting under the powerful in-

fluence of the Holy Spirit there are sure to be signs
following. God's man is never awanting when the national
crisis comes. It was so in the days of Luther and of Knox.
It has always been God's way to single out men through
whom He might reveal His will and power. Fearlessness
will ever characterise that one who is being borne along by
the mighty rushing wind of the Holy Ghost (Acts 4. 13).

IV. Great Deliverance. The summons of Saul met
with a willing and general response—"they came out with
one consent"—for God always works through the Spirit-
inspired message. The relief of Jabesh was both timely
and merciful (vv. 8-11). These besieged citizens were on
the brink of becoming a life-long reproach to all Israel
(v. 2) by being disabled for war and bearing on their
bodies the marks of a shameful defeat. This Spirit-moved
leader was able to roll away the reproach. What a mighty
power for Christ and His cause a Spirit-filled life may be!
Are there not many to-day who, like the men of Jabesh-
gilead, are in jeopardy of losing their testimony for Christ,
and bringing reproach upon the whole Church of God?
O that that sacrifice, which was, as it were, "hewed in
pieces" on Calvary's Cross, might be preached with such
freshness and power throughout all the land that the
people of God would "come out with one consent" to the
rescue of the oppressed and the salvation of the perishing.

V. Magnanimous Intervention. When the people
proposed that all those opposed to the *reign* of Saul should
be put to death (chap. 10. 27), Saul said, "There shall not
a man be put to death this day" (vv. 12, 13). It well becomes those who enjoy great privileges at the hands of God
to extend great forbearance to those who may trespass
against us (see 2 Sam. 19. 22). It ill becomes the servants
of Christ to use their spiritual authority or ecclesiastical
position for the purpose of avenging personal insult.

Remember Him, who though He was reviled, reviled not
again.   The time is coming when Jesus Christ will deal
with those who have opposed His rule (Luke 19. 37).

VI. Happy Result. "They made Saul king before
the Lord in Gilgal, and there Saul and all the people
rejoiced greatly" (vv. 14, 15).   This was the *public* con-
firmation of the *secret* call of God.   Every secret blessing
will have its open coronation (Matt. 6. 6).   The place,
made memorable for suffering and humiliation (Joshua 5. 2),
has now become the place of exuberant joy.   Weeping may
endure for a night, but joy cometh in the morning.   Those
who have received the special anointing must ultimately
rise to special honour.   The kingdom did not come to Saul
because he wrought for it.   It was the gift of God, and
being obedient, he is now crowned with honour and glory.
Blessed are all they that put their trust in Him.

SAUL, THE DISOBEDIENT.
1 Samuel 13. 1-14.

> "None
> Could trace God's will so plain as you, while yours
> Remained implied in it, but now you fail,
> And we, who prate about that will, are fools;
> In short, God's service is established here
> As He determines fit, and not your way—
> And this you cannot brook."—BROWNING.

SAMUEL, in the love of his heart, and in faithfulness to the
Lord, had just sounded a note of warning to Saul and
the people, accompanied with a gracious word of encouragement (chap. 12. 20-25).   But in the day of prosperity we
often fail to *consider*.   "Saul reigned one year."   This
might be rendered: Saul was *like a child of one year* when
he began to reign.   All that we know of Saul up till this
time bears this out.   Like Uzziah, he was marvellously
helped *till he was strong* (2 Chron. 26. 15-16).   The pride

that lifteth up the heart into self-confidence will surely end in destruction. God will never fail or forsake those who trust Him and are little in their own eyes.

I. His Duty was Plain. To get the explanation of verse 8 we have to go back to chapter 10. 8. The word of the prophet was both urgent and explicit. "Seven days shall thou tarry, till I come to thee, *and show thee what thou shalt do.*" Although the time may have been about three years after, still Saul's way was perfectly plain; he was to do as occasion served him (chap. 10. 7) till this present crisis should come, then he was to wait for the ministry and guidance of the man of God. Our responsibility will be according to the *light* we have. If, like Saul, we are conscious of being chosen of God, and of being made partakers of the holy anointing (chap. 10. 1), then surely the *revealed* will of God must become the absolute and unconditional law of our life. This is the way, walk ye in it.

II. His Faith was Tried. The Philistines had gathered in great force to fight with Israel (v. 5). Saul had blown the trumpet thoughout the land, and summoned the Hebrews to meet him at Gilgal. While he tarried there for seven days, according to the set time of Samuel, "the people were scattered from him" (v. 8). His waiting may have appeared to the already distressed army of Israel as a sign of weakness and fear, so many of them took advantage of the delay and *hid themselves* (v. 6). Day by day, as he waited for the prophet, he saw the strength of Israel melting away. Every hour he tarried seemed to make his case all the more hopeless. What a test to his faith and patience! What a struggle there must have been in his soul; what a conflict between *faith* and *sight!* It is always a sore trial to part with the Isaac of our hopes while we are following the bidding of God (1 Peter 1. 7). "He must increase, I must decrease."

III. His Failure was Great. "Saul said, Bring
hither a burnt-offering *to me*; and as soon as he had made an
end of offering Samuel came" (vv. 9, 10). Saul had waited
till *almost* the close of the seventh day, as Samuel had appointed; but ere the full time had come, through pressure
of circumstances, his patience with the will of God had
broken down. He had chosen his own way, and stepped
out of the purpose and favour of God. Every Spirit-
anointed one will have their testing time. As soon as
Jesus Christ was baptised of the Spirit He was led into
the wilderness to be tried (Mark 1 .10-13). If Abraham
had failed when the great testing crisis came he never
would have become the "Father of the faithful." But he
staggered not at the promise of God through unbelief (Rom.
4. 20). The way to abiding honour and usefulness in the
service of God is by "enduring as seeing Him who is
invisible." To fail when we are brought face to face with
the circumstances planned by God for the testing and
developing of our faith is to be a life-long cripple in the
work of the Lord. Whenever, as Christian workers, we
choose our own way rather than wait on the fulfilment
of God's Word, we become as bones out of joint in the body
of Christ. Such can only live a *painful* life.

IV. His Excuse was Vain. "Samuel said, What hast
thou done? Saul said, Because I saw that the people
were scattered from me; . . . I *forced myself* therefore,
and offered a burnt-offering" (vv. 11, 12). His army was
dwindling away, the Philistine host was increasing, Samuel
was long in coming, and his own patience was exhausted.
Yet in taking the place of the priestly prophet he acted
foolishly, and in direct rebellion against the commandment
of the Lord (v. 13). For unbelief and disobedience there
can be no excuse. No argument or reasoning can ex-
tenuate the guilt of doing what *we know* to be contrary to the
mind of God. He that heareth the sayings of Christ, and

believeth them not, is the foolish man that goes on building his life on the ruinous sand (Matt. 7. 26). The most melancholy feature of Saul's attempt to justify himself is that there are no signs of *repentance*. After Samuel's solemn warning he proceeds to *number the people* (v. 15). When we have discovered that we have blundered and failed, and disobeyed, genuine repentance and confession is the only way back to God's favour and fellowship.

V. His Loss was Deplorable. "Now thy kingdom shall not continue: the Lord hath sought Him a man after His own heart, because thou hast not kept that which the Lord commanded thee" (v. 14). Saul has turned away from the Lord, now the Lord seeks another man after His own heart, as an instrument more willing to *abide* in His hand, for the working out of His purposes concerning Israel. All Saul's trumpeting and planning now can no more hinder the kingdom from settling down in David than he could hinder the sun from setting in the west. He may shake himself like Samson, but the power is gone. It is a solemn thought that we may be earnestly keeping up the form of our service for God in the energy of the flesh when the Spirit of power has departed from us. Let us never forget that to choose our own way is to choose loss and defeat. May God work in us both to *will* and *to do* of His good pleasure!

SAUL, THE CASTAWAY.
1 Samuel 15.

"Presume not to serve God apart from such
Appointed channel as He wills . . .
. . . He seeks not that His altars
Blaze—careless how, so that they do but blaze."
—BROWNING.

THERE is a zeal that is not according to knowledge, but which is a defiance of knowledge, a violation of the Word of God and of conscience. In seeking to serve God with our own will, while we reject His, we are as it were offering swines' flesh upon His altar. The Lord will have His altar blaze, but the sacrifice must be blameless. It would seem from these words, *"Now therefore* hearken thou unto the voice of the words of the Lord"* (v. 1), that God was loath to withdraw His favour from Saul. Such is His lingering grace which gives room for repentance. Saul is to have another chance to show himself *faithful* to God. Notice his—

I. **Commission.** "Now go and smite Amalek and utterly destroy all" (v. 3). His orders were plain and explicit. Amalek, like Jericho, was to be entirely devoted to destruction (Joshua 6. 17, marg.). Neither his feelings nor reason must stand in the way of the fulfilment of the divine purpose. When we have the Lord's bidding to go, even though it should be *on the water*, it is ours confidently to obey.

II. **Disobedience.** "But Saul spared Agag, and the best of the sheep, . . . and all that was good" (v. 9). The command was *spare not*, but he spared. He allowed his eye to govern his actions, so he walked not by faith but by sight. His natural instincts, as a judge of and dealer in cattle, overruled the direct Word of God; so he spared *the best*, and utterly destroyed the *vile* and the *refuse*. It is always easy to devote to God that which *we* do not want. Will He be pleased with the vile and the refuse while we spare the best for our own purposes? Whenever self-interest is allowed a place in our service for the Lord it is sure to be at the cost of faithfulness to Him.

III. **Self-Justification.** This is a very sad and melancholy episode in the life of Saul. May we take it as a trumpet-warning against self-deception. The Lord said to Samuel, "Saul *hath not* performed my commandments" (v. 11). And when Samuel met Saul, after he had been triumphantly setting up a monument of his victory, he said with the utmost complacency, "I have performed the commandment of the Lord" (vv. 12, 13). At the same time the bleating of the sheep and the lowing of the oxen that he had spared as spoil were a solemn mockery in the sight of God. Like the crowing of the cock to Peter, they might have reminded Saul of his sin. But this was not all. When Samuel charged him with "not obeying the voice of the Lord," he answered, "Yea, I have obeyed" (v. 20). It is pitiful in the extreme to be seeking at any time to persuade ourselves that we are right with God when He had emphatically declared that we have "turned back." "Be not deceived, God is not mocked" (Gal. 6. 7). The eyes of the Lord are upon us, as they were on Saul, watching whether we are faithful to Him and His Word. Every act of disobedience is an act of rebellion against God.

IV. Confession. Samuel had to be faithful with Saul, although he was deeply grieved at his failure, and had spent the whole night in "Crying unto the Lord" (v. 11). "To obey is better than sacrifice," he said, and "rebellion is as the sin of witchcraft" (vv. 22, 23). Saul discovered that the secret, selfish motives of his heart had blossomed and brought forth fruit that was sure to grow fearfully bitter, so he confessed, "I have sinned: I have transgressed the commandment of the Lord: *because I feared the people* and obeyed their voice" (v. 24). Ah! the secret is out. He feared the people, and the fear of man ensnared his soul (Prov. 29. 25). Are there not multitudes of young, vigorous, gifted lives around us that are wrecked and ruined for the service of God through the very same reason —the fear of man. "Who art thou, that thou shouldst be afraid of a man that shalt die?" (Isa. 51. 12). Any backboneless soul can be a coward. Put on the armour of God, and ye shall be able to stand in the evil day (Eph. 6. 13).

V. Rejection. "Samuel said unto Saul, Thou hast

rejected the Word of the Lord, and the Lord hath rejected thee from being king" (v. 26). To reject God's Word is to be rejected of God (Luke 9. 26). He that believeth not God hath made Him a liar. Saul's seeming repentance and confession had come too late. The moorings of God's guiding presence was cut; Saul's life was now a drifting wreck.

> "There is a line by us unseen,
>   That crosses every path;
>   The hidden boundary between
>   God's patience and His wrath."

"The Strength of Israel will not lie" (v. 29). He abideth faithful. He cannot deny Himself. What a vain show our life must be if it is not lived for the glory of God. Saul may still retain the favour of the people, but, alas, the Spirit of God had departed from him (chap. 16. 14). It is possible to be a Christian, and, like Saul, a "partaker of the Holy Ghost," yet *the life*, through being disobedient to the heavenly vision, may become a wilderness waste to itself, a stumbling-block to others, and an offence to God.

SAUL, THE ENEMY.
1 Samuel 18. 29.

> "Fool that I was! I will rehearse my fault:
>   I, wingless, thought myself on high to lift
> Among the winged! I set these feet that halt
>   To run against the swift."—INGELOW.

LOWELL hath said that "Best things perish of their own excess, and quality overdriven becomes defect." Who would have thought that the beautiful and childlike life of Saul would so soon be transformed and degraded into a purely selfish and God-dishonouring career He began in the Spirit and ended in the flesh. They that are in the flesh cannot please God. Like every other case of backsliding, it had its source in *turning aside* from the revealed will of God (chap. 15. 11-26). One step out of the path of

faith is enough to put us on the way to a self-ruined life.
Saul now becomes the open and avowed enemy of David,
the Lord's anointed. A man possessed by an evil spirit
will rush his head against the thick bosses of Jehovah's
buckler. Saul in becoming the enemy of David became—

I. A Sinner against his own Family. See his dastardly conduct with Michal, his own daughter, who *loved*
David; how he presses and schemes for their union in
marriage, in the hope that she might speedily be made a
widow (chap. 18. 20, 21). Think how often the tender
heart of Jonathan was grieved—for he too loved David—
at his father's heartless and cowardly behaviour. When
any father takes up an attitude of opposition to Jesus
Christ, who is the Lord's anointed, he is always fighting
against the best interests of his own household. Godliness is
profitable for the life that *now is* as well as for the life which
is to come. The love of Christ is meant to sweeten the home
life by enabling us joyfully to bear one another's burdens.

**II. A Sinner against the Testimony of the Holy
Spirit.** The scene at Naioth must have been an exciting
one (chap. 19. 19-24). Saul hears that David is there and
sends messengers to apprehend him, but as soon as they
come within the holy atmosphere of the prophetic band
they are influenced by the Spirit and begin to prophesy.
A second, and even a third company were sent, with the
same result. Then Saul himself went thither, "and the
Spirit of God was upon him also." Surely if ever a man
had evidence that the Spirit of God was opposed to his
present actions that man was Saul, and the time was now.
It would seem as if the Holy Ghost lingered over Saul, as
the Shekinah glory hovered near Jerusalem ere it finally
departed (Ezek. 11. 23). Oh, how loath our God is to give
us up! But this last manifestation of the Spirit of
prophecy fails to turn him from the error of his way.

The effect was only like the morning cloud. **Grieve not the Holy Spirit.**

III. A Sinner against the Servants of God. Saul commanded that the priests of the Lord be slain, "because their hand also is *with* David (chap 22. 17, 18). Saul, in refusing to give David his God-appointed place, is compelled to become the enemy of all who favour him. It is so still. Our relationships to Christ determine our attitude toward our fellowmen. The interests of Jesus Christ and His people are so vitally connected that they cannot be divided. "He that touched you touched the apple of Mine eye." The priestly house of Ahimelech are the first to suffer martyrdom for the cause of David. But the blood of the holy is never spilt in vain; the cause for which it is shed will surelv prosper.

IV. A Sinner against the Best Interests of the Nation. It is worthy of special note that while Saul was pursuing after David, "the Philistines invaded the land" (chap. 23. 27, 28). While he was resisting and opposing the clearly revealed purpose of God the enemy came in like a flood. The will of the Lord was to bless the nation of Israel through David, whom He had chosen. To despise and dishonour him was to obstruct the divinely-appointed channel of blessing and rob the people of the grace of God. Is it otherwise now? God hath sent His Son to bless us, nationally as well as individually. Infidelity and indifference to Christ and His cause will always be a menace and a hindrance to a nation's highest good. Men are slow to acknowledge this, but God is not mocked. In our pride and self-will we may despise and set aside the Lord's anointed, but God knows no other channel through which we can be blessed (1 Tim. 2. 5).

V. A Sinner against his own Conscience. Now when David had shown the kindness of God to his would-be murderer, Saul wept, and said, "Thou are more righteous than I: for thou hast rewarded me good, whereas I have rewarded thee evil" (chap. 24. 16, 17). Yet for all this the bitterness of his heart against David constrained him to play the fool yet again (chap. 26. 21). A man is always playing the fool when he is warring against the revealed will of God, because he is also fighting against the deeper and truer instincts of his own nature. He that sinneth against the light sinneth against *his own soul*. In *submitting* to Christ as our King we justify our own conscience, and there is peace.

VI. A Sinner against the Providence of God. To be out of sympathy with God and His Christ (anointed) is to be out of harmony with the gracious providence of God. In chapter 26 we see the powerful Saul falling once more into the hands of the poor despised David. Oh, the solemn irony of such circumstances! Philip II. of Spain said, after the destruction of the Armada, "I was prepared to conquer England, but not the elements." But the *elements* in the hands of an overruling God have to be reckoned with. Those who are at enmity with the Son of David and His kingdom will certainly find out some time that the unerring providence of the Eternal One has ruled them *outside* His saving grace (Rom. 8. 28).

VII. A Sinner against the Purpose of God. If the mind was not blinded by the Devil, and maddened by the force of a rebellious self-will, no one would ever expect to succeed who was striving against the *"determinate* counsel of God" (Acts 2, 23). "Why do the heathen rage, and imagine a vain thing?" (Psa. 2. 1). It was the fixed purpose of God to exalt David to the throne of Israel, so it is his settled determination that Jesus shall yet become the "Blessed and *only* Potentate, King of kings, and Lord of lords" (1 Tim. 6. 15). Those that fall on this stone shall be broken, and those on whom it shall fall it shall grind them to powder. "Kiss the Son, lest He be angry, and ye shall perish" (Psa. 2. 12). Fall in line with the revealed purpose of God in Christ Jesus, and you will save your *soul* from death and your *life* from failure and everlasting shame.

SAUL, THE SUICIDE.
1 Samuel 28, 31.

> "'*Went* away,' and not *sent* away:
>   Lord! I would lay this word to heart.
> '*Went* away,' and not *sent* away;
>   Lord! give me grace to see my part.
> '*Went* away,' and not *sent* away,
>   Making himself a castaway.
> O heart of mine! this one thing do—
>   At all costs, to THE CHRIST be true."—GROSART.

THE above lines were suggested to the author by reading what is said of the rich young man: "He *went away* sorrowful" (Matt. 19. 22). Like Saul, he was not *sent* away; his turning aside from following the Lord was his own deliberate choice. In turning away from Him who is *the Light*, where else can we go but into the darkness? The way of transgressors is hard. The thirty-seven years that intervened between Saul's first failure through sinful impatience at Gilgal, and his tragic end on Mount Gilboa were most eventful, chiefly because of their extreme sadness and *restlessness*. It is an awful thing to be out of harmony with the holy and merciful God. Let us—

I. **Mark his Trembling Heart.** "When Saul saw the host of the Philistines he was afraid, and his heart greatly trembled" (chap. 28. 5). Samuel was dead, the Spirit of power and of comfort had forsaken him; David was still a fugitive; and the Philistines were growing in numbers and in hopefulness. Saul's poor, desolate, and self-confident

heart began to give way. What is there in us, apart from the grace of God, to sustain when the dark and cloudy day comes? In me, that is, in my flesh, there *dwelleth* no good thing. There is nothing resident in us that will ever in any way compensate the grieving of the Holy Spirit of God. Our own wisdom and strength and youthful vigour are poor substitutes for the "armour of God." "Without Me ye can do nothing" (John 15. 5).

II. **Behold his Vain Inquiry.** "When Saul inquired of the Lord, the Lord answered him not" (v. 6). A *fearful* heart and a *silent* Heaven! What a sorrowful plight for a man to be in who was once a partaker of the Holy Ghost and a companion of prophets! There are times and circumstances when God will certainly close His ears to our entreaties (Prov. 1. 28). If we regard iniquity in our heart, the Lord will not hear. Nothing will more effectually bar our communion with our Lord than *unconfessed* sin. Let us take heed lest there be in any of us an evil heart of unbelief in *departing* from the living God. Not to be obedient to His light is to wander into the blackness of darkness.

III. **Hear his Despairing Cry.** Saul, finding the door of Heaven shut, turns in his desperation to the terrible and useless expedient of witchcraft. "None can bless whom God hath cursed." To the woman of Endor he said, "BRING ME UP SAMUEL" (v. 11). These words are very emphatic in the Hebrew, and betoken tremendous anxiety and determination. In the bitterness of his soul he longs for one short interview with him who had power with God. Oh, for one word more from him who poured the anointing oil upon my head! What value are we now setting upon our God-given privileges? "While ye have the light, walk in the light" (chap. 16. 2). Those who turn away from the truth of God will assuredly be deceived through believing a lie (2 Thess. 2. 11, 12). Take heed to thyself.

IV. Witness his Ruined Prospects. The reappearance of Samuel brought no relief or comfort to the dis-anointed king; it was but the breaking asunder of the last cord of hope. Samuel's message proved to be only Saul's death-knell. "The Lord will also deliver Israel *with thee* into the hands of the Philistines" (v. 19). Saul's sun of prosperity set when he disobeyed the "Word of the Lord" (chaps. 13. 14). Since that time he was living only in the twilight. Now the darkness of midnight is settling down thick and fast. Such is the course of the backslider. The fruits of disobedience, an act of inward rebellion against the "commandment of the Lord," may not appear in all their fearfulness for years; and meanwhile we may be living with comparative ease upon a *past experience*, but all the while our Christian life is but in the Christ-dis-honouring energy of the flesh, which can only bring forth corruption (Gal. 6. 8). "Search me, O God" (Psa. 139. 23).

V. Take Warning from his Tragic End. "The battle went sore against Saul, the archers hit him; and he was sore wounded. Therefore Saul took a sword, and fell upon it" (chap. 31. 3, 4). The *"last battle"* will always go sore against the man who has "rejected the Word of God." The archers, visible and invisible, will be sure to hit him, he will be sore wounded, and the end will be defeat and death. O Saul, thou hast destroyed *thyself*. Saul sought to save his life by taking matters into his own hand, and he lost it (Matt. 16. 25). To forsake the Fountain of living water is to perish of thirst, beside our self-made broken cisterns. The life that is lived in union with Christ will be a saved and *victorious* life, but the life that is not governed and guided by the Spirit of the Lord is already into the *course of this world* and drifting on to the doom of eternal loss. As Christian workers let us give heed to this solemn lesson. To fall out of line with the purposes of God as they march along is to make shipwreck of our usefulness.

It was as *king* that Saul was rejected; it is as *servants* that we may become castaways.

DAVID'S CALL.

1 Samuel 16. 1-13.

"God has other words for other worlds,
But for this world the Word of God is CHRIST."
—HAMILTON KING.

SAUL'S utter rejection and failure through turning aside from the Word of God is a beacon of warning to every servant of Jesus Christ. It is in vain we build if we are not *doing* the *sayings* of our Lord (Matt. 7. 26). The wisdom of *this* world will always be foolishness with God. Let us note—

I. **The Choice.** "I have provided Me a king" (v. 1). Samuel was forbidden to prolong his mourning for Saul. The will of the Lord ought to be more precious to us than the prosperity of our friends. Another king had been prepared and provided for His people. David was being prepared for the throne of Israel by his *faithfully tending* and defending his father's sheep (chap. 17. 34-36). As a well-known preacher has said, "God always begins a long way back." God may choose the foolish things of this world, but He does not choose the lazy things. What we should aim at is not promotion, but *faithfulness* to God. Personal acquaintance with Him, and devotion to His will and work, is the highway to success and open reward. Don't be afraid of your gifts and capabilities being overlooked because you live and move in an obscure sphere of life; the Lord knows where the instrument is lying that is fit for that special work needed to be done. Make thyself a *polished* shaft, and God will surely hide thee in His quiver.

II. **The Commission.** "The Lord said unto Samuel, Fill thine horn with oil and go" (v. 1). Since David, the son of Jesse, has become His chosen one, so He also *chooses* the *means* by which this end may be gained. God's providences will never contradict His purposes. He that hath begun the good work in our behalf will carry it on. The anointing oil for the head of David is put in Samuel's horn at the bidding of God, so it will not be put there in vain. Neither is it in vain when the Holy Spirit fills the heart of any servant of God, as many as are ordained to eternal life through them will believe. Samuel went, as every ambassador for Christ should go, in *God's Name*, with *God's message*, carrying with them the holy *anointing power*. Do we wonder that "the elders of the town trembled at his coming" (v. 4). The true *man of God* will always be a man of authority.

III. **The Search.** "Send and fetch him" (v. 11). Jesse made seven of his sons pass before Samuel; but the Lord cannot be deceived with a man's countenance or the height of his stature. It is with the *heart* man believeth, so "the Lord looketh on the heart" (v. 7). "As a man thinketh in his heart so is he." Because David was the *least* among them, he was the *last* they thought of; but the last shall be first, for nothing could be done till David came. "Not he that commendeth himself is approved, but whom the Lord commendeth" (2 Cor. 10. 18). He who made himself of no reputation was exalted "far above all." Self-defence is often a confession of weakness and self-conceit. In the judgment of men intellectual gifts and outward appearances are of great weight; but in the balance of God the scale goes down in favour of the humble and contrite heart. Eliab and Abinadab may pad their chests and stretch themselves to the full, but they cannot take the place of the herd laddie, whose *heart* is right with God. "Be not deceived, God is not mocked." No amount of pretence or bribery will ever gain that which can only come through being CALLED OF GOD. Make your calling and election sure.

IV. **The Anointing.** As soon as David came the Lord said, "Arise, anoint him: *for this is he.*" So Samuel "anointed him in the midst of his brethren" (v. 13). Perhaps because of envy his brethren show no signs of gladness at their brother's high promotion. This wretched joy-choking feeling is utterly unworthy of any son of God. But the chosen one becomes the anointed one. This is God's order; this is our privilege. "The Spirit of the Lord came upon David from that day *forward.*" It was a definite and memorable experience in the life of David. Is not every truly consecrated life accompanied by the anointing of the Spirit of Power? (Acts 4. 31). We are not sent a warfaring on our own charges. For every special task to which we are called there is a special supply of the Spirit of grace given. David was "a man after God's own heart" (1 Sam. 13. 14) before he was anointed, but just because he was such a man the sacred symbolic oil of power was put upon him. "I thank thee, O Father, Lord of Heaven and earth, that Thou didst hide these things from the wise and understanding, and didst reveal them unto babes" (Matt. 11. 25, R.V.). "To them that have no might He increaseth strength" (Isa. 40. 29).

DAVID'S VICTORY.
1 Samuel 17.

"Faith alone is the master-key
To the strait gate and narrow road;
The others but skeleton pick-locks be,
And you never shall pick the locks of GOD."
—WALTER SMITH.

FAITH is a sword "that smites with more than mortal blow." David learned to use this sword when but a lad tending his father's sheep among the uplands of Bethlehem. Those who win open and public victories for God are those who have triumphed in the lowly sphere of life and in the hidden kingdom of the heart. Goliath is a fit type of the god of this world, who blatantly defies the Lord's people. Tradition credits him as being the one who took the Ark of God. "Choose you out a man, and let him come down to me!" cried this giant prince of boasters. But *they* were utterly unable to choose such a man. The overcomer of Israel's enemy must be the *chosen of God*, the man after His own heart, a true type of Him who came to destroy the works of the Devil, and to bruise the head of the adversary. We shall view David here in this light. Notice his—

I. Gracious Mission. "He went as Jesse had commanded him, and came and saluted his brethren" (vv. 17-22). David, like Christ, came out from his father, rejoicing to do his will, and bringing the love and gifts of the father to his brethren. Grace and truth came by Jesus Christ. As the bright ruddy youth went forth with the ten loaves for his brethren, and the ten cheeses for the captain of their thousand, who would have thought that this (child) was set for the fall and rising again of many in Israel?

II. Motives Misjudged. "And Eliab's anger was kindled against David, and he said, Why camest thou down hither? I know thy pride" (v. 28). This eldest brother, like the kinsmen of Christ, betrays the grossest ignorance of the real character of the pure and generous-minded David. David's motives were so *unselfish* that the proud self-seeking Eliab could not understand him; besides, it was a gratuitous insult to his father who sent him. It is not easy for a man to judge what is white when he persists in looking through coloured glasses. David's sufferings here were akin to the sufferings of Christ, and an example of how we, too, must suffer if we are faithful to the Father's word and will. David's calm reply to this libellous charge is worthy of note. "What have I now done? Is there not a cause?" Yes, there is a *cause*—deep, far-reaching, and God-glorifying.

III. **Solemn Determination.** "David said to Saul,
Let no man's heart fail because of him; thy servant will go
and fight this Philistine" (v. 32). God's *special purpose*
in bringing him into the camp at this time has come upon
David as a rapidly-growing revelation. The Spirit of God
has convinced him that his mission is to overthrow the
defier of Israel, and, like his Lord, "he set his face like
a flint" to do it. If you feel moved by the Spirit to do
even some *unprecedented* thing for the glory of God be not
deterred by the worldly wisdom which says, like Saul,
"Thou art not able" (v. 33). As David, the stripling,
stands before the tall armour-clad king of Israel, with a
sling and a staff in his hands, despised and rejected by his
own brethren, he looks altogether unfit for such a conflict.
But God hath chosen the *weak* things to confound the *mighty*.

IV. **Unwavering Confidence.** "Thy servant slew
both the lion and the bear; and this Philistine shall be as
one of them, seeing he hath defied . . . the living God"
(vv. 34-37). David's past and *secret* experiences of the
power of faith in the living God nerves his soul now with
fearlessness. Was it not so also with the "Greater than
David?" Are there not always secret victories in the life
before we openly triumph in the sight of doubting and
fearful men. Those who *defy* the living God are not to
be feared by those who *trust* Him. Windbags are not of
much account with Him who is a consuming fire. Perhaps
Saul looked upon David as one whose spirit was willing, but
whose flesh was weak when *he* put *his* armour on him (v. 38).
But the armour that suits a man who fights in the energy of the
flesh will never suit a man who wars in the power of the Spirit.
So he put them off, "for he had not *proved* them." The Lord's
anointed must meet the enemy not as a soldier, but as a
shepherd (John 10. 10, 11). As an armour against the sting
of pain they gave Jesus wine mingled with myrrh. But He
received it not. He met the enemy in the strength of faith.

V. Invisible Armour. David said, "I come to thee *in the Name* of the LORD of Hosts, the God whom thou hast defied" (v. 45). Goliath could only see the stripling and his staff; he could not see the mighty NAME in which David was encased as a tower of strength (Prov. 18. 10). His NAME means all that He is in our behalf, and this is "the whole armour of God." Put it on (Eph. 6. 10, 11). Our weapons are not carnal, but mighty *through the Spirit.* Our help is in the Name of the Lord (Psa. 124. 8). ''If ye ask anything in My Name, I will do it'' (see Acts 3. 16).

VI. Decided Victory. "So David prevailed over the Philistine with a sling and a stone" (vv. 50, 51). It was with the sling of faith and the stone of truth that David's Lord prevailed over the enemy of souls in the wilderness (Luke 4. 1-13). As David slew Goliath with his own sword, so Christ conquered death by dying and him that had the power of death, that is, the devil (Heb. 2. 14, 15). David went forth to the fight, as Christ went to the Cross, in the presence of those who doubtless thought that they would see him again no more *alive.* But he came back again, triumphant over the foe, and became the chiefest among the thousands. This great battle was between the *representatives* of two different kingdoms; each nation conquers or falls in their champion. So was it with God's anointed Son. "Thanks be unto God, who *giveth us* the victory *through our Lord Jesus Christ*" (1 Cor. 15. 57). We are "more than conquerors" *through* Him.

DAVID AND JONATHAN.
1 Samuel 18. 1-4; 2 Samuel 1. 26.

"All through life there are wayside inns,
Where man may refresh his soul with love;
Even the lowest may quench his thirst
At rivulets fed by springs from above."
—LONGFELLOW.

"BELOVED, let us love one another, for love is of God" (1 John 4. 7). In this little portion of Scripture we

have "apples of gold in pictures of silver" (Prov. 25. 11).
The love of Jonathan for David seems a pure unclouded
reflection of that love of God which is shed abroad in the
heart by the Holy Ghost. It was wonderful.

I. **His Love was Real.** "He loved him as his own
soul" (v. 1). It was no mere formal business connection.
Jonathan had taken David and all his interests home to the
secrets and carefulness of his own soul. The love that fails
to do this is shallow and selfish. How can we say that we
love Christ if His interests do not appeal as powerfully to
us as our own. Paul had done this when he said, "To me
to live is Christ" (Phil. 1. 21).

II. **His Love was Surpassing.** It passed the love of
women (2 Sam. 1. 26). To say this suggests that it was
supernatural. The highest form of human love is found in
the true motherly heart. The love that excels this is that
"greater love" manifested in the only begotten Son of God
(1 John 4. 9), and begotten in our hearts by the Holy
Spirit (1 John 4. 19). The believer's love to Christ is more
than mere natural love, for the carnal mind is enmity
against God. The natural heart is an alien to the Holy One.

III. **His Love was Inseparable.** "Jonathan and David
made a *covenant*, because he loved him" (v. 3) True love
will always constrain to a closer bond of union; mutual
affection culminates in the marriage tie. The love of
Christ *constrains* us. What to do? Why, like Jonathan,
to yield our life's concerns into the hands of Him whom
God hath exalted to be a Prince and a Saviour (Chap. 20.
14-16). Hear the whisperings of Christ's dying love in
those never-to-be-forgotten words, "Do this in remembrance of Me" (1 Cor. 11. 24).

IV. **His Love was Self-Sacrificing.** "Jonathan
stripped himself . . . and gave to David" (v. 4). Love
will not hide; "It doth not behave itself unseemly: it

seeketh not her own" (1 Cor. 13. 5). Love gives till the giving is felt as a sacrifice. It was so with the love of Christ, who for our sakes stripped Himself and became of no reputation, that we through His poverty might be made rich (2 Cor. 8. 9). The love of Christ was manifested in that poor woman who, when overtaken by a snowstorm, stripped herself to save her child. . In stripping ourselves for the honour and glory of the Christ of God we are proving the reality of our confidence in Him. If He is to triumph for us, let us give Him "even to our sword and our bow." Self-aggrandisement is always inconsistent with the glory of God.

V. His Love was Well Deserved. No doubt there were many personal attractions about David to draw out the full flow of Jonathan's affections, for David *"behaved himself wisely"* (v. 5), and was to Jonathan the fairest and chiefest among ten thousand. But the secret of the strength of his love lay in the fact that he *knew* David as the Lord's anointed and the coming king of Israel (chap. 20. 15). Surely the tenderest affections of his pure soul were well spent when lavished unreservedly on the beloved of God. A greater than David is here! One who spake as never man spake, and whose behaviour has been such that neither God, man, nor devil could find fault in Him. And He says, "Lovest thou Me?"

VI. His Love was Reciprocated. "The soul of Jonathan was *knit with* the soul of David" (v. 1). These two souls were knit together in their desires and motives, as the warp and woof of a web. The *knitting* together shows that the affections of David responded in full measure to the love of Jonathan, so that the vital interests of the one were intertwined with the vital interests of the other. This is something deeper than mere belief in outward conformity; it is the very essence of "the unity of the Spirit." Jesus Christ was moved by that yearning fathomless LOVE when he prayed that "they all may be one, as Thou, Father, art in Me, and I in them." This deep spiritual union can only be brought about where there is the entire surrender of all on both sides for mutual advantage through the constraining power of love. This is what Christ has done for us. What response are we making to Him? "He that loveth not knoweth not God: for God is love" (1 John 4. 8). Our Lord is abundantly willing that His life should be *knit* with our life. Are we equally willing that our life should be knit together with His life, and so become one in heart and purpose for the glory of God?

DAVID IN ADULLAM.
1 Samuel 22. 1, 2; 23.

"When God afflicts thee, think HE hews a rugged stone,
Which must be shaped, or else aside as useless thrown!"
—TRENCH.

IN the closing verses of the previous chapter we have recorded what was perhaps the darkest passage in the experience of David. What a melancholy sight—the Lord's anointed one feigning himself mad through the fear of man. Even anointed ones will be constrained to play the fool when they put their trust in the arm of flesh instead of in the living God (chap. 21. 10). As soon as David lost faith in God he *changed his behaviour*, and took to "scribbling on the doors of the gate" like a lunatic. There is a very vital connection between our creed and our conduct; a change of faith will certainly lead to a change of behaviour. Through fear of King Achish David fled to the cave of Adullam. Solitude with God is better than the friendship of the world. This act of separation was richly rewarded, for "his brethren and all his father's house went down thither to him" (see chap. 17. 28). There came also many others.

I. The Character of those who came to David.

1. THE DISTRESSED. It was one thing to hear about David, and perhaps to sympathise with him in his cause; it was quite another thing to be driven to him by the force of sheer necessity. We are not told what they were distressed about. The cause may have been the sufferings of David or the unsettled condition of the country, or some personal affliction and loss. In any case, it is a blessed distress that constrains us to seek the help and share the fortunes of the Lord's anointed. The self-satisfied heed not the claims of the rejected One (Rev. 3. 20). It was distress that brought the prodigal home to his father (Luke 15. 18).

2. THE DEBTORS. "Every one that was in debt." In fleeing to David, and espousing his cause, those bankrupts found a way of escape out of all their liabilities under the rule of a God-rejected Saul. Under the law we are insolvent debtors, but Christ rescues such sinners, and is willing to bear their blame for ever (Luke 7. 42).

3. THE DISCONTENTED. Those whose souls were embittered through disappointment and harassing circumstances—thirsty, restless, and unsatisfied lives. Oh, how many are smitten with this plague! Yet how few seek refuge in the presence of Him who alone can satisfy (Psa. 23. 5). Around the world's self-made broken cisterns there are great multitudes of such wretched folk who are more inclined to talk of their complaints than to go to the heavenly David, who is the Fountain of Life (Jer. 2. 13). Contentment is learned here (Phil. 4. 11).

II. Why they came to David.

1. THEY CAME BECAUSE THEY BELIEVED IN HIM. They believed that David was God's appointed king, and his was the right to reign over them. They had in fact got converted to David. Faith cometh by hearing. Have we so believed in Jesus Christ as the divinely-appointed and highly exalted King over all?

2. THEY CAME BECAUSE THEY WERE DECIDED FOR HIM. Their belief led them to take definite action. They not only heard the sayings, but did them, according to the ways of the wise (Matt. 7. 24). It is one thing to believe about Christ, as the anointed Saviour and King; it is quite another to take our stand with Him and for Him (John 9. 27). In deciding for David, they, like us, had to go forth unto him, without the camp, bearing his reproach (Heb. 13. 13). Decision for Christ means separation from the world.

3. THEY CAME BECAUSE THEY WERE PREPARED TO SUBMIT TO HIM. Having claimed him as their king, they yielded themselves into his hands, for the honour of his name and the advancement of his kingdom. How can we claim to have acknowledged Christ as our King if we have not surrendered ourselves to Him? Is not this our reasonable service? (Rom. 12. 1).

III. **What David became to Them.** "He became a captain over them." As soon as they took their place as *followers* David assumed his right and power to *lead*. They would thus therefore look to him—

1. FOR GUIDANCE. Their attitude to David now is, "Not my will, but thine be done;" what wilt thou have me to do? Is this the attitude of our heart to Him who hath received us in our dire need, having redeemed us with His Blood? One is your Master, even Christ. He guides by the unerring eye of His Word (Psa. 32. 8). "Lead thou me on."

2. FOR PROTECTION. Having become the disciples of David, they exposed themselves to the wrath and enmity of the followers of Saul. They who obey the god of this world will always be at war in their heart with the followers of the Lord's anointed. But greater is He that is with us than he that is with them. God is for us, therefore

we shall not be moved. David said, "Abide with me, fear not; for he that seeketh my life seeketh thy life: but *with me* thou shalt be in safeguard" (v. 23). "He is able to keep that which I have committed unto Him,".

3. FOR REWARD. The cause of David was no forlorn hope. It was the cause of God, therefore its ultimate triumph was sure. They who suffered with him in the days of his national rejection would, no doubt, be honoured with him in the day of his exaltation. "If we suffer with Him, we shall also be glorified *together*" (Rom. 8. 17). The day is coming when this despised One shall be crowned LORD OF ALL, and those who have followed Him in the rejection will be abundantly rewarded when they enter into the "Joy of the Lord" (Matt. 25. 21). He shall divide the spoil with the strong (Isa. 53. 12).

DAVID AND ABIGAIL.
1 Samuel 25.

"Take love away, and life would be defaced,
A ghastly vision on a howling waste.''—NEWMAN.

"ALL Scripture is given by inspiration of God, and is profit able for *doctrine*" (2 Tim. 3. 16). So that "profitable doctrine" may be found in this chapter if we consider the three prominent persons mentioned as having a typical character—David, as the Lord's anointed, representing Christ and His claims upon men; Nabal in his pride and foolishness is a fit type of the Christ-rejecting men of this world; Abigail is a beautiful example of those who *believe*, in obedience to the deeper and truer instincts of our nature. Let us note—

I. **The Request of David.** "Give, I pray thee, whatsoever cometh to thine hand" (v. 8).

1. THE REASON FOR IT. David and his men had been as a wall of protection unto Nabal's herdmen, both by night and

day (v. 16), while they were keeping their sheep among the hills of Carmel. His presence had saved them from the thievish bands of marauders, therefore his request was reasonable. Surely He who has saved us by the power of His presence has a claim upon us.

2. THE MANNER OF IT. These ten young men, like the ambassadors of Christ, were sent out *in the name* of their lord and master (v. 5). To despise them was to despise him that sent them (Luke 10. 16). They came with a *message of peace* (v. 6), and this peace, like that proclaimed by the messengers of the Gospel, was threefold. "Peace to *thee*, peace to *thine house*, peace to *all thou hast*." Suggestive of peace *with* God, the peace *of* God in the home of the heart, and the peace that *passeth all* understanding, touching all that we have. Truly such a message coming to us, as it came to Nabal, through the servants of God's appointed King, shall constrain us to a *thankful* trust.

II. The Foolishness of Nabal. He is described as a man who was "very great" (v. 2), but great men are not always *wise*. The wisdom of folly of a man will become very apparent when he is brought face to face with the claims of God (1 Cor. 2. 14). The balance of the sanctuary is unerring. His folly is seen—

1. IN REJECTING THE CLAIMS OF DAVID. "Nabal answered, Who is David? and who is the son of Jesse?" (v. 10) Like Pharaoh, he makes a boast of his ignorance (Exod. 5. 2). Like a backslider Peter, he says, "I know not the Man." The servants of Christ often meet with the same ungracious reception in presenting the claims of their Lord. Quibbling questions are asked in such a self-important manner that the messenger is smitten dumb with sorrow of heart. Argument is out of the question, as it is not with the servant they have to do, but with Him who sent them. So they turned back and told David all those things (v. 12). (See Matt. 14. 12.)

2. IN LIVING FOR SELF-GRATIFICATION. "Nabal made a feast like a king, and was drunken" (v. 36). The folly of Nabal is further seen in his making a god of his belly, and seeking the honour and praise of the ungodly rather than that of the Lord's anointed. He had nothing for David, but he had plenty to spend on that which ministered to gluttony and the pride of his own heart. There are many modern Nabals who think all is lost or wasted that's given for Christ while they gorge themselves with surfeiting and drunkenness. Nabal was a fool, and so is he that layeth up for himself, and is not rich toward God (Luke 12. 20, 21).

III. **The Wisdom of Abigail.** "She was a woman of *good understanding*" (v. 3). Surely this was a case of being unequally yoked with an unbeliever. Abigail's wisdom is self-evident when we consider her attitude toward David. "She made haste, and took . . . and fell before David on her face" (vv. 18-23). Thus we see that—

1. SHE YIELDED INSTANTLY. "She made haste" to meet all the demands made by David through his servants. This was to her a work of *faith*, as well as a labour of love. She *believed in David*, that the Lord would certainly establish his cause (v. 28), and although she saw not the messengers sent by him (v. 25), her "good understanding" constrained her to yield a hearty obedience to his will. She knew that this God-appointed king was not to be trifled with, and that there was danger in delay. Have we so believed and yielded to the claims of Jesus Christ our Lord? Or do we rather make haste to excuse ourselves?

2. SHE PLEADED EARNESTLY. She pleaded for her foolish husband, whose way was *right in his own eyes* (Prov. 12. 15), but was utter madness in her's (v. 25). She prayed for herself (v. 28), knowing that the power of life and death was in David's hands. Knowing therefore the terror of the Lord, we persuade men. It is when we believe

in Christ for ourselves, and yield to Him, that we truly see the terrible folly and danger of those who reject Him, and are constrained through pity and compassion to fall down before Him in earnest intercession for them.

3. SHE TESTIFIED COURAGEOUSLY. "In the morning, when she told Nabal these things, his heart died within him" (v. 37). She was wise enough to wait until the wine had gone out of him; she knew the uselessness of reasoning with a drunken man. The night before he could have faced anything under the influence of that wine which is a "mocker." But now, when the stern and solemn truth stares him in the face, the shock of death steals over his heart. Brave Abigail, she acknowledged David as king, and confessed him, fearless of the indifference and spite of her husband against him. Let no wife be hindered from trusting in Christ, and confessing Him, through the folly of her husband.

IV. The Results that Followed.

1. NABAL, THE REJECTER, WAS SMITTEN. "The Lord smote Nabal, that he died" (v. 38). Perhaps Jesus Christ had Nabal before His mind when He gave that parable in Luke 12, "Thou fool, this night thy soul shall be required of thee." The plans and purposes made by the ungodly to escape the claims of Jesus Christ are weapons formed against Him that shall not prosper. The man who refuses to believe in Christ is setting the eternal God at defiance.

2. ABIGAIL, THE BELIEVER, IS EXALTED. "David sent for her, and she became his wife" (vv. 40-42). Assuredly this was a full reward for her faith, and an abundant answer to the desire of her heart (v. 31). Separated from the foolish worldly Nabal, she was now free to be married to another, even to the Lord's anointed. She is now, in the time of David's rejection, as closely related to him as she

was when he sat upon the throne. As she was, so are we now, in Christ Jesus. "Be ye separate, saith the Lord, and I will receive you."

DAVID AMONG THE PHILISTINES.
2 Samuel 37-29.

"In the natural desert of rocks and sands, or in the populous moral desert of selfishness and baseness, to such temptation are we all called."—CARLYLE.

OF all the moral deserts or quagmires into which a Christian may be driven by the force of temptation none is more horrible than that of *selfishness*. Such self-centred lives are scandals on earth and heart-griefs in Heaven. But let him that is without sin cast the first stone. Have we not all at times, in our own hearts' affections, played the prodigal in taking a journey into the far country? Or have we never, like David, while in a fit of cowardliness, sought the comfort and help of the uncircumcised? David finding rest among the Philistines is a greater marvel to us than Saul among the prophets. It is a melancholy spectacle to see the Lord's anointed one depending on a heathen king for protection, or a child of God turning aside to the pleasures of this world for refreshing. Let us note—

I. Why He Went. He was tempted to take this false step because—

1. HE FEARED MAN. "He said in his heart, I shall perish one day by the hand of Saul" (chap. 27. 1). "The fear of man bringeth a snare." When David said this *in his heart* he was denying the holy anointing (1 John 2. 24). This is dangerous ground. It was here where Saul was when he fell from the favour of God (1 Sam. 15. 24).

2. HE FORGOT GOD. If this had not been so, how could he ever have said, "There is *nothing better for me* than that I should speedily escape into the land of the Philis-

tines." Is there *nothing* better for a child of God in the
day of distress than to seek the help of the ungodly? Hath
not he said, "I will never leave thee nor forsake thee, so
that we may boldly say, The Lord is my Helper, and I
will not fear what man shall do unto me" (Heb. 13. 5, 6).
Is that not much better? In Psalm 109. 4 we see David
on his *better* behaviour.

II. How He Succeeds. He—

1. ESCAPED PERSECUTION. "Saul sought no more again
for him" (chap. 27. 4). This is not always an unmixed
blessing (1 Peter 4. 13). There are always two ways by
which we may escape persecution. The one is by the inter-
position of God on our behalf (Acts 5. 19; 12. 7), the other
is by our backsliding into the ways of the world. The
world loves its own.

2. GOT YOKED WITH AN UNBELIEVER. How this came
about is very clear, and was very natural. He first of all
"found grace in the eyes" of the king of Gath (chap. 27. 5).
Then he acknowledged himself as "thy servant," and
so was promoted as "the keeper of the king's head" (chap.
28. 2). In this way, by denying his true character as the
servant of God, and submitting himself to another master,
did David become unequally yoked with an unbeliever.
It was when the prodigal had forsaken his father, and sought
relief in the "far country," that he was constrained to
"join himself" to a citizen of that country. The backsliding in heart will soon be found backsliding in conduct.
It is an infallible evidence that we are "living after the
flesh" when we are more ready to consider what would be
"better for *me*" (chap. 27. 1) than what would be better
for Christ and His kingdom.

3. WAS COMPELLED TO ACT IN A DECEITFUL MANNER.
He and his men had invaded some of the nomadic tribes
up about the borders of Egypt; and when Achish asked

him, "Whither have ye made a road to-day?" David said, "Against the south of Judah." This was a deliberate falsehood (chap. 27. 8-12). Was he not again playing the deceiver when he pretended to the king of Gath that he desired to go and fight with the Philistines against the Israelites? (chap. 29. 8). Was he not, in his heart, glad of this providential way of escape out of the desperate dilemma into which he had brought himself through fear and faithlessness? This is the wretched, double-dealing kind of life that a man is compelled to live who has experienced the saving grace of God, and been made a partaker of the Holy Ghost, when he backslides into the ways of the world and seeks to avoid all suffering for Christ. If he would *please men* he must act the hypocrite, for down in the deeper depths of his being the true light hath shined, although he is inwardly conscious that he is not walking in the light. No man, after receiving the holy anointing, as David did, can ever be the same as he was *before* the anointing, no matter how far he may fall from the enjoyment and power of it. Even salt without its savour is still savourless *salt*. "Wherefore take unto you the whole armour of God, that ye be able to withstand in the evil day" (Eph. 6. 13).

DAVID RECOVERING ALL.
1 Samuel 30.

"Is God less God, that thou art left undone?
Rise, worship, bless HIM, in this sackcloth spun,
As in the purple!"—E. B. BROWNING.

IT is not so easy for us to praise God when our circumstances are to us as a covering of sackcloth and ashes as when they are as the royal robe of unbroken favour and success. Yet the discipline of the one may be as fruitful of blessing as the other if we are found abiding in the will of God. But the wilful prodigal will certainly suffer loss. David's alliance with the Philistines brought him into sore trouble, as all such unholy connections are sure to do. See here—

I. A Crushing Disappointment. "David and his men came to the city, and behold it was burned with fire" (vv. 3, 5). While seeking to help the ungodly he suffers the loss of all that he had. It is the old story in another form of the prodigal son in the far country beginning to be *in want.* "They lifted up their voice and wept," and David was "greatly distressed" (v. 6). In attempting to watch the vineyard of others David failed to keep his own. The enemy's fire is often needed to waken us up to a true sense of our position in the sight of God.

II. A Work of Faith. "But David encouraged himself in the Lord his God" (vv. 6-8). Wives, sons, daughters, cattle, houses, all gone; and the people "spake of stoning him." David now comes to himself, and turns to the Lord as unto a friend in the time of need, for who in such circumstances could *encourage himself* in a stranger. The spirit of faith again sits on the throne of David's heart, as when he faced Goliath, and he is at once another man. Having remembered the Lord his God in affliction, he rises up, like a giant refreshed with new wine, to the dignity of his high calling. Yes. "What time I am afraid I will trust in Thee" (Psa. 56. 3, 4). "He inquired at the Lord" (v. 8). We cannot encourage ourselves much in Him unless we are prepared to submit our way to Him (1 Sam. 28. 6).

III. An Assuring Promise. "Pursue, for thou shalt without fail recover all" (v. 8). This precious word of the Lord sets every fear at rest. Although as yet there is no change in the calamitous circumstances, his heart finds peace. All will be well, for the mouth of the Lord hath spoken it. It is no vain thing, in the day of distress, to encourage yourself in God. Be of good courage, and He shall strengthen thine heart.

IV. A Providential Hap. "They found an Egyptian in the field" (vv. 11, 16). David had the promise of God that all would be recovered. But how was it to be done? Where were now those invading Amalekites? Who will guide them to their rendezvous? This poor unfortunate youth, who had to drop out of the ranks of the Amalekites because of sickness, and was left by his heartless master to perish by the roadside, is the divinely-appointed *means* to the fulfilment of the God-given promise. The means are in His hand as well as the end; and the things that God chooses are "weak and despised" in the eyes of the ungodly, like this dying Egyptian, but mighty to the pulling down of the strongholds of Satan (1 Cor. 1. 27, 28). This little episode, by the way, has a halo of glory about it. Our heavenly David is not ashamed to pick up the world's sick and half-dead castaways, to nourish them into life and health, to engage them as His servants, and to use them for the furtherance of His cause and kingdom, having slain the enmity by the power of His kindness (vv. 11, 12). Such were some of us.

V. A Complete Victory. "David recovered all" (vv. 16-20). Who else could? He had yielded himself to God for this purpose, and having His promise he went in His Name, and proved the faithfulness of His Word. What a prefiguring of Him who was David's Lord, and who encouraged Himself in His God, and came forth to *recover all* that was lost through the sinful failure of the first Adam. His journey was short and the struggle was severe, but the victory was glorious, for Jehovah had laid help upon one that was *mighty*—mighty in sympathy and compassion, mighty in patience and in wisdom, mighty in meekness and in power, mighty in dying and in rising again, mighty to forgive and to save, mighty to burst the gates of death and to open the gates of glory, mighty to RECOVER ALL and to keep and guard all that is recovered.

VI. **A Gracious Offer.** "Behold a present for you" (v. 26). The word "present" is rendered *blessing* in the margin. He who "recovered all" now offers a blessing to all his friends. Those who were not able to go down to the battle, but who faithfully tarried by the stuff, shall in no way lose their reward (v. 24). He who hath redeemed (bought back) the lost inheritance has the alone right to give such gifts to others (Eph. 1. 7). He shall divide the spoil of His unsearchable riches with the strong in faith (Isa. 53. 12). Yes, there is a *blessing for you* in this glorious victory if you claim Him as your Friend and Deliverer, and are faithfully, though feebly, striving to serve Him (Heb. 2. 14, 16).

DAVID CROWNED KING OVER ALL.
2 Samuel 5. 1-5.

"In full and glad surrender we give ourselves to Thee,
   Thine utterly, and only, and evermore to be!
O Son of God, who lovest us, we will be Thine alone,
   And all we are, and all we have, shall henceforth be Thine own."
                                                            —HAVERGAL.

IT was a great day in Israel when all the tribes gathered together in Hebron to make David king over a united people. Perhaps the wisdom and advocacy of Abner had much to do with the bringing about of this happy event (chap. 3. 17-19). The man who had been anointed with the holy oil (Spirit), and who lives by faith in God, will have a path that shineth more and more with the light of His favour. We are reminded here of the time when all the tribes of earth shall confess Jesus Christ as King, and crown Him Lord of all. The turning of the kingdom to David, like the turning of the kingdoms of the world to our God and to Christ, was "according to the Word of the Lord" (1 Chron. 12. 23). We shall note here—

I. **The Confession.** They came to David, as we may come to Christ, making confession of—

1. KINSHIP. "Behold, we are thy bone and thy flesh" (v. 1). To have a "flesh and bone" relationship with a king is surely a great privilege, and a mighty plea in urging a request. Such is the honourable position of every Christian. "For we are members of His body, of His flesh, and of His bones" (Eph. 5. 30). Did not the first Adam say of Eve—a type of the Church—"This is now bone of my bone, and flesh of my flesh" (Gen. 2. 23). This close and living union with Him brings us as members into vital connection one with another (Rom. 12. 5).

2. FAILURE. "In time past, Saul was king over us" (v. 2). There is a ring of sorrowful disappointment in these words. In time past we had an untrustworthy ruler over us, one who broke away from the command of the Lord, and who sought to destroy the influence of His anointed, and to lead us to war against the purposes of God. What a faithful type of the prince of this world, and of the woeful conductor of all those whose minds are blinded by Him. Let the *time past* suffice for the will of the flesh and the work of the Devil.

3. GRACE. "Thou wast he that leddest out and broughtest in Israel" (v. 2). This is a confession of the wisdom and goodness of David's work among them. David, like the Lord Jesus Christ, dealt with them "according to the integrity of his heart and the skilfulness of his hands" (Psa. 70. 72). It is wonderful, in looking back over even our past *sinful* life, how much of the wisdom and grace of our Lord we now see. What we then thought was opposed to our highest interests we can now trace to the skilfulness of His *hands*.

4. FAITH. "The Lord said unto thee, Thou shalt feed My people." By these words the elders made confession of their faith in David as the one appointed by Jehovah to lead them and feed them as a shepherd. He

whom God hath set up shall not be easily overthrown. Hath not Christ, the Shepherd of our souls, been commissioned of the Father to feed His sheep? And shall not we, like these elders, acknowledge our King as He who spreadeth a table for us in the wilderness, and as He who is in Himself the "Living Bread."

5. SURRENDER. "Thou shalt be prince (or ruler) over Israel" (v. 2, R.V.). This language is expressive of perfect subjection to His word and will. Thou shalt rule over us, and our lives are at thy disposal for the carrying out of all the purposes of thy heart. Are we prepared so to yield ourselves as instruments of righteousness to Him who is our Redeemer and King? Can we pray in truth, "Thy will be done *in us*, as it is done *in Heaven*?"

II. The Covenant. "King David made a covenant with them" (v. 3, R.V.). This offer was accepted, and an everlasting bond of union formed. David's league with them was the pledge and promise that his wisdom and power would be exercised for their personal and national well-being. So they anointed David king over Israel. So may it be with us. All who are prepared to crown Jesus King over all will have the benefit of His covenant of promise and power. The crowning of Jesus over our lives means for us a life of victory and blessing.

"CROWN HIM LORD OF ALL."

DAVID RESTORING THE ARK.
2 Samuel 6. 1-16.

"O heart! Weak follower of the weak,
That thou should'st travel land and sea,
In this far place that God to seek
Who long ago had come to thee."—HOUGHTON.

THE Ark was the symbol of the presence of the invisible God among them, and a type of Jesus Christ, God manifest

in the flesh, but Israel had lost it (1 Sam. 4). Sin and iniquity
will always separate between you and your God (Isa. 59. 2).
The same PRESENCE which was the joy and comfort of the
Lord's people was a terror to the ungodly (1 Sam. 5. 8). Separated from Him, "Ichabod" may be written on all we do (1 Sam.
4. 21; John 15. 4, 5). In this chapter we have men taking
up various attitudes towards the Ark, reminding us of the
different positions some take up toward Christ. Notice the—

I. Zealous Formalists. "They set the Ark of God
upon a new cart" (v. 3). The descendants of those carters
are still with us. There is a show of sanctity about
their actions, but they have more pleasure in putting their
religion in new carts—new churches—than carrying it
personally (1 Chron. 15. 15). The Ark had staves, but no
wheels (Exod. 25. 14, 15). The religion of Jesus Christ can
not be driven in a *mechanical* fashion. We may invent
new machinery and organisations and put our faith in them,
but if the *"burden* of the Lord" does not rest on our own
hearts the cause of Christ will make no progress through us.

II. Self-Confident Professor. "Uzzah put forth his
hand to the Ark and took hold of it, and God smote him
for his error" (vv. 6, 7). Familiarity with holy things,
without the heart to appreciate, leads to presumption
(Levit. 10. 1-3). The Ark of God does not need the hand of
man to steady it any more than did the Pillar of Cloud. It is
possible to perish in the place of privilege through putting
forth the *hand* instead of the *heart* (Rom. 10. 3). There be
many like Uzzah, who would defend the faith, and yet show
by their *actions* that they have no faith. They would save the
Bible from falling, and they themselves fall and die unsaved.

III. Timid Seeker. "David was afraid, and said,
How shall the Ark of the Lord come to me?" (v. 9).
David was anxious to have the Ark, as many are anxious
to have salvation, but the holiness and power associated

with it, and a sense of his own unworthiness, made him afraid. How shall this holy, sin-smiting One come to me? How will I ever be able to live in fellowship with such purity and might? Ah, this "how?" has troubled many a seeker after God. The answer is found in the Cross of Christ, for we are reconciled to God by the death of His Son, and our hearts made the habitation of God through the Spirit. Who is able to stand before the holy Lord God? (1 Sam. 6. 20). He who has access *by faith* (Rom. 5. 1, 2).

IV. Humble Believer. "David carried it into the house of Obed-edom, and the Lord blessed Obed-edom and all his house" (vv. 10, 11). Obed-edom's name occurs among the *porters* (1 Chron. 15. 18), but though humble of occupation, he evidently received the Ark joyfully, for from that day salvation came to his house (Luke 19. 5, 6). David was afraid to take the Ark home himself, but he seemingly thought that it would do *no harm* in the humble house of the doorkeeper. The Ark seemed to say, "If any man open the door I will come in, and sup with him, and he with Me." There are many who are afraid to let Christ, the Ark of God, into the home of the heart, lest something else should need to go (Matt. 21. 12).

V. Fearless Witness-Bearers. "They *bare* the Ark of the Lord" (v. 13). They did not invent another "new cart." with elaborate decorations, to help it in its progress, neither did they pay others to do the carrying for them. They boldly took "the *burden* of the Lord," and *bare* it. The cause of Christ is not to be advanced by those who know no more about the personal Saviour than the oxen knew about the Ark. Christ, like the Ark, must be *borne* by those who have been separated unto Him (1 Chron. 15. 14, 15; Acts 9. 15). We need at times to have the Ark on our shoulder, in the street as well as in the house. In the eyes of some the Ark is always out of its place, unless when it is out of sight.

VI. **Joyful Confessor.** "David danced before the
Lord with all his might" (v. 14). His mourning is now
turned into dancing, his sackcloth has been exchanged
for the girdle of gladness (Psa. 30. 11). Obed-edom's
blessing has brought the blessing of a strengthened faith to
him. Perfect love casts out fear. The presence of God
is here triumphing through sacrifice (v. 13). So we joy
in God through our Lord Jesus Christ, by whom we have
now received the reconciliation (Rom. 5. 11, R.V.).

VII. **Sneering Fault-Finder.** "Michal saw King
David dancing *before the Lord*, and she despised him in
her heart" (v. 16). The things of the Spirit of God are
foolishness to the natural man (1 Cor. 2. 14). In their
ignorance and self-conceit they mistake glad men for mad
men (Acts 2. 13). Any fool can be a fault-finder, but it
takes more than the world can give to make a man "dance
before the Lord." The giddy worldlings dance before one
another and become fools before the Lord. Those who
stare through their windows with the eyes of a Michal can
see no beauty or glory in the Ark (Christ) of God, no cause
for joy in its (His) coming. They hide, as it were, their
faces from Him. When Christ comes will He find you among
the formalists, the fearful, the faithful, or the fault-finding?

DAVID AND MEPHIBOSHETH,; OR, SAVED BY GRACE.
2. Samuel 9.

"Man's forgiveness may be true and sweet,
  But yet he stoops to give it. More complete
Is love that lays forgiveness at thy feet,
  And pleads with thee to raise it! Only Heaven
Means *Crowned*, not *Vanquished*, when it says *Forgiven*!"
                                                —A. PROCTER.

MUCH food for reflection might be found in comparing this
chapter with Romans 9-11. The purposes of God concerning

Israel, as revealed in these chapters, ought to be better
known than they are among believers everywhere. We
might observe here—

I. Mephibosheth's Condition; or, The Sinner's Need.

1. FEARFULNESS. From the fact that such inquiry had
to be made, we may learn that Mephibosheth was hiding
from the king. They dread God who know not His love
(v. 1). Hiding from his best friend. So like the sinner
(Gen. 3. 8).

2. DESTITUTION. "In the house of Machir (sold) in
Lodebar" (without pasture) (v. 4). How true! The
rebellious dwell in a dry land (Psa. 68. 6). Away from
God the sinner is but lodging in the house of poverty
(Isa. 44. 20; Luke 15. 16).

3. HELPLESSNESS. "Lame on both feet" (v. 13). At
that time ye were *without strength* (Rom. 5. 6). With regard to the things of God the unregenerated are heartless,
handless, footless. Any ability we have is God-given
(1 Peter 4. 11).

II. David's Purpose; or, The Love of God. He
wished to show kindness to the house of Saul (his enemy)
for *Jonathan's* sake (the gift of God). What an illustration
of 2 Corinthians 5. 19. This—

1. LOVE WAS SPONTANEOUS. It was the voluntary
impulse of a kind and merciful heart. "God is Love."
God takes the first step towards man's redemption (Eph. 1.
4; 1 Peter 1. 2). He *so loved* the world that He gave His
Son. "We love Him *because* He *first* loved us."

2. LOVE WAS GRACIOUS. It sought out the undeserving.
It offered favour to an enemy. While we were yet enemies
Christ died for us. It was, indeed, the "Gospel of Grace"
that David's servant carried to the poor cripple. What

G   Vol. 5

a privilege to belong to such "sent ones" (v. 5). This is
a beautiful illustration of Romans 10. 14, 15. What is
the meaning of John 20. 21?

3. LOVE WAS SELF-SACRIFICING. "I have given all that
pertained to Saul" (v. 9). This was a great gift, but it was
for Jonathan's sake. In John 3. 16 we see a greater gift,
and with this gift comes the pledge of all things (Rom.
8. 32; 2 Peter 1. 3).

III. **Mephibosheth's Faith; or, Salvation Enjoyed.**
He—

1. BELIEVED THE MESSAGE. So proved his faith by
obeying the call. "He came unto David" (v. 6). See
2 Chron. 30. 10, 11). The Master is come, and calleth
for thee. We test the truth of the Gospel when
we believe it.

2. HUMBLED HIMSELF. "He fell on his face." So well
he may. He confesses himself to be as a "dead dog" (v. 8).
You hath he quickened who were *dead in sin*—worse
than a dead dog. The *goodness* of God leads to repentance
(2 Cor. 5. 14).

3. WAS ACCEPTED. "David said, Fear not, I will show
thee kindness" (v. 7). The God who invites will surely
receive (John 7. 37). Think of His kindness towards us
through Christ Jesus (Eph. 2. 7).

4. WAS ADOPTED. "He shall eat at my table as
one of the king's sons" (v. 11). Although he was
lame on both his feet he sat continually at the king's
table. His table of mercy covers many an infirmity
(1 John 3. 1, 2).

5. WAS MADE AN HEIR. "David said, I will restore thee
all the land of Saul thy father" (v. 7). From poverty to
plenty through the grace of the king (1 Peter 1. 3, 4).
By grace are ye saved through faith (Eph. 2. 8).

DAVID'S FALL AND FORGIVENESS.
2 Samuel 12. 1-14.

"The spark, self-kindled from within,
Which, blown upon, will blind thee with its glare,
Or smothered, stifle thee with noisome air."—COLERIDGE.

"LET him that thinketh he standeth take heed lest he fall"
(1 Cor. 10-12). Backsliding never begins with an overt
act of guilt, but in the secret *thought* of the heart. "Thou
hast left thy first *love*, therefore thou art fallen" (Rev.
2. 4-6). Christians may fall out of fellowship with God,
although they may not fall out of their relationship as
children, any more than the prodigal in Luke 15 could fall
from his *sonship*. There was a vast difference in results
between the fall of Saul and that of David, or between the
denial of Peter and that of Judas.

I. **The Nature of it.** David was guilty of adultery
and murder (chap. 11). The killing of Uriah was a subtle
device to cover the shame of his sin with Bathsheba.
Oh, into what depths a child of God may fall in one
unguarded moment! Here note the faithfulness of the
Bible in exposing the faults and failings of its heroes.
David is not the only holy man that has been dragged
into the mire of sin through the influence of a *look* (chap.
11. 2). Eve *saw* before she took the forbidden fruit. Lot's
backsliding began when he "*looked* toward Sodom," and a
look was the ruin of his wife. The first step that led to the
destruction of the old world was taken when the "Sons of
God looked on the daughters of men" (Gen. 6). The
words of Christ are very searching in this connection (see
Matt. 5. 28). As we stand in the glare of this searchlight
from Heaven, who will be the first to cast a stone at David?

II. **The Fruit of it.** "By this deed thou hast given
great occasion to the enemies of the Lord to blaspheme;
the child also shall surely die" (v. 14). The marrying of

Bathsheba before the child was born did not cover the guilt of his sin in the sight of God (chap. 11. 27). How sad when the behaviour of a professed servant of God fills the mouths of His enemies with arguments against Him and His cause! The misdeeds of Christians gives the enemy occasion to say things that blaspheme *His Holy Name*. Has He not said that "the heathen shall know that I am the Lord, when I shall be sanctified *in you before their eyes*" (Ezek. 36. 23; see also Rom. 2. 24).

III. **The Conviction of it.** "Thou art the man" (v. 7). This arrow was not shot at random. Those who are living in sin are not to be convicted with a mere *hint*, they have to be "pierced in the heart" (Acts 2. 37). As Christ was pierced for our sins, so must we be pierced with conviction. David's *secret* sin was naked before God. Like the sin of Cain and Achan, no human device could cover it. The message sent by Nathan was singularly apt, as God's messages always are; and like Latimer and Knox, he feared not the royal wrath. When a man has a message from God his manner will be bold and his speech unequivocal. Was it not thus with Jesus Christ?

IV. **The Confession of it.** "David said, I have sinned against the Lord" (v. 13). He makes no excuse, he mentions no extenuating circumstances, he blames no one for betraying his secret to the prophet. He is too deeply wounded to offer any resistance. He does not say, I have sinned against Uriah, but I have sinned *against the Lord*. When a man has discovered that he has "sinned against Heaven" (Luke 15. 18), he will cease justifying himself (Psa. 51. 4). When the wife of John Brown, the martyr, asked the murderer Claverhouse how he would answer for this day's work, he sneeringly replied, "As for man, I will answer to him; as for God, I will take Him into my own hands." A dead conscience makes a man as arrogant as Satan himself. Job said, "Because I am vile, what shall I answer Thee?" (chap.40. 4). "God be merciful to me a sinner" is the incense that rises from the live coals of a burning conviction (Luke 18. 13).

V. **The Forgiveness of it.** "Nathan said, The Lord hath put away thy sin" (v. 13). It is still true that "If we confess our sins, He is faithful and just to forgive us" (1 John 1. 9). How sweetly David sings of this abounding mercy of God in the thirty-second Psalm. The prophet Micah exults in the same joyful note. "Who is a God like unto Thee, that pardoneth iniquity" (Micah 7. 18).

1. IT WAS IMMEDIATE. As soon as confession was made, so soon was his pardon declared. Behold in this the *readiness* of God to bless, as soon as the heart of man is in a right state to receive it.

2. IT WAS COMPLETE. "The Lord hath *put away* thy sin." Who shall ever find what God hath *put away*? God never upbraids, where there is honest confession, but by the power of His omnipotent grace, He sweeps the hell-born thing for ever from before His face. ''Behold the Lamb of God which taketh away the sin of the world.'' (John 1. 29).

3. IT WAS ACCOMPANIED WITH PROMISE. "Thou shalt not die." The forgiveness of God is associated with the promise of life (Acts 13. 38, 39; Eph. 1. 6, 7; John 5. 24). He forgives, then He *assures* the forgiven one with His Word. Although we should never hear a voice, as it were from Heaven, saying to us as it said to John Bunyan, "Will you have your sins and go to Hell, or forsake them and go to Heaven." Yet are we not justified until we confess our sins and believe on the Lord Jesus Christ.

DAVID AND ABSALOM.

2 Samuel 13-18.

"Seek to be pleasant, seek to be winning,
Rudeness and sourness are kin to sinning;
Seek to bring sunshine wherever you go,
Have faith in a bright word more than a blow.

Seek to be '*care* full' for nothing at all,
Receiving buoyant whatever befall;
Seek still to show that He healeth your scars,
That trials bring joy as night bringeth stars.''

—GROSART.

DAVID'S terrible fall through sin may have had much to do with the fostering of pride and self-confidence in the formation of the character of Absalom. No man liveth unto himself. The fruit of a parent's iniquity may have a resurrection and a judgment in his offspring. The story of Absalom is the story of a prodigal perishing in the far country; it is a beacon of warning to all young men in danger of being lured to ruin through the lust of the eye and the pride of life. Let us take a survey of this young man's career and note his—

I. **Natural Advantages.** These were exceptionally great and favourable. Not only was he the son of a king, but in his personal appearance "There was none to be so much praised as Absalom for his beauty: from the sole of his foot even to the crown of his head there was *no blemish* in him" (chap. 14. 25). But what a terrible contrast there was in his moral and spiritual nature, "From the sole of the foot even unto the head there was *no soundness* in it" (Isa. 1. 6). Hereditary advantages or disadvantages are not sufficient in themselves to make or mar true nobility of character, but a favourable start may count for much in the race of life. Absalom had a wide door of glorious possibilities opened for him in that he was able to command the affections of the men of Israel (chap. 15. 6).

But outward appearance counts for nothing in the sight of God (1 Sam. 16. 7).

II. **Revengeful Spirit.** Absalom's cold-blooded murder of his brother Amnon *"two full years"* after Amnon's vile and cruel deed had been done reveals a dogged and remorseless spirit (chap. 14. 23-28). Time and circumstances had no power to cool the fire of his unforgiving temper. His words were like honey and butter, while deceit lurked in his heart (chap. 15. 4). Outward beauty and inward deformity are for ever characteristic of the hypocrite "whited sepulchres." See the whiting process described in Romans 10. 3.

III. **Renewed Opportunity.** Absalom who had fled to Geshur to escape the wrath of his father is now after the lapse of several years restored to the favour of the king through the influence of his cousin Joab (chap. 14. 33). In the providence of God he has another chance of making a fresh and more honourable start in life. How momentous are the consequences that hang on this renewed day of grace! Will he choose the narrow path that leads to life, or the broad self-made way that leads to destruction? Are there not many young men in our towns and cities to-day who are lightly esteeming a *repeated* privilege that is heavily laden with eternal issues. "Behold, now is the accepted time" (2 Cor. 6. 2).

IV. **Self-Aggrandisement.** "After this Absalom prepared him chariots and horses, and fifty men to run before him" (chap. 15. 1-6). The forgiving grace of the father, instead of mellowing his heart into thankful submission, seemed only to give greater license to his unbridled will and presumption. An *unregenerate* sinner will turn the grace of God into lasciviousness by taking all the favour and blessing God can give him, that these might minister to his own pride and self-glory. In after years

Adonijah played the same proud, ruinous game (1 Kings 1. 5). He that exalteth *himself* shall be abased (2 Cor. 10. 18).

V. Open Rebellion. "Then ye shall say, Absalom reigneth" (chap. 15. 10). The hypocritical mask is thrown off, and the secret purposes of his heart are revealed. He declares himself an enemy to the government of David his father, and an aspirant for the position and authority of the king. It is most suggestive that the two hundred men whom he had called, and who went in their simplicity, *"Knew not anything"* (chap. 15. 11). Open rebellion against the will and ways of God is the ripened fruit of a secret, self-centred life. As long as ungodly men can gain some worldly advantages by their false pretensions they will refrain from manifesting their true inward dislike to the rule of God. But the day is coming when every *hidden thing* will be revealed.

VI. Untimely Death. "Behold I saw Absalom hanged in an oak" (chap. 18. 9-14). In riding into the wood to escape "the servants of David" he rode into the jaws of death, for that head of pride and beauty was caught between two branches of an oak, and the mule in whom he trusted "went from under him." Those who fight against God have forces to reckon with that they know not of; their mule, whatever that may be, will one day *go from under them*, leaving them helpless *"between* Heaven and earth,"* as utterly unfit for either. The man who built his house on the sand had the object of his confidence taken from under him too. It is very different with the redeemed of the Lord (Psa. 40. 2). Joab's treatment of the unfortunate pretender was cruel and ghastly. "Vengeance is Mine, saith the

Lord, I will repay." Surely the triumph of the wicked is short.

VII. **Ironical Monument.** "Now Absalom had reared up for himself a pillar, and called it after his own name" (chap. 18. 18). He had set up this *pillar*, perhaps to mark his last resting-place and to perpetuate his name, but instead they "cast him into a great pit in the wood, and laid a very great *heap of stones* upon him" (chap. 18. 17). His utter disregard for parental and divine authority prepared for him the burial of a dog. His pillar, like the pillar of salt on the plain of Sodom, became a monument of the judgment of God against disobedience. It was another tower of Babel on a small scale. In Luke 18. 11 we see another man busy rearing up his pillar, but their name is legion (Rom. 10. 3).

VIII. **Sorrowful Father.** "O my son Absalom! would God I had died for thee, O Absalom, my son, my son!" (chap. 18. 33). The only one that was able seemingly to shed tears for Absalom was that one who was most grievously insulted by him. What a revelation is here of the depth and tenderness of the love that was sinned against. There were doubtless several elements that went to add pungency to David's grief, viz., his own aggravating fall, the painful circumstances of the death, and Joab's disregard for the king's command (v. 5). But what shall we say of the love of God, who, while we were yet sinners, rebels, sent His only begotten Son to *die for us*? Herein is love, a love that willeth not the death of any, a love that has wept over the erring (Luke 19. 41). A love that is ready to forgive. A love that has already suffered the sharp pangs of death in our stead; but, alas, a love that is as lightly esteemed by many to-day as David's was by Absalom.

DAVID'S SONG OF DELIVERANCE.

2 Samuel 22. 17-20.

"O strengthen me, that while I stand
Firm on the Rock, and strong in Thee,
I may stretch out a loving hand
To wrestlers with a troubled sea."
—F. R. HAVERGAL.

THIS Song of Deliverance is in itself one of the most marvellous deliverances that has ever been achieved by mortal lips. It is the singing of one whose heart has been attuned to the harmony of Heaven. What depth of rich personal experience is revealed in these glowing exultant words (v. 1-7). A full sense of the greatness of God's salvation is enough to make the dumb to sing with a sweetness that even the eloquent worldling cannot approach. Confiding our attention to the few verses indicated above, we remark about this deliverance that it was—

I. Needed. Concerning his enemies, David says, "They were *too strong for me*" (v. 18). Too strong for *him*, but not too strong for the God that was with him. The world, the flesh, and the Devil are all too strong for us, but greater is He that is in us than all who can be against us. Those who fight in their own strength will find out to their sorrowful loss that the enemy is too strong for them.

II. Divine. "He sent from above" (v. 17). The need was so very great that saving help could only come from *above*. Help came from above when God sent Samuel to David with the divine call and the holy oil. He laid help upon One that is mighty when He sent His Son to seek and to save the lost (John 3. 16). "Except a man be born *from above*, he cannot see the kingdom of God (John 3. 3, margin).

III. Personal. "He took *me*" (v. 17). This is a sweet

little testimony. He might have taken others and left me, but *"He took me."* The hand of God's mighty redeeming power was stretched out to grip me and to take me from the "horrible pit" (Psa. 40. 2), and out of the "deep mire" (Psa. 69. 1, 2). The salvation of Christ is a very *personal* matter, and, blessed be His Name, all who trust Him will be taken by Him.

IV. **Great.** "He drew me out of *many waters*" (v. 17). The Lord drew David out of the waters of *danger* when He saved him again and again out of the murderous hand of Saul. He drew him out of the waters of *affliction* when the crown was put on his head. He was drawn out of the waters of *guilt* when Nathan pronounced the forgiveness of his sin (2 Sam. 12. 13). The salvation of God is a *drawing out* of the kingdom of darkness into the kingdom of His dear Son. The waters of affliction and persecution may still flow in upon us, but out of them all our God can draw us. HE *drew me*, or I would certainly have been overwhelmed like the Egyptians. "Salvation is of the Lord."

V. **Hearty.** "Because He *delighted* in me" (v. 20). His salvation was not only a matter of power, but of *love*. "God so *loved* the world that He gave." This a sweet note in the song of the saved, "He delighted in me." We often find this out only after we have had our feet established on the rock of His eternal truth. This *delight* does not spring from anything in us by nature, but has its source in the fathomless generosity of His own character. He delighteth in mercy. Herein is love.

VI. **Satisfying.** "He brought me forth into a *large* place" (v. 20). Some are afraid to be drawn out of the many waters of their sins lest they should be brought into such a *narrow* place that all the joy of their life would be crushed out of them. Those who, by the grace of God, have been brought into the kingdom of God have been brought into a very large place, for this kingdom is bounded by eternity. They have been brought into the family of God, and are the heirs of eternal life. This "large place" may surely be taken as referring also to the enlarged possibilities that open up for us in Christ Jesus as "kings and priests unto God."

DAVID'S OFFERING.
2 Samuel 23. 15-17.

"What Thou has given me, Lord, here I bring Thee,
    Odour and light, and the magic of gold;
Feet which must follow Thee, lips which must sing Thee,
    Limbs which must ache for Thee ere they grow old."
                                                —C. KINGSLEY.

As Herbert hath said, "My God must have my best." There is something sublimely pathetic about this simple act of David in pouring out a drink of water as an offering unto the Lord. It was very natural for the thirsty warrior, while lodging in the hold of Adullam, to long for some water from that crystal spring at Bethlehem, where in earlier days he had so often quenched his burning thirst. First impressions are not easily effaced. The privileges of youth may be eagerly longed for in after days, and a higher value set upon them when they can scarcely be had. See then what David offered. It was a—

I. **Common Thing.** "Water" (v. 15). We may find sacrifices for God in the smallest details of life. We need not be always looking for some great thing to do in order to show our hearts' devotion to our Lord and Master. With every daily mercy there comes the opportunity of glorifying God. Little quiet moments of time may be turned into acceptable sacrifices unto God.

II. **Costly Thing.** It was water secured at the "jeopardy of their lives" (v. 17). A common thing made precious, because purchased with a great price. Such were all of us who have been redeemed with the precious Blood of Christ. David was sufficiently large-hearted not to offer to God as a sacrifice that which cost him nothing (chap. 24. 24). There are those who reserve for God the torn reputation, the *lame* life, and the *sick* days (Mal. 1. 13). They give to God that which they no longer want—a diseased body and a sin-smitten soul. "Honour the Lord with thy substance" (Prov. 3. 9).

III. **Desirable Thing.** "David longed for the water of Bethlehem" (v. 15). In making this offering David was not giving that for which he felt he had no need, for his whole soul longed to have it. It is easy for us to offer God that for which we have no longer any *capacity* to enjoy. Many readily part with their goods for charitable purposes when death is looking them in the face, who while healthy and vigorous held them greedily with an iron hand. There is no *sacrifice* in this. In pouring out the water the royal shepherd was giving to the Lord that which was, at that moment, the *best* he had. Present *yourself* unto God. Perhaps this may be your most *desirable* thing.

IV. **Consecrated Thing.** He "poured it out *unto the Lord.*" He refused to use it for the gratification of his own longings. Even *water* spilt on the ground after this holy fashion is not lost; it brings forth the peaceable fruits of righteousness. It is a making deep the ditches within our own natures for a mightier filling with the "water of life" that comes from the very throne of God. Everything becomes holy that is given to the Lord. "What shall I render unto the Lord for all His benefits?"

V. **Thing that could not be taken back.** "Water spilt; that could not be gathered again." Who ever thought of taking back for their own use the sacrifice that was laid on the altar? What was given to God was His, and His for ever. David was perfectly conscious that in *pouring out* the water *unto the Lord* it could never more be his own. Do we realise what this means? If we have given ourselves unto the Lord, then we are *"not our own,"* and it is the grossest sacrilege to take back for our own self-gratification that which belongs only to God. "Ye are not your own, for ye are bought with a price: therefore glorify God in your body, and in your spirit, which are God's" (1 Cor. 6. 19, 20; see also 2 Cor. 5. 14, 15).

DAVID'S CHOICE.
2 Samuel 24. 1-14.

"God loves to work in wax—not marble. Let Him find
When He would mould thine heart, material to His mind."
—TRENCH.

"WEAK and feeble hands may touch God's great hand while groping blindly in the dark." These are not the exact words of Longfellow, but the suggestive substance. In numbering the people David was groping blindly for the hand of human strength when he touched the divine hand of judgment. In this chapter we have before us a—

I. **Subtle Temptation.** "He moved David to say, Go, number Israel" (v. 1). This *move* evidently came from the Devil, for the author of the Chronicles tells us that "Satan stood up *against Israel*, and provoked David to number Israel" (1 Chron. 21. 1). It was to Israel's own hurt and defect that their number and strength was depended on. It is ever the cunning device of Satan to get us to trust in our own strength, for well he knows that if we do that he will succeed in "standing up against us" (Eph. 6. 11). "It is not by might (numbers), nor by power (human influence), but by My Spirit, saith the Lord" (Zech. 4. 6). We may safely "count our blessings," and count on His promises, but to count on our own wisdom and strength is to lean on a broken reed.

II. Full Confession. "David's heart smote him after he had numbered the people, and he said unto the Lord, I have sinned greatly" (v. 10). Joab's glowing report that there were in David's united kingdom "thirteen hundred thousand valiant men that drew sword" (v. 9) brought no feeling of relief to the sin-smitten heart of the king. What were these if God was not for him? All our natural gifts and powers of intellect however great, all our experiences however rich and varied, will avail us nothing in the work of God if the power of the Holy Spirit is awanting. Perhaps much of our failure in the past has been due to the numbering of our own capabilities, to an ignoring of the Holy Ghost. We number our organisations, our meetings, our people, and our pounds, but say, How much do we count on the POWER OF GOD? Might we not pray with David, "O Lord, take away the iniquity of thy servant, for I have done very foolishly?"

III. Terrible Offer. "Thus saith the Lord, I offer thee three things, choose thee one of them" (vv. 12, 13). The *three* things were all equally fearful, although the length of duration was very different. "Seven years' famine," "three months' fleeing before the enemy," or "three days' pestilence." Yielding to the tempter has brought to David a sorrowful alternative. The wages of sin is *death* in the believer as well as in the ungodly. It would seem that all three judgments were due owing to David's sin; but God, who "delighteth in mercy," gave Him his choice of *one*. The *three* judgments are most suggestive of the fruits of disobedience and dishonouring God. Soul *hunger*, soul *defect*, and soul *disease*. God does not promise to give us our choice as to how He will chastise us for our pride and unbelief, but let us take heed lest there be in any of us such an evil heart, for *sin* will surely find us out.

IV. **God-honouring Choice.** "David said, Let us fall
into the hands of the Lord, for His mercies are great"
(v. 14). David had sinned against God in choosing to number
the people, now he would honour God in allowing Him to
choose for him. God's mighty hand was uplifted to smite,
and the penitent king saw it coming down with terrible
force, but he looked beyond the awful sword-girt arm, into
Jehovah's gracious heart, and took refuge in His mercy.
He would rather anchor his soul in the mercies of a
righteous, sin-hating God than "fall into the hand of man."
He knew that the mercies of the wicked are cruel. The
wounds of a friend are better than the kisses of a traitor.
Although God's *arm* is strong to smite, His *love* is strong to
save. The choice God offers now in grace is between life
and death, between retribution and salvation, Heaven and
Hell. Why should any one now say, "I am in a great
strait," when the only open way of escape from the
vengeance of God against sin is in "His mercies which are
great," in Christ Jesus, who bore our sins in His own body
on the tree. "I flee to Thee to hide me" (Psa. 143. 9).

ADONIJAH; or, THE CONQUERED REBEL.
1 Kings 1. 5-9, 41-53.

"On the verge of never-ending woe
Man doubting stands. Yet plum'd with pride the while,
Folding his arms in self-admired repose,
Cased in self-confidence."—WILLIAMS.

ADONIJAH was a man with a beautiful name, "*My Lord is
Jehovah,*" but with a heart stuffed with grace-withering
pride. David's stormy life was about to close. The
winsome Absalom had been suddenly cut off in the midst
of his vain-glorious career. Now the handsome-looking
Adonijah aspires to the throne of his father. Like many
another child of beauty, he had evidently been half spoiled
through a father's indulgence (v. 6; Prov. 29. 15).

I. See him Exalted. "He exalted himself, saying, I will be king" (v. 5). "He that *exalteth himself* shall be abased." (Luke 18. 14). Satan's lie, "Ye shall be as gods" (Gen. 3. 5), is ever a tempting bait to the proud heart. He prepared him chariots and horsemen, and spread his great bribery feast, but "Solomon he called not." Yet he who was allowed no part in all his plans and purposes was the one chosen of God to prevail. It is ever the sinner's way to exalt himself, to the exclusion of Him whom God hath sent to bless (Acts 3. 26). "Pride goeth before a fall."

II. See him Ignored. David said, "Assuredly Solomon shall reign after me" (v. 30). "And they blew the trumpets and said, God save King Solomon" (v. 39). While Adonijah was exalting *himself*, Solomon, the despised and rejected, was being exalted, and anointed by both priest and prophet (v. 45). There is another King, one Jesus,. whose right it is to reign, and whom God hath exalted Lord over all, blessed for ever. All who exalt themselves against Him will find that their claims and pretentions will be as utterly disregarded by God as were those of Adonijah by David. Those who, in the pride and self-confidence, exalt themselves against the Christ of God will assuredly waken up in the end to find themselves rebels and liars, deceived and defeated. Let the would-be *independent* remember that there is Another who is quite independent of their independence.

III. See him Awakened. It must have been a terrible shock to Adonijah when Jonathan came hastily with the news that, "Verily our lord King David hath made Solomon king, and that he *sitteth on the throne* of the kingdom" (vv. 42-46). Jonathan was a faithful messenger. He told the whole truth, keeping back nothing. And if his message cut the young Pretender to the heart, proving him to be a self-deceived rebel, he was not to blame for that.

The Gospel that was a savour of life to the followers of
Solomon was a savour of death to Adonijah and his ad-
herents (v. 49). The moral is plain. Jesus sitteth on the
Throne of His Father. All who exalt themselves against
Him are rebels. The message is, "He that believeth not
is condemned already." Saul, on the way to Damascus,
had quite as sudden an awakening as Adonijah (Acts 9. 3-5).

IV. **See him Saved.** Here we might note—

1. THE CONSTRAINING CAUSE. "Adonijah *feared* because
of Solomon" (v. 50). Why should he not *fear*? The man
who has been made to see himself an alien to the good
purposes of God has surely great cause for fear. There is
no living creature under Heaven that will not seek safety
through the feeling of fear. Those who sneer at the
thought of being saved through *fear* have usually no
objections to put up their umbrellas through fear of getting
wet when overtaken by a shower. Where there is a true
sense of danger there will be fear. "Noah, moved with
fear, built the Ark" (Heb. 11. 7).

2. THE PLACE OF REFUGE. "He caught hold on the horns
of the altar" (v. 50). Neither the altar not its horns
would have much attraction for him before the fear of
death laid hold on him. It requires a sense of sin and
guilt to make the place of atonement desirable and precious.
"The preaching of the Cross is, to them that perish,
foolishness, but to the sin-convicted soul it is the
saving "power of God." In laying hold of the *horns*
of the altar he was *binding himself*, as it were, a
sacrifice unto God (Psa. 118. 27).

> "Other Refuge have I none,
> Hangs my helpless soul on Thee. "

3. THE CHANGED LIFE. "He came and bowed himself to
King Solomon" (v. 53). In verse 5 we see him *"exalting*
himself,*" but now he *"bowed* himself." The rebel is

suddenly transformed into a servant. Solomon, the king of
peace, bids him go in peace. He has found peace with the
king through the altar of sacrifice. The life that was forfeited because of sin has now been saved by grace, that it
might become the servant of righteousness (Luke 1. 74, 75).

SOLOMON'S CHOICE; or, FULLNESS OF BLESSING.

1 Kings 3. 1-16.

"True wisdom is not gotten, but is given;
Not dug out of the earth, but dropped from Heaven:
Heavenly, not earthly, is the brightness of it."—LYTTON.

IT was said of Solomon that "the Lord loved him" (2 Sam.
12. 24). How fitting it is to find it stated now that "Solomon loved the Lord" (v. 3). Surely the love of God for
us should awaken in our hearts love to Him. It was a
very exceptional opportunity that came to Solomon when
God said to him, "Ask what I shall give thee." Such
special privileges, laden with Almighty and eternal possibilities, don't usually come within the reach of any of
God's servants without some unusually solemn preparation.
It was certainly so with Solomon.

He had gone to Gibeon, a journey of seven miles, and
had a long and solemn time of great sacrificing. "One
thousand burnt-offerings" he has seen laid on the altar.
His whole mind and heart were filled with thoughts of the
holiness of God, the horribleness of sin, and the great holo-
caust atonement. As Solomon lay down that night to
sleep, with a deep sense of his own weakness and unworthiness, God appeared to him in a dream, with such an offer
of grace as was sufficient for all his needs. If we would be
honoured of God, then our souls and in our substance
we must honour him. We shall consider—

I. **The Divine Offer.** "God said, Ask what I shall give
thee" (v. 5). Let us pause and think of who it is that

makes this offer. This *"I"* is the *I* that filleth eternity.
It is the offer of Him who is the Creator and Possessor of
all, whose Name is Holy, and whose nature is Love.
Think again of the abounding generosity of the offer.
"What I shall *give thee."* Only one chance like this is
needed to enrich a soul for time and eternity. In making
this offer God was as it were laying all the wealth of His
Divine Character and Kingdom at the feet of Solomon,
that he might be filled out of all the fullness of God.
But does the Lord come to *us* with an offer like this?
Yea, He has done more, for in the gift of His Son the
whole wealth of "His unsearchable riches" lie *continually
before us* for our daily appropriation. Even without
our *asking,* yea, while we were yet sinners, He gives
His all in dying for us.

II. **The Wise Choice.** "Give Thy servant an understanding heart" (v. 9). It was not enough that he should
have the *opportunity* of choosing; he must make up his
mind and speak out his request. Every Gospel hearer
has the opportunity of making such a choice, but how few
like Solomon seek the *hearing* heart (*margin*). It was a
wise choice, because it—

1. COVERED ALL HIS NEED (vv. 7, 8). A heart quick to
hear the guiding, comforting words of God would strengthen
and sustain him, as a "little child" set by the grace of
God "in the midst of a great people." If any man lack
wisdom, let him ask of God (James 1. 5). "Christ is made
of God unto us wisdom," etc. In choosing Him we choose
that which covers all our need.

2. PLEASED GOD (v. 10). It pleased God, because
what he asked was not for any mere selfish advantage,
but for His honour and the good of His people.
We always ask amiss when we would consume it
on our own pleasures (James 4. 3, *margin*). Are not

our prayers often choked with the cares and anxieties of self-interest?

III. The Abundant Answer.

1. HE GOT WHAT HE ASKED. "I have given thee a wise and an understanding heart" (v. 12). God alone can work in us such a *gift* as this. This is eternal life to *know* Him. The promises of God are meant to be claimed and definitely fulfilled in the experience of the believer. Ask and ye shall receive.

2. HE GOT MORE THAN HE ASKED. "I have also given thee that which thou hast not asked, both riches and honour" (v. 13). He sought *first* the Kingdom of God, and all other things were *added*, and added in such plentitude that Solomon exceeded all the kings of the earth for *riches* (1 Kings 10. 23). He that findeth Christ findeth wisdom, and happy is that man, for riches and honour, and length of days are his (Prov. 3. 13, 16). "If ye abide in Me, and My words abide in you, ye shall ask what ye will, and it shall be done unto you." Lord, give me the "hearing heart," that Thy will may be done *in* me, and that the people may be blessed *through* me.

A ROYAL INQUIRER.

1 Kings 10. 1-13.

"You are not guilty because you are ignorant, but you are guilty when you resign yourself to ignorance."—MAZZINI.

THE coming of the Queen of Sheba to Solomon may be a fore-glimmering of that time when a "Greater than Solomon" shall reign, and when kings shall come to the *brightness* of His rising (Isa. 60. 1-3). The wisdom of Solomon was the wisdom of God, from whom every good and perfect gift cometh (chap. 3. 12). There would be

more anxious inquirers everywhere if there were more
of God's servants in possession of this rare gift—
a *"hearing heart"* (chap. 3. 9, *margin*). The Queen
of Sheba is mentioned by our Lord and Saviour,
as a warning and example to those who, after, should
hear of the wisdom of Him who is the wisdom of
God (Matt. 12. 42).

I. **She Heard.** "The Queen of Sheba heard of the
fame of Solomon" (v. 1). It should be specially noted
that this fame was "concerning the Name of the Lord."
In the report which came to the ears of the "Queen of the
South" the wisdom of Solomon was vitally connected with
the *Name of Jehovah.* Is it not so also with the Gospel
which has been brought to our ears? There is a oneness
between the wisdom and power of Jesus Christ, and the
NAME or character of the Eternal God and Father. The
secret of His fame was concerning the Name of His Father.
Blessed are the ears that so hear (Matt. 13. 16).

II. **She Inquired.** "She came to prove him with hard
questions" (v. 1). She did not make light of it (Matt.
22. 5). She felt that this Heaven-born wisdom of Solomon's
might bring light and comfort to her own beclouded mind;
and although she hardly believed all that she heard she
would satisfy herself with a personal inquiry. So she came
just as she was, with a "very great train" of camels and
servants, and "communed with him of *all that was in her
heart*" (v. 2). She was both an anxious and an honest
inquirer. Go thou and do likewise. You have *heard* of
the saving fame of Jesus. Go and prove Him by telling
Him all that is in thine heart. You have more encouragement than this queen had, for you have a pressing *invitation* (Matt. 11. 28).

III. **She Received.** "Solomon told her all her questions" (v. 3). There was nothing hid from the king that

she required to know.   We cannot believe that her
questions were in the nature of puzzles.   Such trifles
would be entirely beneath the dignity of the wisdom
of God.   We believe that her riddles contained real
intellectual difficulties, and that the darkness in her
mind was dispelled by the light of Heaven.   Oh,
how she would marvel as her difficulties one after
another disappeared in the dawning of the truth of
God as revealed by the Lord's anointed!   So shall it
be when a troubled soul communes with Jesus.   He is
the Truth.   He knows what is in man, and all the
treasures of wisdom and knowledge are hid in Him.

IV. **She was Humbled.**   "When the Queen of Sheba
had seen all there was no more spirit in her" (vv. 4, 5).
When she contrasted Solomon's wisdom, his house, his
table, his servants, and his way up with her own, all her
pride and self-esteem withered up within her.   There was
no room for boasting left; it was excluded by the law of
heavenly grace and wisdom.   When the self-righteous Saul
of Tarsus met the Lord of Life on the way to Damascus,
and was made to see His power and glory, there was no
more spirit in him to think of himself more highly than
he ought to think.   It will ever be a humbling to us when
our own wisdom and righteousness is brought into contrast
with His.

V. **She Confessed.**   "She said *to the king*, It was a
true report that I heard. . . Howbeit I believed not the
words, *until I came*, and mine eyes had seen it; and,
behold, the half was not told me" (vv. 6, 7).   Who hath
believed our report?   The Gospel of the Lord Jesus Christ,
concerning His wisdom, power, and glory, is true, whether
men believe it or not.   Like the Queen of Sheba, we cannot
understand or share personally in this heavenly wisdom
until we come.   But if we have come and got our own eyes

opened, let us not be ashamed or afraid to make full confession to the honour of His glorious Name.

VI. She Testified. "Happy are these thy servants, which stand continually before thee, and hear thy wisdom" (v. 8). ·The enlightened soul covets earnestly the best gifts. The servants of Solomon had a privilege that none others had on the face of the earth. So also has the servants of King Jesus. They see and hear things which many prophets and righteous men desire to see, but did not (Matt. 13. 16, 17). But are there not many to whom this high honour is conferred who are not *happy* in their close relationship to the King of kings? Worldly Christians who have but a poor appreciation of the written Word, which is the wisdom of our God. The *happy servant* hears the words of wisdom from the King's own lips.

VII. She Praised. "Blessed be the Lord thy God, which delighted in thee" (v. 9). It is a comely thing for those who have tasted that the Lord is gracious to render praise and thanks unto His holy Name. Yes, blessed be the Lord our God, who delighted in Jesus Christ as our Atoning Sacrifice, and set Him on the throne, "because He loved *us* for ever." Every manifestation of His grace and wisdom should awaken every faculty within us to praise and adoration. Thanks be unto God for His unspeakable gift.

VIII. She was Abundantly Satisfied. "Solomon gave her all her desire, whatsoever she asked" (v. 13). He supplied all her need. But the grace of the "Greater than Solomon" is greater, for He is able to do exceeding abundantly *above all that we ask.* No seeking soul will ever go hungry away from Him. He satisfies with good. "Ho, every one, Hearken diligently unto ME, and eat ye that which is good, and let your soul delight itself in His fullness (Isa. 55. 2).

A MAN-MADE RELIGION.
1 Kings 12. 26-33.

> "Hope of every sort—whatever sect,
>   Esteem them, sow them, rear them, and protect,
> If wild in nature and not duly found,
>   Gethsemane! in thy dear, hallowed ground—
> That cannot bear the blaze of Scripture light,
> Nor cheer the spirit, nor refresh the sight,
> Nor animate the soul to *Christ-like* deeds,
> (Oh, cast them from thee!) are weeds, arrant weeds."
>   —COWPER.

JEROBOAM, the son of Nebat, although of the race of Joshua, he became a ringleader in sin. Seeds of thought sprang up in his heart and mind rank and wild, but instead of treating them as "arrant weeds" he nurtured and protected them, as if they belonged to the Garden of the Lord. So the seeds of evil spread like thistle down. This religion of Jeroboam is like every other Christless religion.

I. **It had its Origin in the Human Heart.** "Jeroboam said in his heart" (v. 26). There are only, virtually, two religions in the world—the one has its origin in the "I WILL" of God, the other has its source in the "I *think*" of man. "My thoughts are not your thoughts" (Isa. 55. 8), saith the Lord. The heart of man is deceitful and wicked, out of it there can never come a system of worship that meets the claims of God and the needs of the soul. A revelation is needed; a revelation has been given. Anything opposed to this, or a substitute for it, is gross presumption and rebellion.

II. **It was for his own Selfish Ends.** He set up his golden calves—one in Beth-el and the other in Dan—lest the people should go to Jerusalem to worship and the hearts of the people be turned from himself (vv. 27-29). It was a religion that centred on his own personal honour and aggrandisement. SELF is for ever the centre of every godless religion. The pride of life lies at the root of all mere human schemes. The religion of the scribes and Pharisees was just another form of the sin of Jeroboam (Rom. 10. 3).

III. It was Ostensibly for the Good of Others. "It is too much for you to go to Jerusalem" (v. 28). He pretended that it was for their convenience and advantage that these golden gods were set up. The religion that is born in the carnal heart can only make hypocrites. The great scheme of godless socialists are not one whit better than the devices of Jeroboam, they set up calves of *gold*, saying, "These be thy gods, O people." It was a religion of selfish expediency and not of sacrifice. The thought of *self-denial* was carefully excluded.

IV. It was Contrary to the Word of God. "The king said unto them, Behold thy gods, O Israel, which brought thee up out of the land of Egypt" (v. 28). "Thus they changed their glory into the similitude of an ox" (Psa. 106. 20). The command of God was plain, "Thou shall not make unto them *any* graven image" (Exod. 20. 4). The desire of the carnal mind is to walk by *sight*, and not by *faith*. The inventions of the unrenewed heart are sure to be in opposition to the revelation of the mind of God. "I thought," said Naaman, but his thought was not at all in harmony with the manner and purpose of the man of God. Saul was quite in earnest when he thought that he should do many things contrary to the Name of Jesus of Nazareth (Acts 26. 9) The ladder *to* Heaven must come *from* Heaven (John 14. 6).

V. It Became a Snare to Others. "This thing became a sin" (v. 30). The *thing set up* became the *object* of worship instead of a means to help the thoughts to God. Man is always prone to be more taken up with his own works than the works of God. The little ornamental cross or the prayer-book becomes more precious than the things which are invisible and eternal. The products of men's own imaginations are exalted to the throne of the affections, and the presence of God usurped. That thing, whatever it is, that takes the place of God "becomes a sin."

VI. It has no Regard for Purity. "He made priests of the lowest of the people" (v. 31). This is characteristic of all man-made religion; there is no value set on inward holiness of life. Outward conformity and parade are enough to meet all its requirements. The *consecrated* sons of Aaron were not the kind of ministers Jeroboam wanted (Num. 3. 6). Their strict adherence to the Word of God would not suit his purpose. It is so still with those who are satisfied with the form of godliness and deny the power. They wish *their own* will and ways carried out, so they prefer the "lowest" motives as their governing principles; the pure light of God's Word would only reprove and rebuke.

VII. It has the Appearance of Being Right. There was the altar, the priests, and the ordained feast, *"Like unto the feast that is in Judah"* (vv. 32, 33). But the whole thing was a sham and a mockery, a lifeless image of the real. There was all the *outward semblance* of the true, but it had no *foundation* in the sight of God. "No *authority* from Him," no *power* to bless its votaries with pardon, peace, or hope. It was a thing destined to bring disappointment and the curse of God (chap. 13. 2). Examine yourselves whether ye be in the faith. "Without ME ye can do nothing" (John 15. 5).

"ALAS, MY BROTHER!"

OR, THE DECEIVED PROPHET SLAIN.

1 Kings 13.

"Mortal! thou standest on a point of time,
  With an eternity on either hand;
Thou hast one duty, above all sublime—
  Where thou art placed serenely stand."
  —Houghton.

THIS is a melancholy story. It is always infinitely sad to see those who were once mightily used of God tripped up in the end through temptation, and falling a prey to him who goeth about like a roaring lion seeking whom he may devour. But although the lion slew this prophet of God he was not permitted to *devour* him (v. 25). There are seven things about this unfortunate man that we would like to point out.

I. He was a True Believer. He is called "A man of God" (v. 1). He was not a mere "man of the world" whose portion is in this life, but one who has personal dealings with God, and who in heart and life belonged to Him. Not a mere professor or time-server, but a true servant of the Most High.

II. He was a Man with a Message. "He came *by the Word of the Lord* unto Beth-el" (v. 1). He was not a commentator, but he was an ambassador. He had a ministry committed to him by the Lord, a ministry of warning and condemnation. No evangelist was ever more surely called of God than this man. "A man of God" is one whom God has lifted up and fitted as a vessel for His own use, committing to him His own precious treasure (2 Cor. 4. 7).

III. He was a Man of Courage. "He cried against the altar in the Word of the Lord" (v. 2). He testified with a loud voice against this altar built by Jeroboam as a rival of Jehovah's, even while the king "stood by." The Word of God burned in his bones, and he could not but speak the things which he had heard from Him. It was so also with Peter and John (Acts 4. 20).

IV. He was a Man of Power. God bore witness to his testimony by signs and wonders in the stiffening of the king's arm and hand which was stretched out to "lay hold on him," and also in the "rending of the altar" and the spilling of the ashes. "Signs following" are always an evidence that the man is not serving God in his own strength. He had power for service because he spoke in the Name of the Lord. When God works through His servants it is as a *wonder*-worker. We may well question whether GOD is working through us if signs and wonders are not being wrought (Mark 16. 17).

V. He was a Man of Self-Denial. After praying for the restoration of the king's hand (for he had also power in prayer), the king asked him to "come and refresh himself and take a reward," but he would not (vv. 6-9). Like Elijah, he would "receive none" (2 Kings 5. 16). He was no *hireling* in the work of the Lord. He knew what it was to deny himself and take up his cross and follow Him who had called him. Surely such a mighty man as this will never fail! But, alas!

VI. He Fell through a False Professor. This old liar pretended that an angel had spoken to him, saying, "Bring him back" (vv. 11-18). At first he refused, but being tired and hungry (the Devil seemed to take advantage of his physical weakness) he was finally persuaded to turn aside from the revealed will of God and to obey the invention of man. The temptation was sore, but his way was perfectly clear. He had a revelation from God, and so ought not to be turned aside by any private interpretation of man. In obeying the false prophet he must have been quite conscious that in his *conduct* he was contradicting the deeper conviction of his soul. If our hearts *condemn us not* then have we confidence toward God. Hearken not to those prophets who would "make you vain" by ministering to the lusts of the flesh, "they speak a vision of their own heart" (Jer. 23. 16). Beloved, believe not every spirit, but try the spirits whether they are of God, because there are many false prophets gone out into the world (1 John 4. 1). There is one mark by which you may know them, and that is "*lightness*" (Jer. 23. 32). They have little reverence for the "Word of God" or the atoning blood of His Son; they try if possible to "deceive the very elect" (Matt. 24. 24). This man went back and, it cost him his life, for a lion met him and slew him (v. 24). It was the end of his testimony for God. The influence of *false teachers* makes men less faithful to God and His Word. By their fruits ye shall know them.

VII. **He was Mourned over by the One who Deceived Him.** "He laid his body in his own grave, saying, "*Alas, my brother*" (v. 30). Yes, well may he mourn, after tempting him into the net of destruction. Even being buried in the same grave will not atone for the sin of deception. How will he face him in the resurrection whom he had lured from the will of God by the substituting of his own thoughts for God's? How shall it fare with the false teachers (higher critics) of our day when in the presence of God they are face to face with the faith, withering fruits of their self-created visions? "Alas, my brother," take heed how ye hear, stand fast in the truth.

PRAYING IN DISGUISE.
1 Kings 14. 1-17.

"Prayer against His absolute decree
  No more avails than breath against the wind,
  Blown stifling back on him that breathes it forth:
  Therefore to His great bidding I submit."—MILTON.

THE more deeply we are imbued with the spirit of prayer the more simple and child-like shall we become. "Sublimity always is simple," is how Longfellow puts it.

Eloquent prayers may only be the haughtiness of the human heart in disguise. The wife of Jeroboam is not the only one who has put on the mask while making their requests known unto God. Purity of worship was at a very low ebb while King Jeroboam made the "lowest of the people priests" and consecrated "whosoever would" (chap. 13. 33), "I want to" is by no means the only qualification for the service of God. The Lord had sent a warning cry against this unholy altar (chap. 13. 2). Now the jealous God of Israel visits the iniquity with judgment. This attempt to outwit and delude the prophet of the Lord has its lessons for us. There was a—

I. Knowledge of God. Jeroboam could not be a stranger to the great things Jehovah had wrought for His people Israel; and had not the prophet of the Lord foretold him that he should be "king over this people?" (chap. 5. 2). But the *revealed* will of God had been set aside. His acts of worship were now according to his own *thoughts* and convenience, so he made Israel to sin by the substituting of his own ways for the ways of the Lord (chap. 12. 33). There may be a *knowledge* of the ways and will of God, while the *daily life* is a presumptuous denial of the divine revelation.

II. Feeling a Need. "Abijah the son of Jeroboam fell sick" (v. 1). They were very anxious to know "what shall become of the child" (v. 3). Our dearest and our best are never beyond the withering touch of God's finger. Every sorrow and disappointment may be to us as goads to drive us nearer our God if our hearts are right with Him. There is bitterness of heart that cannot be spoken into the ears of ordinary mortals; that needs the touch of the Eternal. The yearning of the soul at such times is to know what the will of God is concerning us.

III. Disguising of Character. The wife of Jeroboam changed her appearance and went to inquire of the man

of God, *"feigning herself to be another woman"* (vv. 2-5).
Perhaps the king knew that the old prophet Ahijah was
blind by reason of age, but both he and his wife seemed
to forget that God was not blind. It is utterly needless
for any one to come to God feigning themselves to be
different from what they are; and yet this disguising of
the true character, while making requests known unto God,
is a common pious fraud. On our knees we may pretend to
believe all that the Lord hath spoken, then among our
fellowmen we put on our self-magnifying glasses, and forget
the Lord that bought us. God looks on the heart, and as
a man thinketh in his heart so is he before Him.

IV. **Complete Failure.** As soon as she came to the
door of the prophet she heard these mask-scathing words,
"Come in thou wife of Jeroboam, why feignest thou thyself
to be another" (v. 6). The veil of her disguise was rent
from the top to the bottom, and the light of God's presence
shone in upon her. Saul had his disguise torn off him
while on the way to Damascus. The Pharisee that went
up to the temple to pray feigned himself a righteous man,
but he went away as he came, with his mask untouched
and his soul unblessed (Luke 18. 14). Jeroboam and his
wife were desirous of knowing the mind of the Lord about
their child, but they were afraid to face the will of God
concerning *themselves* and their ungodly lives. The *disguise*
was evidently an attempt to avoid the dreaded prediction of
the "man of God" in the preceding chapter. Is there anything in the background of our lives that we are afraid God
should deal with, things which make us put on a mask when
we venture to seek for divine light or guidance? It will not
improve matters to hide them, God will deal with us according to our daily life before Him. Therefore come to the
light that the evil deeds may be reproved, confessed, and
cleansed (John 3. 19-21), for be sure your sin will find you out.

ELIJAH, THE SEPARATED ONE.
1 Kings 17. 1.

"If thou could'st trust, poor soul,
In HIM who rules the whole,
Thou would'st find peace and rest,
Wisdom and sight are well, but trust is best."

—A. PROCTOR.

AHAB, the haughty king of Israel, had taken Jezebel, the pretty but wicked Zidonian to wife. Through her influence the prophets of God are slain, and the worship of Baal is established in the land as the national religion. Only seven thousand among all the thousands of Israel remain true in heart to God, and these, through fear of the king, hid themselves and their testimony. The whole nation seems overwhelmed with this flood-tide of idolatry. But away in the village of Tishbe, among the uplands of Gilead, there is a man, perhaps a poor peasant, whose heart has become hot with indignation, and whose jealousy for the honour of Jehovah burns with holy zeal. We fancy we hear him in secret pleading with God for His own Name's sake to rebuke the iniquity of His people and bring Israel to its knees by sending some arresting judgment upon the land (James 5. 17). God answers the earnest cry of the Tishbite, and there and then chooses him to be the instrument in His hand, to turn the nation back to the worship of their Divine King. To accomplish this great work he is invested with all authority. "There shall not be dew nor rain these years but according to my word." The interests and the power of God are committed to this servant, because he is wholly devoted to Him. Having been equipped with power, he goes forth to Samaria to declare the message of God in the ears of Ahab. No man will ever accomplish much for God who has not had in some respects a similar training. Note—

His Standing. "The Lord God of Israel, *before whom I stand*." He stood as one—

1. WHO BELIEVED IN GOD. His faith gave him the victory over all fear of Ahab. Those who have set God before them will not play the coward in the presence of any earthly monarch. It was this consciousness of the presence of God that stiffened the moral backbone of Luther and John Knox. After Pentecost Peter and John were filled with the same holy boldness as Elijah (Acts 4. 19, 20).

2. ACCEPTED BY GOD. Elijah had yielded Himself unto God that he might be a channel through which His words might come to the hearts of the ungodly, and through whom the power of God might be manifested. The Lord accepted his offer, and filled him as an earthen vessel with His divine treasure (2 Cor. 4. 6, 7). He had got the victory with his God in *secret*, now he is rewarded *openly*. Many of God's notable servants have come suddenly out of unexpected places.

3. IN FELLOWSHIP WITH GOD. The whole force of Elijah's moral and spiritual being was on the side of the God of Israel. There was a oneness of purpose between them. All idea of self-seeking was withered up by the fire of Jehovah's presence. Those who would serve the Lord will have very unpleasant work to do if they are careful about their own personal interests and honour. The secret of courage and power in the work of Christ lies in knowing His will and delighting to do it.

4. WHO WAITED ON GOD. As the eye of the maid is turned to her mistress, watching for the next indication of her will, so stood the life of Elijah before the Lord God of Israel. So may our souls wait on Him. The Moravian motto is most suggestive with the ox standing between an altar and a plough, "Ready for either." Ready

for either sacrifice or service, as the Lord may appoint. But Elijah's standing before God was not in idleness, but in the fearless attitude of one whose life was a protest against the popular sin of the nation—idolatry. "Let your light so shine" (Matt. 5. 16).

5. WHO HAD THE AUTHORITY OF GOD. He speaks as if the power of God and the resources of Heaven were at his disposal. "There shall not be dew nor rain these years but according to *my* word." The keys of Heaven had been given to him, and the treasures of dew and rain would only be poured out when he was pleased to open the door. This was a terrible and most effective weapon which God had put into the hand of His faithful servant. Those who fight the battles of the Lord are never sent to warfare on their own charges. Is not the gift of the Holy Spirit equally effective now for the carrying out of God's purposes in the reclaiming of men to the fellowship of His Son? Elijah, like Jesus Christ, spoke as one having authority, because he had the authority of God for that which he spoke. Elijah was a man "subject to like passions as we are." But have we the faith of Elijah? (Mark 9. 23).

Some Other Lessons.

1. That God can easily find the man He needs.

2. That the man chosen of God is often prepared in secret.

3. That great men often come out of unexpected places.

4. That those sent by God have always a definite mission.

5. That the secret of holy boldness is, "Standing before God."

6. That judgment is sure to overtake those who defy God.

ELIJAH, THE HIDDEN ONE.

1 Kings 17. 2-6.

"Yet not in solitude! if Christ is near me,
  Waketh Him workers for the great employ!
  Oh, not in solitude! if souls that hear me
  Catch from my joyance the surprise of joy."—MYERS.

WHEN Elijah had delivered his God-given message to the idolatrous king of Israel it would seem as if he did not know which way to turn next. Perhaps it was in answer to a prayer for guidance and protection that God said, "Get thee hence, and hide thyself by the brook Cherith." He who had slain so many of the Lord's servants was not likely to spare a man like Elijah. The servants of Christ still find it a testing time *after* the delivery of some unwelcome death or life message in the Name of God. How sweet it is at such times to find the Lord Himself a refuge and a hiding-place to the troubled soul! We observe that Elijah's hiding-place was a place of—

I. **Divine Appointment**. The Lord said, "Hide thyself by the brook Cherith." How could he feel safe or satisfied hiding in a place of his own choosing or making? What a sigh of relief would escape the heart of the obedient prophet as he sought and *found* the God-appointed place of rest, such a feeling of relief as the sinner knows, when in obedience to God's Word he flees for refuge to that appointed place called "Calvary." It matters not where the man-slayer ran for safety, he could have no assurance of it until he ran into the God-appointed city of refuge. Are we resting *where* God has bid us rest, in Jesus Christ, His beloved Son?

II. **Perfect Seclusion**. He was completely hid in the secret of the Lord's presence from the pride of Ahab and the strife of Jezebel's tongue (Psa. 31. 20). The place of God's salvation is a place of separation and seclusion.

Your life is hid with Christ in God. What an honour to belong to "Thy hidden ones" (Psa. 83. 3). All such hidden ones abide under the shadow of the Almighty (Psa. 91. 1). They are saved from the fear of man, from the slavery of fashion, and from the harassing anxieties of the ordinary worldly life. *"Thou* art my hiding-place" (Psa. 32. 7).

III. **Assuring Promise.** "Thou shalt drink of the brook: and *I have commanded* the ravens to feed thee *there*" (v. 4). God never sends us a warfare on our own charges. This promise could not be separated from that hallowed place "Cherith." All the promises of God are in Christ Jesus Yea and Amen. To know that *His Command* had gone forth was enough to allay every doubt and fear as to all his needs being supplied. All things work together for good to them that love God, to them that are the *called according to His purpose.* We are saved by His grace and assured by His Word.

IV. **Wonderful Experience.** "The ravens brought him bread and flesh in the morning and in the evening" (v. 6). The prophet could not have such a manifestation of ·the loving-kindness of God anywhere else; being in God's way He met him and blessed him. So is it at the Cross of Christ. The provision was—

1. PLENTIFUL. Not only had he "bread and water," but flesh also. The life of faith will always be met with His "exceeding abundance." The young lions in the full vigour of their own strength do suffer lack; but they that *trust* the Lord shall not want any good. At that holy place appointed by God, the Cross, there is sufficient for all.

2. REGULAR. "Morning and evening," as long as it was needed. He who hath begun the good work is able to carry it on. He who gave you the first mouthful of grace is able to make His grace sufficient for you all

the way (Exod. 16. 35). In the secret place of His presence you may have "day by day your daily bread."

3. MIRACULOUS. Every morsel of Elijah's food while here came to him in a supernatural fashion. "Man shall not live by bread alone, but by *every word that proceedeth out of the mouth of God.*" The life that has been begotten by the Word of God must also grow thereby. Miracles are an everyday occurrence to the man who lives by faith in the Son of God. When Jesus asked those who had gone out in His Name, "Lacked ye anything?" they said, "Nothing" (Luke 22. 35). God's ravens are everywhere, and His *command* is enough to make them the ministers of mercy and blessing to any of His hidden ones.

ELIJAH, THE FAITHFUL.
1 Kings 17. 7-16.

"Reason unstrung the harp to see
　　Wherein the music dwells;
Faith pours a hallelujah song,
　　And heavenly rapture swells.
While Reason strives to count the drops
　　That lave our narrow strand,
Faith launches o'er the mighty deep
　　To seek a better land."—HAVERGAL.

WE walk by faith, not by sight. Elijah had a long rest beside the secret brook—perhaps about twelve months. This would serve as a test both to his faith and his *patience.* We must learn to wait on God if we would do exploits for Him. Moses waited in the Midian desert forty years before the divine call came. But what could he have done to save Israel *before* that? The man who had to face the testing ordeal of Carmel must be a man approved of God. Precious faith, like precious gold, must needs pass through the refining fires. The prophet now receives another call.

I. **The Time of this Call.** "After the brook dried up" (v. 7). We may be perfectly assured of this, that when God in His providence closes one door against His servants He will open another. It will be a trying time to witness in the channel of our present comforts being gràdually narrowed and the stream slowly drying up. It may be the drying up of the brook of worldly prosperity, but especially when the much-loved brook of self-confidence has dried up do we feel how utterly helpless we are. But man's extremity is God's opportunity.

II. **The Command Given.** "Arise, get thee to Zare-phath" (v. 9). When the brook became silent then God spoke. When the mountains of our boasted strength shall depart and the hills of our carnal hopes be removed the *kindness* of the Lord shall not depart, neither shall the covenant of His peace be removed (Isa. 54. 10). Zarephath means a smelting-house, a place of fiery trials. It was meet that the prophet of fire should pass through the refining furnace. All who would live godly must suffer persecution. Elijah's journey of one hundred miles through a famine-stricken country would afford him ample oppor-tunities for faith. Away from the shady brook, this must have been to him as a baptism of fire. Did not the New Testament Elijah say of Christ that He will baptise you with the Holy Ghost and with fire?

III. **The Promise Made.** "I have commanded a *widow* to sustain thee" (v. 9). Perhaps the prophet thought that she must surely be a *wealthy* widow that was to supply his need during the remaining time of the famine. In any case, God's "commands to the ravens" had not failed him, neither would His Word to the widow. How the message came to this poor widow we don't know, but doubtless this Zidonian was prepared in some way; it may have been

through earnest prayer, like Cornelius (Acts 10). He is
faithful that hath promised.

IV. **The Test of Circumstances.** This widow, as we
suppose, with some secret God-given premonition that all
her wants would be supplied, is now face to face with
starvation. As far as her *reason* could go there was only
"an handful of meal" between her and death. She went
out with a heavy heart to gather fuel to cook her last meal
when the crisis came (vv. 10-12). Her circumstances
seemed to belie the "command of God." Abraham was
similarly tried when commanded to offer up his son Isaac,
the child of promise. But see, Elijah comes, looking for
the wealthy widow with whom he was to lodge. He meets
her gathering sticks, and when he asks "a morsel of bread"
he is told that all she possesses for her and her son is "an
handful of meal and a *little* oil." Here, again, circumstances seem to make the Word of God of none effect. But,
like Abraham, "he staggered not at the promise of God, but
was strong in faith, giving glory to God, being fully persuaded that, what He had promised, He was able also to
perform" (Rom. 4. 20). He shows his faith in the divine
promise by persisting in having the *first* share of the little
store, and saying to the half-bewildered woman, "Fear
not." Did not our Lord ask a drink of the woman of
Samaria, knowing that He had something better to give
her, even that blessing which, like the widow's meal,
"shall not waste?"

V. **The Obedience of Faith.** "She went and did
according to the saying of Elijah" (vv. 14, 15). The
prophet gave her the promise of the Lord God of Israel, that
the meal in that barrel would not waste nor the cruse of oil
fail until the famine would cease. She believed the Word,
and took what seemed her last handful of meal, and even
with a hungry soul prepared it for Elijah. She practically

gave away, at God's bidding, all that she had, and cast herself entirely upon His promise. She had neither precedent nor example for such an act and for such a hope, but she had faith in the Word and power of God. Blessed are they who have not seen and yet have believed.

VI. The Fulfilment of Promise. "The barrel of meal wasted not, neither did the cruse of oil fail, according to the Word of the Lord" (v. 16). Thus for a full year (v. 15, *margin*) did they eat bread, day by day, that was miraculously given them. Truly theirs was a life of faith on the promise of God. If the meal was always at the *bottom* of the barrel, yet was it never awanting. They who trust Him wholly will find Him wholly true. "Said I not unto thee, that, if thou wouldest believe, thou shouldest see the glory of God?" (John 11. 40).

ELIJAH, THE REVIVER.
1 Kings 17. 17-24.

"Whene'er a noble deed is wrought,
Whene'er is spoken a noble thought,
　　Our hearts, in glad surprise,
　　To higher levels rise.
　The tidal wave of deeper souls
　Into our inmost being rolls,
　　And lifts us unawares
　　Out of all meaner cares."—LONGFELLOW.

THERE were many widows in *Israel* in the days of Elijah, but unto none of *them* was he sent, but unto this widow in a city of Sidon. Why did our Lord refer to this at the time He did (Luke 4. 25) if it were not just to show them that salvation is through the *grace* of God, delighting to lift up the despised among men, and the unworthy in the sight of God. It was a marvellous work the God of Israel had wrought for this poor lonely widow, not only in supplying her daily need, but in raising her son from the dead. Truly

might she sing, "Oh! to grace, how great a debtor!" What
hath the grace of God that *bringeth salvation to all men*
taught us? (Titus 2. 11, 12). Now we see in this highly
favoured home—

I. A Severe Trial. "The son of the woman fell sick,
and there was no breath left in him" (v. 17). The light of
her eyes, the joy of her heart, and the hope of her future
life has been suddenly cut off. She sits with the dead boy
"in her bosom" (v. 19), but the *natural* warmth even of a
mother's heart is utterly unavailing to bring back to these
vacant eyes the light of a living soul. No more can we, by
the strength of natural affection, nurse back to life those
of our loved ones who are dead in their sins. "Without Me
ye can do nothing."

II. A Bitter Complaint. "She said, What have I to do
with thee, O thou man of God? Art thou come to call my
sin to remembrance?" (v. 18). The death of the child had
awakened within her some sad memories of the past. What
this sin was we cannot positively say. It may have been
connected with the birth of the child. Anyway, her soul
was deeply moved. The presence of the "man of God,"
the manifestation of the power and goodness of God in the
daily multiplying of the handful of meal, and this vivid
remembrance of *her own sin* filled her soul with the deepest
anguish. It is an awful sight to see one's sinfulness in the
light of the great goodness of God. When Simon Peter
saw it, he cried, "Depart from me, for I am a sinful man,
O Lord" (Luke 5. 8). It is infinitely worse to remember
one's sins, like the rich man, where there is no "man of
God" to help, or message of hope for a self-ruined soul
(Luke 16. 25).

III. A Gracious Request. He said unto her, "Give me
thy son" (v. 19). Although the sharp words of the afflicted
and sin-wounded woman must have deeply stung the

sensitive heart of the "man of God," yet he betrays no impatience. He utters no complaint, but with the tenderness of a father, and with the faith of a Heaven-born giant, he says, "Give me thy son," and he took the dead boy "out of her bosom." Oh, man of God, what canst thou do with the *dead*? A MAN OF GOD will always act differently from an ordinary mundane mortal, by facing difficulties that seem unsurmountable and tasks that are impossible with men.

IV. **A Place of Blessing.** "He carried him up into a loft where he abode, and laid him upon his own bed" (v. 19). The loft must have been a very humble place in appearance, but to this prophet, priest, and prince it was the "Holy of holies," the audience chamber of the Prince of Life and Glory. The little window of this "closet" looked right into the throne-room of the Eternal. Blessed is that man whose "closet" is filled with the warmth of the breath of God. "When ye pray, enter into thy closet and shut the door. Thy Father seeth in secret" (Matt. 6. 6).

V. **A Prevailing Prayer.** "The Lord heard the voice of Elijah, and the soul of the child came into him again" (vv. 21, 22). In asking that the "child's soul might come into him again," he was surely asking a *great thing*. But men who claim to "stand before God" must expect great things from God. The life of faith cannot be limited to the natural, and circumscribed by precedent. Above what we ask or think, God is able to do. But not only did he *ask*, he also *"stretched himself* upon the child three times."* With the faith of his heart he gave also the whole warmth of his physical body. His body, soul, and spirit were all consecrated to this great work of *reviving*. There are many who *pray* for reviving who would not stretch their little finger to lift a soul out of the ditch of sin. In "stretching himself" he gave *himself* wholly to the work. When Paul wished to recover Eutychus he *embraced* him (Acts 20. 10).

There be many who *stretch themselves* without the prayer of faith, but it is as vain as when Samson "shook himself" without the power of the Holy Spirit (Judges 16. 20).

VI. A God-honouring Confession. When Elijah had brought down the child and delivered him unto his mother, she said, "Now *by this I know* that thou art a man of God, and that the Word of the Lord in thy mouth is truth" (v. 24). The miracle in the barrel did not convince her like the miracle in her son. The overwhelming evidence of the truthfulness of the "Word of the Lord" is, that by it souls pass from death unto life, born again by the incorruptible seed of the Word. The death and reviving of her son was the means in the hand of God of bringing her into the knowledge and love of God; so out of our deepest trials there may come our highest blessings, and when they do come let us honestly and joyfully confess them.

ELIJAH, THE FAITHFUL WITNESS.
1 Kings 18. 1-39.

> "Could we but crush that ever-craving lust
> For bless, which kills all bless, and lose our life—
> Our barren unit-life—to find again
> A thousand lives in those for whom we die,
> So were we men and women! and should hold
> Our rightful rank in God's great universe."—KINGSLEY.

THE third year of the famine was now running its course. All this time Elijah, as the mouthpiece of God, had no message for the guilty nation. Jehovah Himself was speaking through those barren fields and sealed-up heavens, calling for confession and repentance. There are times when God's servants have to be silent, when He is speaking loudly by some crushing providence. Elijah had a long silence before he made that bold and tragic declaration on Carmel. In this chapter we get a fuller view of the faithfulness of this prophet of fire in his—

I. **Readiness to Obey.** When the call came, "Go, show thyself unto Ahab," immediately "Elijah went to show himself" (vv. 1, 2). He had been commanded to *hide* himself (chap. 17. 3). Now he is to *show* himself. He was equally ready for the one or the other. The man who is set on witnessing for God, as Elijah was, and is willing to *hide himself*, is sure to be lifted up, brought out, and set before the people as one having authority. To show himself to Ahab was to show himself to one who had been eagerly hunting for his life (v. 12). But the *righteous* are bold as a lion (Prov. 28. 1).

II. **Boldness to Rebuke.** When Ahab found Elijah he seemed as if he had found a "pestilent fellow." But was there not a tremor of fear in that question so awkwardly put, "Art thou he that troubleth Israel?" How could *he* trouble Israel by shutting up the heavens when the *king* was utterly helpless? The prophet's answer was straight and piercing as an arrow to his heart from the quiver of the Almighty. "I have not troubled Israel, but thou . . . in that ye have forsaken the commandments of the Lord" (v. 18). What constitutes a *troubler*? "Forsaking the Word of the Lord." Every backslider is a troubler in the Church of God. Achan's secret sin brought trouble into the whole camp of Israel. What should be said of those infidel "critics" who pose as religious teachers and are troubling the whole land with their soul-damning heresies? The need of the age is Elijahs.

III. **Call for Decision.** The prophet commands the king, and his eight hundred and fifty false prophets are summoned, with the nation, to meet Elijah on Mount Carmel. It was a big order, but the man who "stands before God" will go in for great things. "How long halt ye between two opinions?" is the pointed question rung out as soon as the people had gathered themselves together.

This solitary man of God was intensely practical. Well he knew that "no man can serve two masters," and that indecision about the service of God was ruinous. Their decision for God or Baal was to be evidenced by their *"following* Him." The outward life must declare the inward purposes of the heart.

IV. Desire to put God to the Test. "Let them choose one bullock, and I will dress the other, . . .and the God that answereth by fire, let Him be God" (vv. 23, 24). Better test our theories and principles in time than to have them breaking down on the border of eternity. The man of faith is never afraid to risk his all on the honour of God (Heb. 11. 17). An "answer by *fire*" was quite a reasonable test for them, as they worshipped Baal, the god of fire. Surely the great "sun god" would not fail such a multitude of prophets. At *midday*, when the sun was at its hottest, they got frantic, and "leaped upon the altar" as if they themselves were ready to be sacrificed for their faith, but there was "neither voice, *nor any to answer.*" Their god was the voiceless myth of their own imagination. The "two opinions" between which they halted were MAN's and GOD's. "My thoughts are not your thoughts, saith the Lord." Prove your own selves.

V. Believing Prayer. There is no fuss, no excitement betrayed by the man of God, as he calmly builds the altar and drenches the sacrifice and the wood with "barrels" of water from the sea (Jer. 46. 18). He does not seek to make it easy for God to answer by fire, but to make it sure that the fire is from God. His prayer is simple, because it is the prayer of faith. "Let it be known this day that Thou art God in Israel," etc. (vv. 36, 37). The prophet urges a fourfold reason for this special miraculous manifestation of His power.

1. That it might be known that THOU ART GOD.

2. That I AM THY SERVANT.

3. That I have done all these things AT THY WORD.

4. That the HEART of the people might be TURNED BACK.

It was a cry for the vindication of God's own honour, a cry that was immediately answered, for *"Then* the fire of the Lord fell" (v. 38). This was a Pentecostal day for Israel. Those who are truly faithful to God must expect great things from Him, that His own Name may be glorified in them and by them. It is because of our unbelief that signs and wonders are not still being wrought among us. "Command ye me."

VI. Bringing Others to Confession. "When all the people saw it, they fell on their faces; and they said, The Lord, He is God" (v. 39). It was such a revelation as Thomas had when he said, "My Lord and my God." There is nothing like the down-coming of the fire of God— the Holy Ghost—to burn off the masks from the faces of self-deceived religionists. The "one man ministry" of Elijah was an overwhelming force in the kingdom of Israel. The man that "stands before God" has always God to stand by Him. There is no other way to bring deluded sinners to their knees but by the power of God in answer to the daring faith of His believing servants.

ELIJAH, THE INTERCESSOR.
1 Kings 18. 41-46.

"Surely, too, some way
He is the better of my love! I'll believe
His very eye would never sparkle thus,
Had I not prayed for him this long, long while."
—BROWNING.

THE falling of the fire of the Lord from Heaven, and the cutting off of the prophets of Baal, had effectually arrested the rising flood-tide of idolatry that threatened to overwhelm the whole land. Now that the people were on their faces confessing that "the Lord He is God" (v. 39) showers of blessing are at hand. The quick ear of the man of God is the first to hear the "sound of abundance of rain." The heavens will soon be opened to pour out its treasures upon thirsty souls when they bow in humble confession before Him (Isa. 44. 3). It was a welcomed Gospel that Elijah preached to Ahab when he said, "Get thee up, eat and drink, for there is a sound of abundance of rain." There are those to whom times of refreshing from the presence of the Lord mean nothing more than *eating and drinking*—personal enjoyment. It was far otherwise with Elijah. To him the sound of coming blessing was an urgent call to prayer. He—

I. Prayed Believingly. He heard the "sound of abundance of rain" (v. 41). The *sound* may have been that of the assuring *promise of God* ringing in his soul (v. 1). So faith cometh by such hearing. The secret of a bold, courageous life lies in the hearing of faith. When the ear of faith is dull, the feet of service will be tardy and the tongue of testimony will stammer. To prevail in prayer, "hear ye the Word of the Lord."

II. Prayed Humbly. "He cast himself down upon the earth, and put his face between his knees" (v. 42). The believer who is the boldest before men will be the humblest before God. To cast *ourselves down* is the best way of preparing ourselves for the fulfilment of the promise of God. The greatest in the kingdom of Heaven may be the littlest in the eyes of men (Matt. 18. 4). The greatest of all masters was the humblest of all servants. It was the man who could not lift up his face that received the benediction of God (Luke 18. 13).

III. Prayed Perseveringly. "There is nothing. And he said, Go again" (v. 43). Elijah had heard the sound of a coming abundance, but his servant could *see nothing*. It is not easy *seeing* that which as yet can only be apprehended by *faith*. But although nothing could be seen that did in no way discourage the prophet, he said, "Go again, seven times." He had the sure Word of God's promise, and he kept believing and pleading although *appearances* were all against him. Like Jacob, he will not let go till the blessing come (Gen. 32. 26). Elijah walked by faith, while his servant walked by sight. The importunate pleadings of faith will never be sent empty away (Luke 18).

IV. **Prayed Definitely.** He prayed for rain (James 5. 17, 18). This mighty man of God seemed never to have more than one arrow in his quiver at a time. Prevailing prayers have always been definite. David said, "In the morning will I direct (set in order an arrow in the bow) my prayer unto Thee, and will look up," confidently expecting the answer (Psa. 5. 3). The *general* prayer is generally powerless. Who would come into the presence of an earthly king with a string of generalities, not one of which was immediately wanted or expected? Prayer meetings are often strangled to death by the numberless petitions offered which are never expected to be answered. As a rule the prayer that prevails with God and is answered by floods of blessing springs out of some definite promise of God, received by faith, and perseveringly pleaded before His throne of grace (Ezek. 36. 37).

V. **Prayed Successfully.** "Behold there ariseth a little cloud, . . . and there was a great rain" (v. 44, 45). Let us take heed when the *little cloud* appears that we do not despise the day of *small things* (Zech. 4. 10). God's "little cloud" can be made broad enough to cover the whole sky and to meet all our need. The few loaves and small fishes are sufficient in His hands to satisfy the cravings of a multitude. Elijah asked, believing that he would receive, and he did have (Mark 11. 24), and God was glorified in so answering. "Whatsoever ye shall ask in My Name, that will I do, *that the Father may be glorified in the Son*" (John 14. 13). Seeing that it is the chief desire of the Son to glorify the Father in answering our prayers, surely this is one of the most powerful of all reasons why we should "ask in prayer, believing that we shall receive" (Matt. 21. 22).

ELIJAH, THE DOWNCAST.
1 Kings 19. 1-8.

"Art thou alone? and dost thy soul complain
    It lives in vain?
Not vainly does he live who can endure!
    O, be thou sure
That he who hopes and suffers here can earn
    A sure return."—PROCTOR.

"GREAT men are not always wise." Elijah failed just at that point where we would have expected him to take an unflinching stand. Yet it may be good for us to know that God's greatest servants were men of "like passions with ourselves." As they, like our Lord and Saviour, were made sharers of our infirmities, so we might be made partakers of their virtues and glories. All things are possible to him that believeth. We observe here a—

I. **Cowardly Flight.** "When he saw that, he arose, and went for his life" (v. 3). When he saw that Jezebel's pride and hatred were unsubdued after all that he had done—in proving his authority on Carmel by calling fire from Heaven and praying floods of rain upon the parched land, and showing his loyalty to King Ahab by running as a herald before the royal chariot all those eighteen miles through the drenching storm. As he waits outside the gate all the reward he gets is a message that because he had slain the prophets of Baal his life would be taken "by

to-morrow about this time." So he "went for his life."
Exhausted and disappointed he forgets God and the present
need of Israel for a spiritual teacher, and takes to preserv-
ing his own life. By faith he boldly stood before Ahab
and all the prophets of Baal; by fear he fled before the vain
threats of an unprincipled woman. How are the mighty
fallen! "Let him that standeth take heed."

II. **Despairing Cry.** "He requested for himself that
he might die" (v. 4). He found it a very unprofitable
business that of seeking merely to *save his own life*. A self-
centred life is sure to come to grief. When one steps out
of the current of God's will and purpose concerning us our
chariot wheels are sure to "drive heavily." Jonah prayed
the same prayer while he was in a bad mood (chap. 4. 3).
Paul was animated by a different spirit when he wrote,
"Nevertheless to abide in the flesh is more *needful for you*"
(Phil. 1. 24). At that moment the kingdom of Israel was
in desperate need of that very man who was counting his
life a worthless thing. Has the cause of Christ no need
of thee?

III. **Gracious Touch.** "As he lay and slept, behold,
an angel touched him, and said unto him, Arise and eat"
(v. 5). Elijah's merciful Master did not send a messenger
to thrash him, or even to rebuke him for his fearfulness.
His loving heavenly Father knew best what his tired and
weary child needed. "Arise and eat." The terrible strain
of Carmel, the wearisome run before Ahab, the long journey
into the wilderness had no doubt brought upon him complete physical and nervous prostration. The remedy provided by God was "a cake baken on the coals and a cruse of
water." He knows the frailty of our frame (John 21. 9-12).
How long he slept before the angel touched him we cannot
know, but perhaps he was, through utter weakness, in
danger of sleeping the sleep of death had not the angel

wakened him up to *eat*.   Are we not reminded here of that
other angel of His presence, the Holy Spirit, whose gentle
touch awakens many of God's downcast ones, and whose
tender voice bids them arise and eat of Him who is the
Living Bread.   That angel may be touching you even now.

IV. **Wonderful Discovery.**   "He looked, and, behold,
there was cake *baken on the coals*; . . . and he did eat and
drink, and laid him down again" (v. 6).   It is not for
naught that the angel of God touches any one.   For every
Spirit-awakened soul there is a much-needed miraculous
feast awaiting them.   He was not disobedient to the
heavenly touch.   "He looked," and seeing the divine
provision he appropriated it.   It must have been a very
palatable breakfast, cooked by an angel, and all for himself.
But God's provision is always suitable to the needs of the
soul.   It did not concern Elijah how the cake was formed
or the coals kindled.   It was enough for him that this was
God's gift to him, and that he needed it and was invited to
take it.   So it is with the salvation that is in Christ Jesus.

V. **Second Blessing.**   "The angel of the Lord came a
second time, and touched him" (v. 7).   He had already
got as much of the gift of God as to save his life, but not
so much as would strengthen him for the journey that
lay before him.   So in mercy he was called again to
"arise and eat, because the journey is too great for thee."
Are there not many who have received of the Lord Jesus
Christ as the gift of God that which has saved their souls
from death, but who, like Elijah, have "lain down again"
in selfish ease, and who need a second awakening that they
might arise and so partake of Christ, that they may be able
to *go on* in a life of suffering and testimony?   Some people
don't believe in a *second* blessing, but Elijah did.

VI. **Supernatural Power.**   "He went on the strength
of that meat forty days and forty nights unto Horeb, the

mount of God" (v. 8). Elijah's first meal saved his soul, but the second enabled him to witness for God. That forty days' journey was not accomplished in his own strength, but in the strength of the gift of God. This grace ministered to him was sufficient to bring him unto the mount of God (a journey of about two hundred miles). All this is most suggestive of what the gift of His grace is able to do for all who will obey the call to "arise and eat" (2 Cor. 12. 9). Who has ever yet found out the full "strength of that meat" which is within the reach of every child of God in His blessed Word? Downcast and discouraged soul, this call is for you. "Arise and eat." "Thy words were found, and I did eat them," etc. (Jer. 15. 16; Psa. 119. 111).

ELIJAH REBUKED.

1 Kings 19. 9-16.

> "Who can come near to God with a heart not on fire?
> Souls must tire upon earth who in Heaven would rest.
> Is it hard to serve God, timid soul? Hast thou found
> Gloomy forests, dark glens, mountain tops on thy way?
> All the hard would be easy, the tangled unwound,
> Would'st Thou only desire as well as obey."—FABER.

On the strength of the Heaven-sent meat, Elijah reached "Horeb, the mount of God." "They that wait on the Lord shall . . . walk and not faint" (Isa. 40. 31). Horeb was pre-eminently the mount of the revelation of God, because here the unconsumed bush was seen ablaze with a divine fire; here the law was given with its terrible accompaniments, and perhaps it was in this very cave that Moses stood while the glory of God's goodness passed by (Exod. 33). It must have been with mingled and solemn feelings that Elijah found himself in the midst of surroundings crowded with such striking and holy memories. Will there be any such manifestation of the divine presence to him? Surely he has come here to meet with God! Will those who

seek Him not find Him? If men would go to the "house
of God" as Elijah went to the "mount of God" what signs
and wonders would be wrought!

I. A Searching Question.   "What doest thou here,
Elijah?" (v. 9).   By this question was the Lord sternly
demanding of the prophet why he was *here*, instead of en-
couraging the nation to stand firm for the God who had
answered by fire on Carmel, or was it a question full of grace
and tenderness seeking to call out the needs and fears of
his heart that He might in mercy satisfy and comfort?
In any case, it is always God's method to go to the
root of the matter and deal with the *motives* of the life.
Throughout the Scriptures divine questions are frequently
accompanied by marvellous revelations (Gen. 32. 27;
Exod. 4. 2).

II. An Honest Answer.   "I have been very jealous for
the Lord God of hosts; . . . I only am left, and they seek
my life" (v. 10).   All those who would faithfully serve
the Lord will have many heart-searching questions to
answer.   As a *defence*, Elijah's reply was a very poor one,
but as a *confession* it was simple and sincere.   He had
been very jealous for the Lord, now he was afraid of
his own life.   All Israel had gone astray, he only was
left.   Perplexed and despondent he had come here
partly through fear and partly to hear what God the
Lord would speak to his soul.   Any one who truly loves
the Lord, but who, through unusual temptation and
bodily infirmities, has given way to fear, can easily
understand the feelings of this man of God at this
particular time.

III. A Wonderful Manifestation.   There came now the
divine call to "Go forth and *stand before the Lord*" (v. 11).
Is he not reminded by this that through unbelief he had
lost his standing (chap. 17. 1).   Let us *keep on* the whole

armour of God that we may be able to stand (Eph. 6. 13). The prophet is now made a witness to the marvellous power of the Lord in a fourfold manner. He sees it in the *wind*, the *earthquake*, the *fire*, and the *still small voice*. But in the *rending* wind, the *shaking* earthquake, or the *melting* fire there was no message from the Lord for the trembling servant. "The Lord was not *in* them." The Lord would teach us as well as Elijah that there is something more needed to bring men to Himself than a mere display of *natural* powers. The strong *wind* of words, the *earthquake* of argument, and the *fire* of enthusiasm may do mighty and terrible things, yet if the still small *voice* of the Lord, the Spirit, is not in them there is no message from God to the souls of men. It is "not by might, nor by power, but by My Spirit, saith the Lord" (Zech. 4. 6). The mightiest of all the forces that are at work in this world is that "still small voice" of the Holy Spirit that whispers God's Word of truth and life into the listening heart. A *voice* is something more than a sound or an influence, it is an assurance of the presence of a living PERSONALITY (Song of Sol. 2. 8). "My sheep hear My voice" (John 10. 27).

IV. **A Powerful Effect.** "When Elijah heard it he wrapped his face in his mantle and went out" (v. 13). The terrific effects of the wind, the earthquake, or the fire had evidently driven him back into the depths of the cave (v. 11); but the sweet wooing voice lured him from his dismal hiding-place, with his face hid in his mantle because it was burning with shame. Men will be all the more likely to be *constrained* by the sweet voice of love *after* they have heard the thunderings and felt the burnings of that law which is holy, just, and good. The terrible trumpet of Sinai made men stand "afar off," while the voice of Calvary constrains men to draw nigh with a shame-mantled face.

Here, but in very altered circumstances, the same question is again put, "What doest thou here, Elijah?" And, alas, the very same answer is given. Has he profited nothing by all those revelations of divine resources that he adds no petition for grace or strength to go on overcoming in the Name of Him who doeth wondrously? It would seem as if this *repeated* question was his last chance of getting fully restored to the power and authority of the prophetic office, but he failed to take advantage of it. He is not allowed to become a *castaway*, but it would seem that from this time the purposes of God concerning him are changed, and another is chosen to take his place. Has he now become a marred vessel in the hands of the Great Potter? Let us take heed lest we should come short. How shall we escape the same failure if we neglect the great opportunities that God in His infinite mercy brings within our reach?

V. A Humbling Confession. "Go, return, . . . and Elisha shalt thou anoint to be prophet in thy room" (vv. 15, 16). When Elijah persisted in saying "I, even I, only am left," it was an evidence that he had climbed down from his walk of faith and was now walking by *sight*. Was the Lord not rebuking his unbelief when he said to him, "I have left Me seven thousand in Israel which have not bowed unto Baal" (v. 18). God could easily have made Elijah sufficient to do the work of the three men whom he was now sent to anoint. Who can tell all that the Lord is able to do through one life that has been entirely and continuously yielded to His will? It was surely a self-humbling work to go and call a man to take his own place so soon after accomplishing such a mighty work for God as was witnessed on Mount Carmel. "Let him that standeth take heed lest he fall." "Let no man take *thy* crown" (Rev. 3. 11).

THE CALL OF ELISHA.
1 Kings 19. 16-21.

"Jesus calls us from the worship
Of the vain world's golden store;
From each idol that would keep us,
Saying, 'Christian, love ME more.'"
—C. F. ALEXANDER.

THERE is a self-evident vein of irony in these words of C. Kingsley:

"I was not good enough for man,
And so was given to God."

How ready we are to think and act as if the prime of our days was too valuable *for us* to be given to God, and that the fag end of our life is best suited for surrendering to the will of God. Where in all the Bible do we find any one called of God to do service for Him when infirm with age? Were not the Levites *disqualified* for the work of God at the age of fifty? (Num. 8. 25). Are there not now comparatively few being saved beyond that age? Elisha was undoubtedly a young man, whom Elijah, at the bidding of God, came without a murmur to anoint him as prophet "in his own room." Observe the—

I. Significance of his Name. Elisha means *God is Salvation*. This was a name well suited for the man who was to take the lead at this time of national crisis. While in a despondent mood Elijah said, "I, even I, only am left," but the Lord rebuked his pessimism by saying, "I have left Me seven thousand," and Elisha was one of them. The after life of Elisha shows him to be strong where Elijah was inclined to be weak—in being faithful and careful down to the smallest events in life. Elijah's faith was mighty in Mount Carmel, but it failed him under the juniper tree. The man who knows that the presence of *God is Salvation* will surely be steadfast and immovable in the work of the Lord.

II. **Time of his Call.** It was while he was "ploughing" (v. 19). He was only a ploughman. Yes, but who can tell what depth of soul exercise and heart agony he may have had over backsliding Israel while following the oxen across the fields. There was One who did know, and who answered the secret longings of his heart by calling him out as a witness for Himself. The Lord knows where and when to lay "His hand on that *hidden one* who has in secret been prepared for a more honoured place in His service." The divine call came to Moses while he kept the flock of Jethro (Exod. 3. 1); to Gideon while he thrashed wheat (Judges 6. 11); to David when in the sheepfold (Psa. 78. 70); to Amos while a herdman (chap. 7. 14). All Christ's disciples were called from very common occupations. He found Bunyan among the pots and pans. "If *any man* hear My voice" (Rev. 3. 20).

III. **Manner of his Call.** "Elijah passed by him, and cast his mantle *upon him*" (v. 19). It came *suddenly*, although Elisha's preparation may have been going on for several years. It came *unmistakably*. The mantle or spirit of the prophet had now fallen UPON HIM. This was to him an holy *anointing* from the Lord (v. 16). The mantle of Elijah was the symbol of the Spirit of power. Elisha could do no mighty works for God without this definite baptism. No more can we. "Tarry until ye be endued with power from on high" (Luke 24. 49). The sudden encircling of the prophetic mantle about him was an experience he could not possibly forget or ignore (Acts 19. 1).

IV. **Effects of this Call.** It was followed by—

1. AN INSTANT RESPONSE. "He left his oxen and ran after Elijah" (v. 20). He did not wait for a more convenient season, or he too might have been startled some day with the question, "What doest thou here, Elisha?" His call, like ours, is a *passing* one. The prophetic power will

not abide with him unless he follows and keeps, as it were, in touch with that mantle which, in grace, had fallen upon him. So if we would abide in the power of His anointing we must be willing and ready to be *led* by the Spirit, and to walk in Him and with Him. An instant recognition of God's call, by the coming upon us of the Holy Spirit, should be made. "Set *thine heart* upon all that I shall show thee" (Ezek. 40. 4).

2. A REVELATION OF FILIAL TENDERNESS. "Let me, I pray thee, kiss my father and my mother, and then I will follow thee" (v. 20). These words, we think, do not in any way betray the spirit of that man who said, "Suffer me first to go and bury my father" (Matt. 8. 21). The call came to Elisha in the form of an *offer* instead of a command. An offer which he instantly accepted. Perhaps his *love* for his father and mother was one of the chief evidences of his righteousness with God and fitness for service. Those who would feel it no sacrifice whatever to leave home, even for the service of God, are not likely to be sent by Him (Matt. 19. 27-29).

3. A WILLING AND DEFINITE TESTIMONY. "He took a yoke of oxen and slew them . . . and gave *unto the people*" (v. 21). What would the people think of such an act? Killing the useful oxen and making a fire of the agricultural instruments! It was an indication to them that he was now done with this business, as he had deliberately accepted the gracious offer of the prophetic office at the hand of Elijah. All that Elijah said to him was, "Go back again, for what have I done to thee?" As much as to say, If there is no correspondence *in your heart* to this outward call then go back. But there was, and he fearlessly obeyed.

4. A PERSONAL SEPARATION AND SERVICE. "Then he arose and went after Elijah, and ministered unto him" (v. 21). As a vessel he has been cleansed, and made meet

for the Master's use. He forsook all and followed Him.
He began his great life's work in a very humble fashion,
by "pouring water in the hands of Elijah" (2 Kings 3. 11).
He sought not great things for himself, but only to please
and help his Master. Oh, that the words of our gracious
Master might be true in our lips when face to face with the
needs of men! "I am among you as he that serveth."
"Whatsoever He saith unto you, do it" (John 2. 5).

ELIJAH, THE REPROVER.

1 Kings 21. 15-29.

"Life is beautiful wholly, and could we eliminate only
  This interfering, enslaving, o'ermastering demon of craving,
  This wicked tempter inside us, to ruin still eager to guide us,
  Life were beatitude."—CLOUGH.

IF spotless angels fell through the sin of ambition, how can
a sinful man hope to succeed by it? The scheming Jezebel
had brought the honest Naboth to an untimely death, that
her weak but ambitious husband might get possession of
his inheritance. The *greed of gain* has driven others than
Jezebel into terrible deeds of darkness. The love of the
world is as cruel as the grave. It is as the nursing of a
beautiful serpent that will one day send its poisonous
fang into the soul. There was a—

I. **Seeming Success.** "When Ahab heard that Naboth
was dead, he rose up to take possession of the vineyard"
(v. 16). It was nothing to him how Naboth had died
as long as he was now out of his way to the taking possession of his valuable garden. *"Get, get,"* by hook or by
crook, is the creed of iron-heeled selfishness. What better
are those drink-dealers, who by their craft and cunning
have enticed multitudes to ruin and death that they might
get possession of their money, which was their only
vineyard?

II. **Forgotten Factor.** The Lord said unto Elijah, "Behold, Ahab is gone down to possess the vineyard of Naboth" (vv. 17. 18). That secret chamber has never yet been built where a plot can be formed without the eyewitnessing of God. The forgotten factor in the schemes of worldly men and women is GOD. God is not in all their thoughts. Such may succeed for a time, like Ahab and the Babel builders, but all man's works, to be a *final* success, must pass muster with a righteous God (Gen. 11. 5; 1 Cor. 3. 13).

III. **Stern Command.** "Go down to meet Ahab, and speak unto him, saying, Hast thou killed, and also taken possession? In the place where dogs licked the blood of Naboth shall dogs lick thy blood, *even thine*" (vv. 17. 19). This was a terrible message that Elijah got from the Lord Almighty, who is so infinite in love and compassion. God is love. Yes; but while he "keepeth mercy for thousands" (Exod. 34. 7) He will by no means clear the guilty impenitent. The prophet might have preferred to have taken a more *gracious* message to the king, but to tone down the solemn warnings of Jehovah would be to prove himself a traitor to God and a deceiver of souls (Acts 20. 20-27).

IV. **Startling Question.** "Ahab said to Elijah, Hast thou found me, O mine enemy?" (v. 20). The messenger of God found out Ahab, as the writing on the wall found out the profane Belshazzar. Sudden surprises are sure to overtake the secret sinner (Luke 12. 20). "Be sure your sin will find you out" (Num. 32. 23). But why was the prophet of God his *enemy*? Just because he was living at enmity with God. Was Elijah His enemy because he told Him the truth? (Gal. 4. 16). If the sinner is not found by the servant of God he will one day be found by God Himself. Will it then be as an enemy? Light is always the enemy of darkness.

V. **Straight Answer.** "I have found thee; because thou hast sold thyself to work evil in the sight of the Lord"

(v. 20). When a man has *sold himself* to the work of the
Devil it is surely high time that he was "found out," and
what a mercy it is to be arrested in such a fatal course.
Ahab, in selling himself, like every other such sinner, had
stifled his conscience and deliberately become the abject
slave of lust and pride. To sell one's self "to work evil in
the sight of the Lord" is one of the most culpable and
dastardly transactions of which a human soul is capable.
Yet for greed of gain and love of the world how many there
be who are daily doing it.

VI. Terrible Prospect.   "The dogs shall lick thy
blood; . . . evil upon thee and upon thy posterity; . . . the
dogs shall eat Jezebel" (vv. 21-24). What a dismal out-
look for wealthy royal sinners! The woe that slumbereth
not against the covetous has come (Hab. 2. 9). "With what
measure ye mete, it shall be measured to you again"
(Matt. 7. 2). These judgments were of God's appointment,
not the prophet's. All workers of iniquity have a fearful
future, which sooner or later will reveal itself in awful
reality (Rev. 21. 8). "The hope of the wicked shall be
cut off" (Prov. 2. 22).

VII. Merciful Deliverance.   "When Ahab heard those
words he rent his clothes, and fasted, and lay in sackcloth,
and went softly. Then when the Lord saw that Ahab
humbled himself before Him, He promised not to bring the
evil in his days" (vv. 27-29). Repentance and humility
before God is the only way whereby the guilty may hope
to escape Holy and fiery indignation. There is nothing like
a discovery of our sinfulness before Him to make us go
softly. Here is another proof of God's readiness to forgive
the penitent. He *delighteth* in mercy; judgment is His
strange work. The great outstanding and unfailing testimony to God's willingness to save is the Cross of Christ
(Isa. 57. 7).

BĔN-HADAD'S FALL AND RESTORATION.

1 Kings 20. 30-34.

"Jesus, who to Thy Father prayed
For those who all Thy love repaid
With this dread cup of woes,
Teach me to conquer, Lord, like Thee,
By patience and benignity,
The thwarting of my foes."—FABER.

THE cause of the defeat of the great host of Syrians was a *denial of God*. They did not believe that the God of Israel had any power in the *valleys* (v. 28). An imperfect and false idea of God has been, and is still, the source of ruin to many. "They that *know* their God shall be strong" (Dan. 11. 32). To the believer God is the God of every hill and valley of their daily life. We do not attempt here an *exposition* of the above Scripture, but wish to use it only as an illustration or historical *picture* of the great salvation. Notice then a—

I. Fearful Condition. "Ben-hadad fled into an inner chamber" (v. 30). The marginal reading of the Revised Version is "from chamber to chamber," as one convicted of danger and seeking safety, but finding no place to rest. How like this is to an *awakened* sinner, running as it were from place to place, from sin to sin, and from pleasure to pleasure, seeking rest and relief to his troubled soul, but never getting any assurance of salvation. "Not by works of righteousness which we have done."

II. Hopeful Proclamation. "We have heard that the kings of the house of Israel are *merciful* kings" (v. 31). These servants who had heard this good news did not hide the tidings from the anxious Ben-hadad, but carried them at once to him. Have we not heard that the King of Heaven is merciful, and that He *"delighteth* in mercy," and is *"ready* to pardon?" Are we hiding the good news, like the lepers of Samaria, from those timid and fearful souls who, like Ben-hadad, have been crushed and defeated in the battles of life, and who run to and fro *secretly* seeking a place of rest?

III. **Self-humbling Intercession.** "They put sackcloth on their loins, and ropes on their heads, and came to the king of Israel, and prayed for him" (v. 32). In praying for Ben-hadad they were praying for one who had forfeited his life through open rebellion. These intercessors identified themselves with the guilty one for whom they prayed. The sackcloth and the ropes spoke of repentance and a readiness to die for his sake. The way to pray for others is to put ourselves in their position and circumstances. Did our Lord Jesus Christ not do this? Where is our sackcloth and ropes when we make intercession for transgressors before our merciful King? Is our *sympathy* manifested?

IV. **Heartening Revelation.** "He is my brother" (v. 32). When the king of Israel deigned to call him, who had been his enemy, *his "brother,"* it was the throwing open of the door of grace and mercy to the petitioners. They were quick to catch it, and take advantage of it, by saying, *"Thy* brother." What an encouragement we have in praying for others when we know that He *loves* His enemies and is prepared to receive them and treat them as brothers!

V. **Peaceful Reconciliation.** "He caused him to come up into the chariot" (v. 33). A little while ago he was fighting against the king of Israel, now he is reconciled to him, and having fellowship with him in his own chariot. Once we were enemies to the Son of God by our wicked works, but now, through grace and a mighty intercession, we have been brought nigh, and lifted up, and made to sit with Him in heavenly places. Our fellowship is now with the Son in the chariot of His salvation.

VI. **Voluntary Restitution.** "Ben-hadad said, The cities which my father took from thy father I will restore" (v. 34). Now that he had been "saved by grace" he was prepared to yield up to him all that beforetime had been taken from him. Should not the saving grace of the Lord Jesus Christ constrain us to yield up to Him that life which was beforetime taken from His service and spent in opposition to His will? (Rom. 12. 1). "Thou hast loosed my bonds. . . What shall I render unto the Lord?" (Psa. 116. 12, 16, 17).

VII. **Blessed Consummation.** "So he made a covenant with him" (v. 34). They made a mutual agreement to seek one another's welfare in time to come. Surely all self-seeking should end when we have been forgiven and reconciled unto God through the death of His Son. Is there not also a mutual understanding between the saved sinner and the Son of God, that while He looks after our interests in Heaven we should look after His interests on earth? As He has brought us into sonship shall we not agree to be His bond-slaves? "I determined not to know nothing among men save Jesus Christ and Him crucified" (1 Cor. 2. 2). So said Paul, whose whole soul had been captivated by the covenanting grace of God.

MICAIAH, THE FAITHFUL.
1 Kings 22.

"When gathering clouds around I view,
And days are dark and friends are few,
On Him I lean, who, not in vain,
Experienced every human pain;
He sees my wants, allays my fears,
And counts and treasures up my tears."—GRAN

UNION is not always strength, for an unequal yoke with unbelievers is shown in this chapter to be utter weakness. God is willing to use *weak* things, but not *unclean* things.

The godless Ahab was quite pleased to have the help of the God-fearing Jehoshaphat, but such compromising on his part could only end in shame and defeat. However, he was anxious that some true prophet might be consulted, and at last Micaiah was called. Micaiah is a noble man, with some of the daring of Elijah about him. Let us ask—

I. Who was he?

1. HE WAS A HOLY MAN, a man who knew the mind of the Lord (v. 8). The meaning of his name is *"Who is like Jehovah?"* In his *character* he was like God, and in his *testimony* there are *none like God*. He was Jehovah's mouthpiece and representative, a light to shine in a dark place. All who have been called of God into the fellowship of His Son have been called to a like life and work.

2. HE WAS TEMPTED. The messenger that was sent from the king to call him tried to persuade him to speak words pleasing to the king, as the other prophets had done (v. 13). The temptation was to please man rather than God. Paul said, "If I *yet* pleased men, I would not be the servant of Christ." The king's four hundred false prophets had all spoken smooth things, but the man who stands in God's stead must be prepared to stand alone. The workers of iniquity always like to hear good said concerning them, and men-pleasers are always found speaking smooth things.

3. HE WAS FAITHFUL. "Micaiah said, What the Lord saith unto me, that will I speak" (v. 14). When Luther was told that all the world was against him, his answer was, "Then I am against the whole world." The faithful preacher will never shun to declare the whole counsel of God" (Acts 20. 27). "He that hath My Word let him speak My Word faithfully, saith the Lord, for what is the chaff to the wheat?" (Jer. 23. 28). A man handles the Word of God deceitfully when he turns its sharp edge away from the hearts of the people (see v. 17).

II. How was he Treated?

1. HE WAS HATED. "There is yet one man, Micaiah: but I hate him" (v. 8). Why did the king hate him? Because of this faithfulness to God. "He doth not prophecy good concerning *me*." His words were not smooth enough for the royal ear. Christ and His disciples were hated for the same cause. The carnal mind *is* enmity against God. It is quite clear that if Ahab had loved God he would not have hated His servant because he spoke the truth. "Every one that doeth evil hateth the light" (John 3. 20).

2. HE WAS MOCKED. "Zedekiah smote him on the cheek, and said, Which way went the Spirit of the Lord from me to speak unto thee?" (v. 24). What does false prophets or men-pleasing professors know about the Spirit of God? He has no place in their ministry. They are always ready to *smite* with the tongue when grace has not been poured into their lips. But smiting the speaker does not break the teeth of the truth. In our testimony for Christ we need never forget that our position is outside the camp of worldly-mindedness, bearing His reproach.

3. HE WAS IMPRISONED. "Put this fellow in the prison" (v. 27). He became the enemy of the self-seeking because he spoke the truth. It is easy to bind the servant of God, but the Word of God is not to be bound; its Spirit, like the wind, bloweth where it listeth. When they imprisoned John Bunyan "The Pilgrim's Progress" came out of the jail, and has been wandering through the world ever since.

III. What Became of his Prophecy? (v. 17).

1. IT WAS FULFILLED, ALTHOUGH SOME BELIEVED IT NOT. The king had ordered him to be shut up until he would return from the battle in peace. He was peaceful enough when he came back, for he was carried back dead (v. 37) according to the word of Micaiah (v. 28). The

unbelief of some could never make the Word of God of none effect.

2. IT WAS FULFILLED, ALTHOUGH THE UNBELIEVER DISGUISED HIMSELF TO ESCAPE IT (vv. 30, 34). No man has ever yet been able to disguise himself so that God could not find him out. The "bow at a venture" became the divine detective to apprehend Ahab. God's arrows never miss the mark. There are many ways by which unbelievers disguise themselves, with the hope of escaping the judgment of God. Be sure your sin will find you out. The cloak of morality or religion will never hide from God the sin of an unbelieving heart (1 Sam. 16. 7).

3. IT WAS FULFILLED, BECAUSE IT WAS GOD'S WORD (v. 14). His Word shall not return void, as an empty, fruitless thing. Every Word of God is pure, incorruptible, and unfailing. He never *speculates*. There is no shadow of doubt about God's shalls. The prophet who speaks in the Name of the Lord and whose word does not come to pass is a fraud (Deut. 18. 21, 22). It is impossible for God to lie. *"How* shall we escape if we *neglect* so great salvation?" (Heb. 2. 3).

——

CHRIST NEAR, BUT OUTSIDE.
Revelation 3. 20.

1. A Present Saviour.   "At the door."

2. A Waiting Saviour.   "Behold I stand."

3. A Seeking Saviour.   "And knock."

4. A Pleading Saviour.   "If any man open the door."

5. A Promising Saviour.   "I will come in."

6. A Providing Saviour.   "And sup with him, and he with Me."

EXPOSITORY OUTLINES.
New Testament.

A GREAT FAILURE.
Luke 12. 13-21.

"Give us Thy grace to rise above
    The glare of this world's smelting fires;
Let God's great love put out the love
    Of gold, and gain, and low desires.
Still sweetly rings the Gospel strain
    Of golden store that knows no rust;
The love of Christ is more than gain,
    And heavenly crowns than yellow dust."

              —Alexander.

This parable of the rich and prosperous fool was given to rebuke the covetousness of the man who said to the Master, "Speak to my brother that he divide the inheritance with me." But the Lord could see that under the mask of justice there gleamed the greedy eye. Who made Me a judge or divider over you? Take heed and beware of covetousness, for a man's life consisteth not in the abundance of the things which he possesseth. This socialistic brother, who wanted the *inheritance divided*, misunderstood the mission of Christ, who came to save us from our *sins*. But the time is coming when He will be made both Judge and Divider over all the earth, for He shall judge His people and divide to every man according to his works. In turning our attention to the "certain man" referred to in the parables we would note his—

I. **Prosperous Condition.** "The ground of a certain rich man brought forth plentifully" (v. 16). He was on the highway to worldly honour and applause. "For men will praise thee when thou *dost well thyself*" (Psa. 49. 18). He was evidently a land proprietor, the *ground* seemingly belonge'd to himself. He could pull down his barns at will, without consulting any one. The day of prosperity is perhaps a greater test to a man's character than the day of adversity. The Rev. Mr. Jay once had this request handed to him: "The prayers of this congregation are asked for a man who is prospering in trade." He needed them.

II. Present Dilemma. "He thought within himself, saying, What shall I do?" (v. 17). Ah! this thought *within himself* was not hid from Him who is a discerner of the hearts of men. He had probably just gone for his night's rest, after having surveyed those fields so heavily laden with a plentiful harvest. The vision of lavish abundance is before his eyes, the tide of good fortune is coming in like a flood. "What shall I do?" He is quite unconscious of the tremendous importance of this crisis. What he does *now* will fix and determine his eternal character. Let us also take heed.

III. Settled Purpose. "He said, This will I do: I will pull down my barns and build greater" (v. 18). The die is cast. He is weighed in the balance and found wanting. There is no recognition of God in all his plans, no acknowledgment of His goodness. God is not in all his thoughts. He has made the greatest miscalculation that any scheming mortal can make in allowing the GIVER OF ALL no place in his reckoning. We may deliberately vote God out of our lives by our "This will I do," but every "I will" of self has to do with the "Thou wilt" of God (Acts 9. 6).

IV. Self-Congratulation. "And I will say to my soul, Soul, thou hast much goods; . . . take thine ease," etc. (v. 19). This rich pauper's life was entirely absorbed in his own selfish ease and gratification. A self-centred life is for ever a lost life. *"Much goods."* O, soul, be these thy gods? They will certainly be deaf and dumb to thy cry in a famishing eternity (Luke 16. 19-25). The writer once received a one-pound note with these words written on the back of it, "This is the best friend I ever had." So that poor unknown soul had to part with his *best friend*. Not so with those who have the living unchanging Christ as their Friend.

V. Terrible Awakening. "But God said unto him, Fool, this night thy soul shall be required of thee" (v. 20). This sudden handwriting of God on the wall of his self-satisfied soul was a fearful interruption to his godless plans. This night "THEY require thy soul" (R.V., *margin*). They! Who? They by whose spirit he had been ruled (Eph. 2. 2), and to whom he had yielded himself a willing servant (Rom. 6. 16). God does not require such world-sodden souls in the kingdom of Heaven. "Lo, this is the man that made not God his strength; but trusted in the abundance of his riches" (Psa. 52. 7). Covetousness is a kind of lunacy that makes men fools in the sight of God. Blessed are they who are fools for Christ. Then notice lastly—

VI. The Lord's Application. "So is he that layeth up treasure *for himself*, and is not rich toward God" (v. 21). To make it our life's business to live only for self-interest is pure unadulterated madness. Not to be rich toward God when He hath brought within our reach the "unsearchable riches of Christ" (Eph. 3. 8); riches of His grace and glory is to play the fool. Sell not your soul's birthright to heavenly and eternal treasure for the "much goods" of this world, which, if you set *your heart* on them, will only be to you as Esau's mess of pottage. There is a poverty that maketh rich (2 Cor. 6. 10). "Covet earnestly the best gifts" (1 Cor. 12. 31).

LESSONS FROM A BANKRUPT.
Luke 12. 22-34.

"Heart-buried in the rubbish of the world—
The world, that gulph of souls, immortal souls."
—YOUNG.

OUR Lord never lost an opportunity of letting the light of
truth shine into dark sin-beclouded souls. He had just
spoken the parable of "a certain rich man" to expose the
sin and folly of covetousness. Then, in these verses quoted
above, He presses home upon the hearts of "His disciples"
the needlessness of *harassing anxiety* about worldly and
material things. The "rich man" who suddenly died a
spiritual pauper should teach us to lay up treasures in
Heaven. The Great Teacher come from God bases his
application on a sevenfold argument—

I. **The Value of Life.** We should not be troubled with
anxious thoughts about our life, for "*the life* IS MORE *than
meat*" (vv. 22, 23). We do not live to eat, but eat to live,
and life is the gift of God. This thought is specially
precious to the children of God by faith. They have been
made partakers of the divine nature, a new creation,
through the incoming of this new and eternal life. This
life is surely more than the meat that supplies it with fresh
energy. *Your* life, as the followers and servants of Christ,
is of more value to Him than the food and raiment needed
to sustain that life. Therefore take no thought for your
life. He who gives the greater will not fail in the less.
"Cast all your care upon Him" (1 Peter 5. 7).

II. **The Manner of the Ravens.** "Consider the ravens:
they neither sow nor reap, . . . and God feedeth them ; . . .
ye are better than fowls" (v. 24). The second reason
Christ gives us why we should rest ourselves in God, concerning the things of this present life, is, "God feedeth the
ravens, and ye are *better than they*." They were not re-

deemed by the Blood of His Son, nor called with an holy calling. The ravens, with neither "storehouse nor barn," were happily unconscious of their poverty; the rich man who would "pull down his barns and build greater" (v. 18) was equally unconscious of his spiritual bankruptcy. The raven's ignorance is its bliss; the rich man's ignorance was his curse. Christ's next argument is drawn from—

III. **The Growth of the Lilies.** "Consider the lilies how they grow. . . . If God so clothe the grass, . . . how much more YOU?" (vv. 27, 28). If God clothes and adorns the grass that may go to the oven to-morrow with the lilies, how much more carefully will He clothe you who are going into the Father's house above? The lily-glory of the grass was greater than Solomon's; the righteousness which is unto all, and *upon all* who believe is the righteousness of God. Therefore, with regard to *supply* and *adorning*, the disciples of Christ must rest in the Lord. This rest does not mean idleness (1 Tim. 5. 8). Neither can it mean failure (Phil. 4. 19).

IV. **The Knowledge of the Father.** "Your Father knoweth that ye have need of these things" (v. 30). Oh, the sweetness of these words to the care-burdened heart! *"Your Father knoweth."* Coming as they do from the lips of Him who is the eternal Son, they are unspeakably precious, for He does know the deep, real love and faithfulness of the Father's heart toward those who are His blood-bought children. Your Father knoweth that ye have need of these things. Then why harass your hearts with anxious thoughts about them, as if your Father neither knew nor cared about your need? If you can say, "The LORD is my Shepherd," you may confidently add, "I shall not want." Be content, for He hath said, "I will never leave thee" (Heb. 13. 5).

V. **The Promise of Christ.** "Seek ye the Kingdom of

God, and *all these things will be added unto you*" (v. 31).
Those who seek first the Kingdom of God as the object
of the soul's life will have all those things which "the
nations of the world *seek after*" added as a matter of course
and of necessity.   It is a small matter to give the clothing
when we have parted with the child.   Those things which
the restless worldling seek after are to be *added* to the
servants of God as things that are as needful for the life as
the sunshine of Heaven or the air we breathe.   Solomon
asked that he might have *understanding*, for the Kingdom
of God's sake, and there was added both *riches* and *honour*
(1 Kings 3. 11-13).   Godliness has the promise of the life
that *now is* and of that which is to come (1 Tim. 4. 8).

VI. **The Littleness of the Flock.**   "Fear not, little
flock; for it is your Father's good pleasure to *give you* the
Kingdom" (v. 32).   The more weak and helpless the child
is the more love and care will the mother lavish upon it.
Our felt and confessed weakness is the secret of our
spiritual strength (2 Cor. 12. 10).   It is not to those wise
in their own eyes, but "unto *babes*," to whom the Father
reveals His great and precious secrets, and for this Jesus
was thankful (Matt. 11. 25, 26).   It is the poor of this
world that are most frequently the rich in faith (Jas. 2. 5).
The flock may be very little, as the word means, but the
pleasure of the Father-Shepherd towards them is very good.
Therefore, take no anxious thought about your life.

VII. **The Character of the Heart.**   "Where your
treasure is, there will your heart be also" (v. 34).   It is
not so much *what* the treasure is as *where* it is that de-
termines the nature of it.   The human *heart* has always
a something that is dearly coveted as treasure.   So the
affections of the heart and that real or imaginary treasure
will always be wedded together.   Seeing, then, that the
things needful for this present life are freely promised us,

we are thereby relieved from any *anxious thought* about
them, that we might be entirely free to set our whole
hearts' affections on things above (John 8. 36). "Whatsoever He saith unto you, do it" (John 2. 5).

HE IS COMING.
Luke 12. 35-48.

"Thou art coming, O my Saviour!
Thou art coming, O my King!
In Thy beauty all resplendent,
In Thy glory all transcendent,
    Well may we rejoice and sing.

Coming in the opening east,
Herald brightness slowly swells;
Coming! O my glorious Priest,
Hear we not Thy golden bells."—HAVERGAL.

IN this portion there are several lessons which are of
tremendous importance in these latter days in which we
live. We learn that—

I. **The Lord is Coming.** "He *will return* from the
wedding" (v. 36). This is not the coming of death—at
death we go to Him—but the coming of the "LORD HIM-
SELF," who said, "I will come again" (John 14. 3). Were
the disciples not told by the heavenly messenger that "this
same Jesus shall in like manner come again?" (Acts 1. 11).

II. **He will Come like a Thief** (v. 39). He will come
suddenly, like lightning (Matt. 24. 27), and like a thief,
unexpectedly to the many. A thief would never think
of telling the day and the hour when he was coming to
break through and steal. The day of the Lord cometh as
a thief *in the night*. This terrible Christ-dishonouring night
is fast settling down upon us. "But *ye, brethren,* are not in
darkness that that day should overtake you as a thief"
(1 Thess. 5. 2-6).

III. **We should be Looking for Him.** "Blessed are

those whom the Lord, when He cometh, shall find *watching*"
(v. 37).   We are not to look for death, but for the "glorious
appearing of our great God and Saviour Jesus Christ,
who gave Himself for us" (Titus 2. 13).   It is said to the
credit of the Thessalonian converts that they "turned
to God from idols to serve the living and true God, and to
wait for His Son from Heaven."   Do we not always watch
and long for the return of loved ones when they go away
from us for a season?   If Christ is precious to us we cannot
but look and long for His personal appearing.

IV. **We should be Ready to Meet Him.**   "Be ye
therefore ready" (v. 40).   This readiness consists in having our "loins girded and our lamps burning" (v. 35).
The "girding" and the "burning" speaks of *teaching* and
testimony, the twofold need of these latter days, when many
are turning away from the faith and giving heed to fables
and the traditions of men which make the *Word of God of
none effect* (Mark 7. 13).   The loins of the mind are to be
"girt about with TRUTH,"   the speculations of critics will
never do this.   The lamp of *life* is to be trimmed and
brightly burning through the oil of the Holy Spirit.

V. **The Faithful shall be Rewarded when He Comes**
(vv. 41-44).   All the servants of Christ are *"stewards* of
the mysteries of God" (1 Cor. 4. 1), and as such are expected to give to the household of faith "their portion
of meat in due season."   We, as servants, "must all appear
before the judgment-seat of Christ, that every one may
receive according to that he hath done" (2 Cor. 5. 10).   His
"Well done," will never be spoken to those who have lived
only for themselves.   A selfish life is a cowardly God-
dishonouring existence.   Such verily have their reward.

VI. **The Unfaithful shall Suffer Loss at His Coming.**
He will be cut asunder, separated from the faithful ones,
and appointed the portion of the unbelieving (v. 46).

The portion of the unfaithful is *shameful* disappointment (1 John 2. 28). Looking for the coming of the Lord Jesus Christ has a powerful effect upon the daily life. It was the man who said, "My lord delayeth his coming," that began to smite his fellow-servants (v. 45). Children in school will be on their good behaviour when they know that the master is just at the door, coming in. It is possible to be saved and yet to suffer the loss of every reward by having our *works* burned up in the fire of His testing judgment (1 Cor. 3. 12-15). But there will be degrees of punishment, because there are degrees of privilege. To whomsoever much is given, of him shall be much required (vv. 47, 48). Whether the stripes be many or few, the Judge of all the earth shall do right. Let us praise His Name, "that with His stripes we are healed" (Isa. 53. 5).

THE BARREN FIG-TREE.
Luke 13. 6-9.

"Praise, O Lord, for grace bestowed,
If fair graces in me have showed;
Praise for growth as of leaf or flower
By Thy Spirit's quickening power;
But fruit, 'much fruit,' O Lord, I ask
As 'neath Thy sweet shining I bask;
Enrich me as I urge my suit,
With nothing less than plenteous fruit."

THE Jews as a nation were more highly favoured than any other. Taken out of barren Egypt and planted by the hand of God in fertile Canaan, with all the care and protection that divine wisdom and power could bestow, much fruit was naturally expected. But the heart of Him who planted was grieved and disappointed. For three years GOD IN CHRIST sought fruit and found none. Yet the compassionate Saviour interceded, crying, "Father, forgive them" (Luke 23. 34). And though spared for a season to get the "digging" of His teaching and proofs of His resurrection, yet remaining in unbelief they were cut off (Rom. 11. 20). Cumberers will not always be permitted in His vineyard. This parable contains solemn and searching lessons for every Christian.

I. The Tree Mentioned. Observe its—

1. HOPEFUL CHARACTER. "A fig-tree" (v. 6). It is the right kind of a tree for a garden. It was a fruit tree. It belonged without doubt to a valuable *class* of trees. None could dispute its good connection. This fig-tree represents one who has been born from above, who has received a new nature, and who is a new creature, one who belongs to the *family* of God. He is perfectly assured of his honourable connection. Once he had another name and a more disreputable character, but now he is classed as a Christian.

2. GREAT PRIVILEGE. "Planted in the vineyard" (v. 6). This fig-tree did not grow by the wayside. It was more highly favoured. It was *chosen* by the Lord of the vineyard and carefully *planted* in the most favourable place, under the immediate *eye* and *hand* of the skilful dresser, and within the enclosure of the separating walls. In short, it was chosen, planted, supplied, and protected. Such is the privilege of every chosen one. "I have chosen you, and ordained you, that you should bring forth fruit" (John 15. 16). Ye are the Lord's planting, and in the place of blessing has He put you "by the rivers of water" (Psa. 1. 3).

3. BARREN CONDITION. "Fruitless" (v. 7). Fruit sought and none found. Is it possible? A fruit tree in a vineyard and yet no fruit? Quite possible, and, alas, far too common. Then who is to blame? Neither the dresser nor the ground, but the tree, which refuses or neglects to rise up to its great privilege. It was planted there not for an ornament, not merely to be fed, but to *bear fruit*, failing this all is failure. It might boast of its life, leaves, and opportunities, but there is nothing to satisfy the Lord.

Many are fruitless Christians just for the same reason. Failing to *prove their nature* by their fruits they fail to rise to their high calling. The Lord seeks fruit, and has a right to expect it from every fruit-tree in His vineyard. Your presence in the vineyard proves His claim.

II. The Master's Complaint. "Behold these three years I come seeking fruit on *this* fig-tree" (v. 7). From His own language we have suggested three thoughts. His—

1. LONG SUFFERING GRACE. "These three years. " (v. 7). "He is long suffering to usward, not willing that any should perish" (2 Peter 3. 9). The three years suggest something like a threefold failure. Yet hitherto no judgment was passed. It stands by grace alone. How his heart must have been grieved at seeing such great grace bestowed in vain, or worse, only used for *self- aggrandisement.* How is it with you? What about all your privileges? Has the Master found fruit in your life? He, no doubt, has been seeking fruit. How long is it since you was converted, or planted in the vineyard? Have you only been a receiver, drinking up the sap and the sunshine of His gifts, while he, the Master, receives nothing? Oh, ungrateful heart!

2. WEARIED PATIENCE. "Cut it down" (v. 9). "Hope deferred maketh the heart sick" (Isa. 7. 13). The trees in the vineyard are judged by their *works*, those outside by their *nature*. By our works are we justified or condemned. Fruit-bearing constitutes the only title we have to our continuance in the vineyard (Isa. 15. 2). "My Spirit will not always strive with men. " Privileges abused will be privileges lost. He that *hid* his lord's money lost it, and suffered besides. Shall we sin that grace may abound? God forbid! for the grace of God teacheth us to deny ungodliness and to live soberly and righteously in this present world. Mere lip profession will not save us from becoming a castaway as a servant (1 Cor. 9. 27).

3. SOLEMN QUESTION. "Why cumbereth it the ground?"
Every *fruitless* tree is a cumberer. Why should *it* be a
hindrance? Who can reply against this? Who can defend
the *fruitless*? Every unfruitful professor is a burden and
a hindrance. Their roots, or motives, get intertwined with
those of the fruit-bearing, and drink up that which should
have gone to the fruit-making. And how often we spread
forth our barren branches over others, hindering the bright
sunshine, and so affect their fruit-bearing. The incon-
sistencies of professing Christians have been the destruction
of much fruit; they act as a biting frost upon the tender bud.

III. The Dresser's Intercession. He—

1. PLEADS FOR MORE GRACE. "This year also" (v. 8).
How interesting that he who had been at all the labour and
watchfulness, without receiving any credit or honour
through it, should yet advocate its cause and plead in its
name. Here Jesus is seen, and His voice is heard. He
maketh continual intercession for us. "I pray not that
thou shouldst take them *out of the world*" (John 17. 15).
That some Christians are still in the *place of* fruit-bearing,
but in a barren condition, living only for self, how much is
this owing to the priestly work of Jesus? "This year also."
This may be your last.

2. PROMISES MORE WORK. "I shall dig about it, and
dung it" (v. 8). This speaks of grace more abundantly.
If fruit is found at all it must be the result of grace alone.
Other trees are not to be impoverished for the sake of this,
hence the extra digging, etc. The unfruitful Christian has
often been perplexed and amazed at the unusual digging
about the roots of his being, which looked very much like a
removal at the time. Such times of affliction and trial are
solemn warnings. They seem to whisper, "More fruit," or less
privilege. The shaking of the roots indicate the presence of
the Gardener. After the digging comes the additional supply

3. Agrees that the Results should be Final. "After that" (v. 9). Oh, how very solemn is this *"after that!"* This is known only to themselves, the owner and the dresser. The last effort grace may expend in order to fruit-bearing may be a season of affliction, a searching sermon, or some providential incident. In the case of many this may have already taken place. The present may be the brief season of His waiting. Waiting on God, and God waiting on us, are widely different thoughts. The fruit of a fig-tree is figs, the fruit of a Christian is Christ.

MADE STRAIGHT.
Luke 13. 10-16.

> "I would not champ the hard cold bit
> As *thou*—of what the world thinks fit,
> But take God's freedom, using it."
> —E. B. Browning.

Coleridge's definition of freedom is, "The unfettered use of all the powers which God for use hath given." Before all the powers that God hath given us can be used for Him the fetters of sin and the power of Satan must be broken. The woman before us here, "whom Satan had bound," and whom Christ set at liberty, is a perfect example of how a sin-bound soul may enter into the freedom of God. She was—

I. Crooked. "Bowed together" (v. 11). She had been bound by Satan for eighteen years (v. 16). Completely *deformed* by the power of the Devil. It is always Satan's business, wherever he can, to bow down the souls of men to the earth. Sin never fails to make a crook in the will and thoughts of those under its dominion. Their name is legion, who are so bound together by the love of the world that they cannot lift their faces to Heaven. Crooked through the constant use of the muck-rake.

II. Helpless. "She could in no wise lift up herself"

(v. 11). It was utterly impossible for her to break the cords that bound her face to the earth. She had been so long bowed down that her deformity had become fixed, like a crooked tree of eighteen years old. She was perfectly conscious of her outward disfigurement, and had often tried to straighten herself up, but "she *could not.*" How like this is to those who are morally "bowed together" through drink, lust, or temper, and who again and again have attempted to *lift themselves* up, but they cannot, back they go to their *natural* deformity.

III. Anxious. She was in the synagogue on the Sabbath day, when Jesus was there (v. 10-11). Perhaps it was because He was there that she was there; at anyrate she was putting herself in the way of getting blessing. It does not matter where we take our sin-crooked souls, there is no deliverance for them so long as we avoid the presence of the Son of God and refuse to hear His Word. If Bartimeus had bolted over the fence when he heard that Jesus was passing by, instead of praying, he would have certainly remained in his blindness.

IV. Invited. "Jesus called her to Him" (v. 12). He *saw* many in the synagogue, but He *called* her, for He came not to call the righteous, but sinners to repentance. The Spirit of the Lord was upon Him to proclaim *liberty* to the captives, and the opening of the prison to them that are *bound* (Isa. 61. 1). True to His mission, He searches out this helpless one "whom Satan had *bound,* lo, these eighteen years." Jesus Christ alone hath the keys of all the prison houses of Satan (Rev. 1. 18). When He opens no man can shut.

V. Touched. "He laid His hands on her" (v. 13). Jesus Christ comes into *personal* contact with every soul whom He saves. He cannot delegate this great work to another. He is ready to lay His healing and fetter-breaking hand upon all who accept His invitation, as this poor woman did. The woman mentioned in Luke 8. 44 came without any special invitation, and touched His garment, and was instantly delivered. The results are the same, whether He condescends to touch us, or suffers us to touch Him, it is all of grace on His part. His hands are the hands of infinite love and power, they are never exercised in vain.

VI. **Delivered.** Notice the terms used, "Loosed from thine infirmity,...made straight,...loosed from this bond" (v. 12). It was to her a *full* salvation. It consisted of a deliverance from her own weakness, a freedom from the binding power of Satan, and a being made straight for future life and work. She was now a monument of His gracious wonder-working power. Such is His salvation. A *loosing* of the soul from the bondage of Satan and moral infirmity, and a making of the heart *straight* for an *upright* life and loving service. Therefore the song of the saved is, "Unto Him who loved us, and...*loosed* us from our sin by His own blood" (Rev. 1. 5, R.V.).

VII. **Thankful.** "Immediately she glorified God" (v. 13). A new song was put into her mouth as soon as her feet had been taken out of the horrible pit of her eighteen years' bondage through Satan (Psa. 40. 2, 3). The snare was broken by the power of Him who came "to heal all that were *oppressed* by the Devil" (Acts 10. 38), and now her soul had escaped like a bird, and was singing her song of praise high up in the wide, pure Heaven of God's redeeming love.

THE GREAT SUPPER.

Luke 14. 16-24.

"My need, and all my need, Thou wilt supply;
I take Thee at Thy Word, and ask not why."
—GROSART.

THE supper *time* is this present dispensation. The *supper* refers to the blessings and privileges provided for men in

the sacrifice of God's Son.   The *many* bidden (v. 16) are
the Jews who received the *first* invitation, and who had been
advised a long time beforehand.   The *excuses* are the silly
objections brought by them against Jesus and His claims.
The *poor and maimed* are the publicans and sinners among
both Jew and Gentile who accepted the invitation.   Those
compelled to come in from the highways and hedges are the
strangers afar off who had no hope.   Those who shall *never
taste* of this supper are the unbelieving Jewish nation, who
have been "cut off" (Acts 13. 46; Rom. 11. 20).   Such
may be the dispensational teaching of the parable, but let
us look at some practical thoughts.   A—

I. Threefold Reason for Coming.

1. "COME, FOR ALL THINGS ARE NOW READY."   "All
things."   Every spiritual and temporal blessing for time
and eternity is *now ready* in Christ Jesus.   We often see a
notice about some new book being in the press or *now ready*.
Here is an advertisement that all things pertaining to a
sinner's salvation is "NOW READY."   Do you need a *substitute* ?   Then behold the Lamb of God.   Do you need
forgiveness?   Then this is ready (Acts 13. 38).   Do you need
peace ?   Then "Peace is made," etc.   Do you need *power*?
Then "Power is offered" (Acts 1. 8).

2. "COME, FOR ALL CLASSES ARE INVITED."   Surely these
four classes include all sorts.   First, *the poor*—those who
feed on stale scraps, and who have never known what it is
to have a thoroughly satisfying feast.   Those who go from
door to door of the world's pleasure-haunts, begging for
something to satisfy and getting nothing.   Second, *the
maimed*—those who have been deprived of some of their
limbs, and have become hopelessly mutilated.   Morally,
this class represents those whose conscience has been seared,
and whose will-power may have been cut off.   What a helpless object!   Yet come, for all things are ready.   Third,

the halt—those who have all their limbs, but in a crooked and deformed condition, whose manner of walk is neither straight nor steady. They do their best to appear all right, but they cannot possibly conceal their deformity. Fourth, *the blind*—those who can walk pretty straight, but are in the blackness of darkness all the time. Their outward life may be all right in the eyes of men, but they know not where they are going and are unconscious of their danger. You may explain the truth to them, but their answer is, "I cannot see it."

3. "Come, for yet there is room." The house is being rapidly filled, but yet there is room. How much room still remains none can tell. We know not the hour when the Master may rise up and shut to the door. *Yet* there is room —room in the Father's love, in the Saviour's atoning death, in the ministry of the Spirit, and in the offer of the Gospel.

II. **Threefold Excuse for not Coming.** To put them briefly, they may stand thus—

1. "I have something else to see." "I have bought a piece of ground, and must needs go and *see it*" (v. 18). Why is it that men *must needs* go and see after their earthly possessions, and have no time to *look* at the provision God hath made for their eternal safety and inheritance? There are certainly many interesting things in the world to be *seen*, but what can be compared to the saving glory of the Cross of Christ?

2. "I have something else to do." "I must go to prove them" (v. 19). He was more anxious to prove the oxen than to prove the riches of the kingly offer. Some people seem to think that the time to obey the call of God will be when they have *nothing else* to do. There are those who will persist in going on proving their own worldly interests until they finally prove themselves to be fools. While they are "busy here and there" their chance for eternal life is gone.

3. "I HAVE SOMETHING ELSE TO ENJOY." "I have married a wife, and therefore I cannot come" (**v. 20**). All *new* relationships, whether they be business or matrimonial, are sure to have a powerful influence in one way or another. There may be no sin in marrying a wife, in buying a house, in forming a new companionship, or looking forward to some coming event; but if the affections of the heart are so centred on these that the Gospel of God's grace must take a secondary place, then the life becomes a positive insult to the Son of God. God will not be mocked, He has emphatically declared that those who treat lightly His gracious invitation "Shall not taste of My supper." They who prefer to make their own suppers in time will in the end feel the pinch of that poverty which is eternal. No man has ever yet been able to form a God-satisfying excuse for not accepting His Son as their Saviour. It is *you* God invites, not *your excuses*; these can never stand for YOU.

THE LOST SHEEP.
Luke 15. 1-7.

"Blame not thy thought, that it cannot reach,
    That which the Infinite must teach;
Bless thy God, that the Word came nigh,
    To guide thee home to thy native sky."—MacDonald.

THE murmuring of self-righteous scribes and Pharisees drew from our Lord those three pet parables that have brought healing under their wings to many a sin-laden soul. They said sneeringly, "This man receiveth *sinners*," and with merciless feet they sought to trample on the *grace* of Christ. But all the more did this "plant of renown" send forth its heavenly fragrance. The obvious meaning of this parable is to reveal Christ's personal interest in the *salvation of sinners*. It brings before us—

I. A Painful Discovery. "One is lost" (**v. 4**). Whether this one represents a world, a nation, or an individual, the underlying thought is that the Shepherd's restfulness of heart has been disturbed by the discovery that He has lost *one*. The *lost* one immediately draws out the sympathy and longing desires of His soul. When this discovery on Christ's part was first made it may be difficult to say (Eph. 1. 4), but it has been made.

II. **An Altered Purpose.** "He leaves the ninety and nine, and goes after that which was lost" (v. 4). He counted ninety and nine, but He did not count the lost one. To be out of His count is to be lost. The ninety and nine *left* in the wilderness may represent the Jewish nation, who are in the *wilderness* still, being without a Shepherd and without a home—a separated people, having neither king nor country, and priding themselves in their righteousness. But the Shepherd of Israel goes forth in humiliation, agony, and death to seek and save that which was *lost*. He does not seek the lost sheep merely because of *its value*, but because of *His love*. Fallen angels might have been of more *value* than fallen man, but God so *loved* the world.

III. **A Patient Search.** "He goes after the lost *until* He finds" (v. 4). There is no turning back with Him until His purposes are fully accomplished. "He shall see of the travail of His soul, and shall be satisfied." Christ's determination is to find the lost ones, and every lost one He will yet find, if not in His saving mercy certainly in His righteous judgment. Has He not said, "I, if I be *lifted up* from the earth, will draw all men unto Me" (John 12. 32). If sinful men are not drawn to Him by the grace of His Cross they will be drawn by the power of His throne. Every human soul the atoning Son of God must find, either as Saviour or as Judge. Don't you hear the gentle footfall of His blessed presence in His Word even now?

IV. **A Joyful Finding.** "When He hath found it He layeth it on His shoulders rejoicing" (v. 5). To *find* the lost, while He is a seeking Saviour, brings gladness to His gracious heart. Oh, the infinite tenderness of this self-sacrificing Shepherd! there is no word of reproach or of blame uttered. What a wonderful moment this is when the weary sin-worn sinner finds himself *alone* with the gentle Shepherd, and feels His tender yet mighty hands raising him up into the great bosom of love! At this blessed crisis the sheep is everything to the Shepherd and the Shepherd is everything to the sheep. Each rejoicing in each, and having nothing else besides. What a picture of the great salvation! Until the lost ones meet the Saviour they are living solitary, selfish, hopeless lives.

V. A Restful Journey. "He layeth it on His shoulders" (v. 5). The weary, aimless wanderer has now found a resting-place on the shoulders of Him who came to seek and to save. The Lord neither drives nor drags those whom He saves, but undertakes to carry them every step of the way to the home beyond. The way of salvation for this lost one was very simple—just "abiding." The sheep did absolutely nothing but rest on Him who was able and willing to save. His shoulders is the place of strength and safety; the government of the universe rests upon them, then surely they are strong and broad enough for thy weary soul.

VI. A Happy Home. "When He cometh home, He calleth His friends, ... saying, Rejoice with me" (v. 6). As surely as the Shepherd goes home, so surely will He take His trustful sheep with Him. "Where I am, there shall ye be also" (John 14. 3). While in the wilderness, seeking to save the lost, the Son of Man was away from home. But He comes back rejoicing, bringing His sheaves with Him. The "friends and the neighbours" may represent the redeemed; and the angels in glory, who must be everlastingly interested in all that glorifies the Lord Jesus

Christ as the Saviour of men. Are we sharing **Heaven's** joy just now by *rejoicing with Him* over sinners repenting?

THE LOST SILVER.
Luke 15. 8-10.

"I would be missed when gone;
I would not—my life done—
Have no eyes wet for me,
No hearts touched tenderly,
No good of me confessed;
Dead—and yet not missed."

THERE is no exaggeration or false colouring in the word-picture of this heavenly artist. Every touch bears the impress of what is absolutely true. The pictures of ordinary mortals look best in the shade, but Christ's always improve in loveliness as the light increases. This little gem of a parable has been lightly esteemed, because its true meaning and value have not been generally understood. In the *first* parable we have the love of the *Son* in seeking the lost; in the *third* the love of the *Father* in seeking the lost; in this *second* we surely have the love of the *Spirit* in seeking the lost. The woman is a fit emblem of the Holy Spirit in search of a lost but precious thing that might be put to some honourable use. The small silver coin referred to here was a drachma, about the value of a shilling. As representing a human soul, we would point out that it was—

I. Precious. To a poor woman, whose fortune consisted of ten shillings, it was a great privation to lose one. It was a loss that was keenly felt. It also bore the *image* of the king, and so was good *current* coin. Such are souls redeemed by Christ in the estimation of the Holy Spirit. They are precious to Him, and fit for circulation in the interests of the Kingdom of God.

II. Lost. It had slipped *out of her hand*, so that now she had no control over it. It is a sad, sad thing for any one who has known what it is to be in the hand of the Spirit to slip out of touch with Him through pride or unbelief. To be out of His hand is to be *lost* to Him. The *fall* may have been in a moment, but the *grief* created was intense. "Grieve not the Holy Spirit, whereby ye are sealed until the day of redemption" (Eph. 4. 30).

III. **Lost in the House.** It was not like the sheep, lost far away from home. It was *in* the house, but as utterly useless as if it had been in the depths of the sea. It is possible to be in the house of God's salvation, in the place of safety and privilege, and yet to be lost to the *management* of the Holy Ghost.   It is one thing to be justified by faith before God; it is quite another to be ready for service in the hand of God. We may be in the home of the Spirit for salvation, and yet *not* be in the hand of the Spirit for service.

IV. **Lost to Usefulness.** As long as this silver coin was not in the hand and at the disposal of this woman it was lost to all the good it might do. If you throw a sovereign into the sea it would not be only so much gold that would be lost, but all the good that gold might do is lost. So is it with our *lives* after we have been brought into the household of God.   If we are not in the hands of the Holy Spirit, that He might use us by spending us for the glory of God, then our lives are *lost*. Christ seeks to save, but the Holy Spirit seeks to find that He might *use*. No one is able to get so much out of our lives as He.   Be assured He will spend you to the best advantage, whether it be at home or abroad.

V. **Lost in the Dust and Darkness.** In seeking to find she had to "light a candle and sweep the house." The candle of God's Word and the besom of providence are needed before He can get a hold of His lost treasure. The dust of sin and the darkness of unbelief always hinder the Spirit of God from rejoicing over us as a means in His hands for bringing glory to the Lord Jesus Christ. Though the *sweeping* process may be attended with much that is painfully unpleasant, as the dust of our unconfessed sin gets stirred up and the covering of our guilty darkness is being taken away, there must be a disturbance in the house if the Lord the Spirit is to get possession of His lost treasure.

VI. The Cause of Great Joy in the Finding. "Rejoice with me, for *I* have found the piece which *I* had lost" (v. 9). As Jesus, the Shepherd, rejoices over the saving of the sinner, so the Holy Spirit, like this woman, rejoices over the recovery of a precious soul that had been lost to communion and service. It is worthy of notice that the woman does not say, "*My* piece which was lost." The very omission of the *my* (see vv. 6, 24) is strong evidence that the work of the Holy Spirit is here indicated. Believers are the *property* of Christ, but are to be used by the Holy Spirit (Acts 1. 8).

THE LOST SON.
Luke 15. 11-24.

"Alas! how have I served the Devil,
 Still lusting after all things evil;
 For, O my God, I saw the light,
 Yet plunged into the foulest night."

In studying the *three* parables (so-called) in this chapter we should not overlook the fact that they were spoken by our Lord as *one* parable (v. 3) to show how God, as Father, Son, and Holy Ghost "receives sinners" and companies with them. The Son, like the shepherd, seeks the lost that He might *save* them; the Spirit, like the woman, seeks the lost that He might *use* them; God, like the father, seeks the lost that He might have *fellowship*

with them. This is the threefold aspect of this great
and perfect salvation. This parable of the prodigal
has been called "the prince of parables." It has been
the door of hope to many a weary wanderer. Let us
consider his—

I. Selfish Demand. "Give me the portion of goods"
(v. 12). Like many in our own day, he wanted to have all
the goods and blessings that the father could give him, that
they might minister to his own personal gratification,
utterly regardless of the father's wisdom or feelings. It is
dishonouring to God that we should seek to manage our
own lives with His gifts.

II. Wayward Journey. "Into a far country" (v. 13).
The "far country" represents that condition or sphere of
living where God the Father is unknown. A *son* must have
got into an awful sad and sinful state of soul when he feels
that he must leave a rich and gracious *father* in search of
pleasure. The self-will is a rebel against God.

III. Reckless Living. "And there wasted his substance" (v. 13). The sweet fellowship of the father was
exchanged for the "riotous living" of the ungodly, and the
result was, as it ever is with a backslider from God, a
wasting of His precious gifts. We cannot keep the
substance of God's forgiveness—peace and joy—when
we wilfully forsake Him for the pleasures of sin. All
will be wasted; the enjoyment of them will speedily
die away.

IV. Miserable Plight. "When he had spent all, there
arose a mighty famine" (v. 14). A "mighty famine" is
sure to overtake all who have wandered away from God.
Hunger of soul will certainly come upon those who
spend their gifts for that which is not bread. He found
out by bitter experience that "the *rebellious* dwell in
a dry land."

V. Despairing Effort. "He went and joined himself to a citizen" (v. 15). He had willingly given away his substance, now he is compelled to give *himself*. Such is the course of sin. If we waste our gifts and privileges we ourselves will finally become bond-slaves. Lot took the same foolish and fruitless step when he became a ruler in Sodom.

VI. Friendless Condition. "No man gave unto him" (v. 16). He had sold himself for naught. Wretched and self-ruined, he longs for even the satisfaction enjoyed by the beast, envying the swine. "No man gave him." No *man* ever will give a sin-wasted sinner what he needs. You might as well expect heat from an iceberg.

VII. Noble Resolve. "I will arise and go to my father" (v. 18). This is the language of one whose pride had driven him to acts of madness, but is now "come to himself." He *remembers* the "father's house" and the provision there, and the fire of hope springs up from the smouldering embers of his wasted life.

> "While the lamp holds on to burn,
> The greatest sinner may return."

He not only said "I will arise," but he *did it*. Herein was the evidence of his sanity.

VIII. Gracious Reception. "He fell on his neck and kissed him" (v. 20). The father's love at once cast out the prodigal's fears. He began to confess, but his *coming* home was to the father the best confession. What value is there in confession if there is no turning away from sin? (Isa. 55. 7). No one *gave* him in the far country, but now all that the father hath is at his disposal. By taking *his portion* he had forfeited all *right* to further blessing, but he is saved by GRACE, and the father is happy. "By grace are ye saved through faith" (Eph. 2. 8). His grace is sufficient for all who come.

LOST SYMPATHY.

Luke 15. 25-32.

"I ask Thee for a thoughtful love,
　　Through constant watching wise,
To meet the glad with joyful smiles,
　　And wipe the weeping eyes;
And a heart at leisure from itself,
　　To soothe and sympathise."—A. L. WARING.

In its wider scope we think this part of the parable (the
elder brother) is brought in to illustrate the attitude of
the Jewish nation towards that manifested GRACE of God
which hath brought salvation to all men.　The Gentile
prodigal is being saved by grace, while the self-righteous
Jew is angry and will not go in.　Yet all the while, whether
he will or not, this religious *elder* is the *prodigal's* brother—
both alike in need of the Father's forgiveness.　There are
some things about this *elder brother*, so often neglected, that
are worthy of special attention.　He stands before us here
as one—

I. **Who was Willing to Work.**　"Now his elder son was
in the field" (v. 25).　Whatever else he was, he was not
lazy, he had a mind to *work*.　While others were feasting
and dancing he was busy looking after the flocks or the
crops.　He is a type of those who like to be doing, and
whose hands are constantly filled with some kind of good
and useful work.　So active are they that they would much
rather be *in the field* of service than in the *closet* of prayer.

II. **Faithful to Duty.**　He could say, "Neither transgressed I at any time thy commandment" (v. 29), and he
was quick to say it.　As regularly as the clock, does he go
the round of his daily task.　His motto is, "I must do my
duty."　This type of Christian is as straight as an arrow,
as regular as the post, and equally as formal.　He speaks
and acts from a sense of duty and prides himself on doing
the right thing, although it may be done with a heart as

cold as an icicle. The other brother was the *sinner*, but this one is the Pharisee (Luke 18. 11). It is not duty but *love* that constrains the true servant of Christ.

III. **Who had never Received a Mirth-making Gift from the Father.** "Thou never gavest me a kid, that I might make merry with my friends" (v. 29). The reason why he had never received even a kid was doubtless because that in his self-complacency he had never asked it nor even felt the need of it. He was working away without ever seeking any definite token of the father's grace and love, serving without receiving his *mirth-making* GIFT. What about those who week by week go the round of religious performances, but have never at any time received the soul-gladdening gift of God (John 1. 12). It was not the father's fault that his son's service had been so joyless. "Ask and ye shall receive" (John 16. 24). It is honouring to the Lord Jesus Christ when others are constrained to say, like the Queen of Sheba, "Happy are these thy servants" (1 Kings 10. 8).

IV. **Grievously Offended.** "He was angry, and would not go in" (v. 26). His pride was wounded to think that one whose life had been a public scandal should now receive more honour than himself who had never done anything very bad. He *would not go in* with this way of doing things, so he gets entirely out of sympathy—

1. WITH HIS FATHER. The father's heart was brimful of joy at the finding of the *lost* one, but it brought no gleam of gladness into the selfish soul of the elder brother. The conversion of sinners brings no mirth into the heart of those who are out of fellowship with God.

2. HE GOT OUT OF SYMPATHY WITH HIS BROTHER. If he had had any love for his wandering brother he would have rejoiced over his home-coming. To get out of sympathy with God is to get out of sympathy with sinners. How

can a man say that he loves God if he love not his brother also?

3. HE GOT OUT OF SYMPATHY WITH THE SERVANTS. The servants were evidently sharing the joys of the feast, for this one that he questioned had to be *called* (v. 26). The true servant of God must and will rejoice in all that brings gladness to His heart and glory to His Name. To be out of sympathy with the Lord's happy servants, and to refuse to *go in* and share their joys in the saving work of God is a sign of haughtiness of heart and grievous backsliding.

V. Graciously Intreated. "Therefore came his father out and intreated him" (v. 28). The *love* and longsuffering patience of the father in his willingness to receive the *prodigal* has always been recognised and confessed, but his love in plying with melting intreaty this prodigal in *heart* has not been generally acknowledged. It is often more easy to pity the profligate sinner than the self-righteous one. The pleading of the father with the offended son was that he might enter into real hearty *sympathy with him* in his desire after and joy in the salvation of the lost. Are we, as His servants,-in full sympathy with the Lord in His desire to seek and to save?

VI. Greatly Encouraged. Could the father have given him any greater inducement to cast aside all coldness and indifference to his highest interests than this, "Son, thou art ever with me, and *all that I have is thine*" (v. 31).

The return of prodigals unto God is not going to lessen your inheritance in Him any more than the opening of a blind man's eyes can hinder your enjoyment of the sunshine. Christian workers, are you offended because the grace of God lavishes such blessings upon the really *unworthy*? Are you out of sympathy with soul-saving work? Out of sympathy with God? Be intreated, come in, all the fullness of God is awaiting you.

LESSONS FROM A LOST SOUL.
Luke 16. 19-31.

"Sin, not till it is left, will duly sinful seem;
A man must waken first, ere he can tell his dream."
—TRENCH.

THIS "RICH MAN" had to waken up in eternity before he could tell the dream of a wasted life.

"No man can serve two masters" (Matt. 6. 24), especially when the masters differ in character as much as "God and Mammon." Mammon stands for the "love of riches" and the "pleasures of sin." Both God and Mammon demand the *mastery* of our beings. If the love of God does not master us the love of the world will. If we hold to the one, we must of necessity despise the other. The *covetous*, in the pride of their heart, are always ready to "justify themselves in the sight of men," forgetful that they may esteem things very highly which are an abomination in the sight of God (vv. 14, 15). The words which follow about "a certain rich man" and "a certain beggar" are heavy laden with solemn and weighty meaning. The Lord does not call this a parable. His meaning is clear and unmistakable. Then what are the lessons we may learn from this portion?

I. **That a man may have a beautiful appearance in the sight of men, and yet be utterly corrupt in the sight of God** (v. 19). The "purple and fine linen" of man's righteousness will never beautify in the eyes of God. There are those who think that they have need of nothing, and know not that they are wretched, and miserable, and poor, and blind, and naked (Rev. 3. 17).

II. **That a man may be poor and loathsome in the eyes of his neighbour, and yet be rich and beautiful in the sight of God** (vv. 20, 21). The poor beggar may have been an object of disgust to many, but the Lord looketh

not upon the *outward* appearance. It is no uncommon
thing for the character of a poor afflicted child of God to
stink in the nostrils of the covetous and wealthy man of the
world. But the soul of Lazarus was a precious jewel to
God, although the casket was in a *broken* condition.

III. **That a man may have but the burial of a dog,
and yet be attended by the angels of God** (v. 22). No
poorhouse inmate ever got a more unceremonial funeral than
Lazarus.

> "They rattle his bones over the stones,
> He is only a pauper whom nobody owns!"

Yes, God owns him, and white-robed angels bear his
emancipated spirit to the Father's bosom.

IV. **That a man may have a pompous funeral, and
at the same time be a miserable soul** (vv. 22, 23). There
would be more *real mourners* at some funerals if only they
could see within the veil. Men eulogise the *past* of the
world's departed great ones, but what about their *present*?
The wail of the "Dead March in Saul" is mockery compared
with the wail of a lost soul in eternity.

V. **That a man may have abundance of this world's
goods, and yet, in the world to come, be utterly
destitute of the commonest mercy** (v. 24). This wor-
shipper of Mammon on earth has found out in eternity that
a "smiling providence" is no evidence that the soul is right
with God. This everlasting *thirst* for a drop of water is an
awful experience to a man who never knew what want meant,
and who only lived for the gratification of his own desires.

VI. **That if a man neglect his opportunities in this
life, in the life to come he will have good cause to remember his folly** (v. 25). "Son, remember thy lifetime." The remembrance of a wasted *lifetime*, in the
midst of many "good things," will be, in the world to come,
the undying worm of remorse.

VII. **That though saints and sinners may meet together now, the time is coming when they must be eternally separated** (v. 26). Earthly relationships will avail us nothing when the "great gulf is fixed." Everything depends on our relationship to God and His Christ. All the prayers and penance of the Papacy or of purgatory will never bridge this gulf, for it is FIXED (Matt. 13. 30).

VIII. **That the prayers of the lost can avail nothing, neither for themselves nor others** (vv. 24, 27, 28). Those who set no value on prayers in this life will have no value set on them in the life which is to come. It is not enough to be in earnest when the day of grace is past. "Behold, now is the accepted time."

IX. **That those who will not hear and believe the Word of God shall perish without remedy** (vv. 29-31). Signs and wonders would profit us nothing if we will not *hear Him* whom God hath sent to bless us (Luke 9. 35). The Israelites saw His wonders, and murmured against Him. Many saw the miracles of Christ, and yet hated Him; even Lazarus "rose from the dead," and they sought to kill Him (John 12. 10, 11). "Believe in the Lord Jesus Christ, and thou shalt be saved" (Acts 16. 31).

TEN LEPERS CLEANSED.
Luke 17. 11-19.

"Sin is established subtly in the heart
  As a disease, like a magician foul,
  Ruleth the better thoughts against their will.
    Only the rays of God can cure the heart,
  Purge it of evil, there's no other way,
  Except to turn with the whole heart to God."
                                        —ALLINGHAM.

WHEREVER Jesus went He always found occasion for the exercise of His infinite compassion and power; and what is better, He was constantly on the look out for the distressed

and the despairing, supremely conscious that in Himself He
was all-sufficient to meet the need of all.   In Jesus Christ
all the fullness of the Godhead tabernacled among men, and
when He laid down *His life* for us on the atoning Cross, it
was the paying down of His unsearchable riches as the
redemption price of our souls.   His miracle of healing in
this nameless village while on the way to Jerusalem (vv.
11, 12) has for us heart-searching thoughts.   Let us see the—

I. **Pitiful Sight**.   "There met Him ten men that were
lepers" (v. 12).   Ten men bound together by a common
misery, and utterly unable to save themselves.   Although
there were *ten* of them, that did not lessen the sufferings and
dangers of each.   Although we may have many companions
in sin, that does not in any way detract from the guilt of each.
In Scripture *leprosy* is the outstanding type of sin.

1. Like sin, it brings UNCLEANNESS.   The true cry of
the leper, with his shame-covered lip, was to be "Unclean, unclean" (Lev. 13. 45).   We are only *taught*, like
the leper, to speak the truth when we are asked to make
confession of our sins.

2. Like sin, it leads to SEPARATION.   "They stood afar
off" (v. 12).   The place appointed for them by the law of
God was "without the camp" (Lev. 13. 46).   "Far off" is
the position of all those who have not been made nigh by
the blood of Christ (Eph. 2. 13).   Their very character
alienates them from the life and fellowship of God.

3. Like sin, it is humanly INCURABLE.   Man has no remedy
for leprosy; he can only attempt to alleviate their sufferings
while the dreadful plague runs its death-working course.

II. **Earnest Prayer**.   "Jesus, Master, have mercy
on us" (v. 13).   This may have been a hoarse cry through
throats diseased with leprosy, but there was music in it to
the ear of Jesus, for it came from the heart, and was for the

one thing needful. "Mercy"—that mercy which in Jesus Christ was wedded to Omnipotence, and that had its abode in the tenderest and purest of men.

III. **Simple Remedy.** "Go, show yourselves unto the priests" (v. 14). This seems a strange command, but the meaning is clearly this: "The priests have condemned you as lepers; then, if you believe that I can heal you, and am healing you, go and show yourselves, that they may see that you are healed" (Lev. 14. 2-4). "And *as they went* they were cleansed." Two things were absolutely needed:

1. *Faith* in the WORD of Christ (v. 19).

2. *Obedience* to the WILL of Christ.

If they had waited till they *felt better* before they went, they never would have gone. It is while we believe and obey that we enter into life.

IV. **Grateful Recipient.** "And one, when he *saw* that he was healed, turned back and glorified God" (v. 15). Personal healing is something we can only *see* by experience, and a something for which we should be instantly and profoundly thankful. It was a moral impossibility for this man to *glorify* God while in the terrible bondage of leprosy. It is only when we are made free from sin that we can give glory to God. The healing mercy of Christ not only made this Samaritan very thankful, it also made him *humble*. "He fell on his face at His feet." Humility and thankfulness are characteristic of those saved by the grace of God.

V. **Searching Inquiry.** "Were there not ten cleansed? But where are the nine?" (vv. 17-19). He who counted the stars will not fail to *number* those who have been cleansed by His Word. He knows them every one. "Where are the nine?" Surely our Lord expects that those who have been saved by Him should glorify God by making a public acknowledgment of His cleansing power. It is quite possible for us, like those nine, to be very anxious to get salvation merely for our own comfort and happiness, and to be utterly indifferent about honouring the Saviour with our new life. Such *secret* believers—we cannot call them disciples—are ungrateful cowards. This despised "stranger" who turned back to give God the glory got something that the thankless nine did not get. He got the Lord's *assurance* that the work wrought in him was perfect (v. 19). The belief of the heart should always be accompanied with the confession of the mouth (Rom. 10. 9). Where are the nine? Are you one of them?

CHRIST'S SECOND ADVENT.
Luke 17. 20-37.

"Surely the time is short,
Endless the task and art,
To brighten for the ethereal court,
A soil'd earth-drudging heart.
But HE, the great Proclaimer of that hour,
Is pledged to thee in love, as to thy foes in power."
—KEBLE.

THE Lord Jesus Christ did in no way rebuke those Pharisees who demanded of Him "when the Kingdom of God should come" (v. 20). It has been clearly revealed that the *Messiah* would redeem His people, and establish the throne of David. So powerfully did this truth lay hold on the people that at one time they were about to take Jesus by force and make Him King (John 6. 15). But Jesus did not commit Himself to them, knowing what was in man. Even after His resurrection the disciples asked Him, "Lord, wilt Thou at *this time* restore again the kingdom to Israel?" (Acts 1. 6). But even then it was not fit for them to know *when*. We are here taught something of the—

I. **Nature of the Kingdom.** "The Kingdom of God is *among* you" (vv. 20, 21, *margin*). They asked when it should come. The Kingdom, as the *Rule of God*, was already among them in the Person of His Son. There can be no kingdom without a king (see Matt. 12. 28). But as to its outward visible glory, it was still hidden, because He was not yet glorified as Prince and Saviour.

1. It will come SUDDENLY.. "As the lightning" (v. 24). The lightning does not *"come* with observation,*"* that is, men do not see the lightning before it becomes a present reality. "So shall also the Son of Man be *in His day*."

2. It will be UNMISTAKABLE when it does come. When we pray, "Thy Kingdom come," we pray for the coming of the King. When *He comes* there will be no need for saying, "Lo, here," or "Lo, there," for the shining of His influence will be like lightning from one part under Heaven unto the other, that is, from one hemisphere to the other (vv. 21,24).

II. **State of the World at His Coming**. "As it was in the days of Noah, so shall it be" (vv. 26-30). Most certainly the world was *not* converted in the days of Noah. Neither will it be converted at the coming of the Lord (Luke 18. 8). The days of Noah were characteristic of backsliding and unbelief (Gen. 6. 1-7). They ate, and drank, and married, and *rejected* the testimony of Noah until the flood came. God had said, "My Spirit shall not strive with man for ever" (R.V.), indicating that in the days of Noah the voice and pleadings of His Spirit were resisted. "So shall it be in the days of the Son of Man." "In the last days perilous times will come, for men shall be lovers of themselves, . . . heady, highminded, lovers of pleasure more than lovers of God" (2 Tim. 3. 1-4). And our rationalistic *lower* critics are doing what they can to complete this dark picture, striving against the Spirit of God (see 2 Tim. 4. 3, 4), and "turning the truth into fables." From such turn away. Whatever teaching does not *exalt* the Lord Jesus Christ and honour the Holy Ghost is not of God.

III. **Results of His Coming.** The results will be very many, but there are two definite effects brought before us here.

1. SEPARATION. When Noah, who had been condemning the world by his righteous works (Heb. 11. 7), was taken into the Ark and shut up then the flood came. When Lot was taken out of Sodom, then the fire and brimstone fell from Heaven. "One shall *be taken*, and the other left" (vv. 34-36). So shall it be when the Son of Man cometh. There shall be a taking away of those who are the Lord's. "Caught up to meet the Lord in the air" (1 Thess. 4. 16-17).

2. JUDGMENT. The taking away of the righteous prepares the way for the judgments of God upon the unbelieving. The Lord declared that He could "do nothing" till Lot was brought out of Sodom. When the "salt of the earth" has been removed, then there is no hindrance to the process of death and corruption. When the Church of God has been taken out of this Christ-rejecting world, then the Lord shall take "vengeance on them that obey not the Gospel of our Lord Jesus Christ" (2 Thess. 1. 7-10). Wheresoever the *lifeless* and corrupt body is, thither will the eagles of God's judgments be gathered together (v. 37).

SUCCESSFUL PRAYER.
Luke 18. 1-14.

"Pray, though the gift you ask for
  May never comfort your fears,
 May never repay your pleading,
  Yet pray, and with hopeful tears!
An answer—not that you long for,
  But diviner—will come some day;
Your eyes are too dim to see it.
  Yet trust, and wait, and pray."—A. PROCTER.

THERE is as much difference between the mere form of prayer and the spirit of prayer as there is between a dead body and a living one. The one is but the breathless skeleton of the other.

I. Prayer is a Great Privilege. How black the heavens would be if there were no opening to the cry of human need; how hopeless our lives, in the day of distress, if we had no access to the ear of God. Even this sin-blotched world may become to us the audience chamber of the King of kings; thy closet may be gilded with the glory of God. Let your requests be made known unto Him.

II. Prayer is a Necessity. "Men *ought* always to pray, and not to faint" (v. 1). It is "impossible to believe in God and not feel the need of prayer." It is the Christian's "vital breath." It is absolutely needed to spiritual life and health. We ought always to pray, because we are always dependent upon Him in whom we live and move. If we had more delight in prayer we would have less inclination to grumble; if we loved the presence of the Lord more we would quarrel with our neighbours less.

III. Prayer must be Urgent. "Because this widow troubleth me, I will avenge her" (vv. 3-5). Her "continual coming," which prevailed over the indifference of this "unjust judge," is used by our gracious Lord as an argument for persistent prayer. If your desire is for things *needful*, or for the glory of God, do not be afraid to "trouble the Master" about them. His silence for a time may be but the testing of your faith. If you can possibly be satisfied *without* this definite answer to your prayer, the likelihood is that no answer will be given. Be *importunate*, and you will certainly get all you need (chap. 11. 8).

IV. Prayer must be Void of Self-confidence. The parable of the two men that went up into the temple to pray was spoken to those that "trusted in themselves" (vv. 9-12). Prayer is a solemn mockery on the lips of the self-righteous. It was quite true that he was not "as other men," for he was neither a saint in the sight of God nor a sinner in his own. The man who would be justified by his works has whereof *he* might glory, but not before God. The fact is, the spirit of pride and self-sufficiency is at enmity with the spirit of prayer. This Pharisee *said* his prayers, but he did not *pray*. The spirit of prayer is the most humble spirit on the face of the earth; compared with other earthly spirits, it is as a lily among thorns.

V. **Prayer must be Honest.** The publican smote upon his breast saying, "God be merciful to me a sinner" (v. 13). Out of the heart are the issues of life. The Pharisee compares himself with others, and justifies himself; the publican compares himself with God, and makes confession of his sin. No prayer can be perfectly honest before God which does not express the true conscious condition of the heart. The Lord has an open ear for our cry, but he has also an open eye for our heart. Those are God-pleasing prayers that smite our own breasts; but there are others that smite the breast of God.

VI. **Prayer will be Answered.** "I tell you that He will" (v. 8). "I tell you that he went down justified" (v. 14). True prayer will never be sent empty away. The prayer of the poor, friendless, but importunate widow, and the prayer of the honest, sin-conscious publican were *prevailing* prayers, while that of the self-righteous Pharisee only insulted God and ministered to his own pride and self-deception. Our own righteousness will neither save ourselves nor our prayers any more than counterfeit jewels would save a drowning man. The way to get up in the estimation of God is to get down in our own. "He that humbleth himself shall be exalted" (v. 14), and he that is so exalted shall ask what he will, and it shall be given him.

THE PHARISEE AND PUBLICAN AT WORSHIP.
Luke 18. 9-14.

"Even as Elias mounting to the sky,
   Did cast his mantle to the earth behind,
So when the heart presents the prayer on high,
   Exclude the world from traffic with the mind."
                                        —SOUTHWELL.

THIS parable was spoken as a rebuke to all those who "trusted in themselves that they were righteous, and despised others." In the preceding parable He taught that "men ought always to pray, and not to faint," but here He shows clearly that while all men ought to pray, everything depends on the spirit and motives which constrain us to pray if we are to have the answer of God to our petitions. These two men represent two classes of worshippers.

I. **A Self-satisfied Professor.** Here are some of the general characteristics of such—

1. HE BELIEVES IN BEING RELIGIOUS. This Pharisee goes up to the temple to pray. Like his modern descendants, he goes regularly to his place of worship, and keeps up a kind of bowing acquaintanceship with all the ordinances of God's house. He has a great respect for religion, and thinks that everybody should say prayers. As for himself, he can always pray like an unfallen angel, for he is not like "other men."

2. HE HAS GREAT FAITH IN HIMSELF. "He trusts in *himself*" (v. 9). If ever there was a righteous man on the earth, he is that man. His brown penny is worth anybody's shilling. He glories in what he *is*, "not as other men," in what he *does*. "I fast twice a week." In what he *gives*, "I give tithes." His every sentence begins with a capital "I." He *trusts* in *himself*, not in God. He attends the Church because he likes to patronise things that are honourable. He believes that as long as he is able to trust in

himself there will be no cause for His faith getting shaken. He has made himself what he is, so he worships a god of his own making.

3. HE HAS NO SENSE OF PERSONAL NEED BEFORE GOD. "He trusts in himself that he *is* righteous" (v. 9). He is rich in religious works, and increased with the goods of personal qualifications, and has *need of nothing* (Rev. 3. 17, 18). He belongs to that famous generation "that are pure in their own eyes" (Prov. 30. 12). The Cross of Christ makes no appeal to him. He is quite independent of any such provision. He would not bemean himself by classing himself with *sinners*. His eyes are so very innocent that they cannot see anything very bad in anything that he has ever done.

4. HE HAS NO LOVE FOR OTHERS. "Despised others" (v. 9). This is quite consistent with his hypocritical profession. *Others* have so many faults and imperfections that his self-righteous soul cannot esteem them. There is no true religious uprightness but in his own pride-puffed bosom. *Others* may, through weakness, fall, and be caught in a whirlpool of disaster, or may be slowly drifting toward the precipice of eternal ruin, but what is that to him. Such drift-souls are unworthy of his notice. His creed is, Let every man care for himself.

II. A Self-abased Confessor.

1. HE BELIEVES IN PRAYER. He may have gone up with the Pharisee, but not *like* him. The one went up to perform a work, the other to enjoy a privilege. Custom constrained the one, while a deep-felt need moved the other.

2. HE IS SENSIBLE OF GOD'S HOLINESS. "He stands afar off" (v. 13). He realises that there is a great moral distance between God's character and his own. "Afar off" describes our true position as sinners before God (Eph. 2. 13).

But while the prodigal was yet "a great way off" the father ran and met him. He came not merely to pray, but to have a personal dealing with a personal God. "He that cometh to God must believe that *He is.*"

3. HE IS CONSCIOUS OF HIS OWN SINFULNESS. "He smote upon *his breast*" (v. 13). He is convinced that the source of his guilt lies deeper down than mere words or acts, that his *heart* was "deceitful, and desperately wicked." He stands before God a self-condemned man, so overwhelmed with shame that he could not "lift up so much as his eyes unto Heaven." He takes his true place as one "condemned already" (John 3. 18).

4. HE PLEADS THE ATONING SACRIFICE. We infer from the word used, "God be *merciful*"—be *propitiated* for me the sinner—that this sin-smitten one had his eyes on the sacrifice smoking on the altar when he uttered this prayer (v. 13, R.V., *margin*). When a man is thoroughly convinced of his guilt before God he has no difficulty about the doctrine of substitution. He feels that this is his only hope, and thanks God for the Cross of Christ.

III. **An Infallible Judge.** This "I tell you" of Jesus is the final pronouncement of God upon the attitudes of these two classes as before Him (v. 14).

1. THE SELF-EXALTED SHALL BE ABASED. No man can lift *himself* up into the favour of God by his own works. "God *resisteth* the proud" (James 4. 6). As long as a man covers his own sin he shall never prosper in the sight of the heart-searching God (Prov. 28. 13).

2. THE SELF-ABASED SHALL BE EXALTED. "Humble yourselves in the sight of the Lord, and He shall lift you up" (James 4. 10). The story of Haman and Mordecai is a perfect illustration of this truth. In Luke, chapter sixteen, we see a proud rich man abased to hell, while the

humble beggar is exalted to Heaven. This word is settled in Heaven, that if *you* save your life you will lose it, and if you lose it for Christ you will save it.

ONE THING LACKING.
Luke 18. 15-30.

> "Lord, by Thy grace I have made my choice,
> In Thy Salvation I rejoice,
> I empty was, I'm empty still,
> Thy full Salvation doth me fill,
> Transient are all things that move,
> But Thine is everlasting love."—GROSART.

JESUS is equal to the need of all, from the ruler of the Synagogue down to the infant in the mother's arms (v. 15). Blessed are those mothers who seek for their children the *touch* of the life-giving Christ, and who will not be discouraged in this good work by the forbidding or mocking looks of ignorant and cold-hearted disciples. The Kingdom of God must be received in the simple, *unquestioning* spirit of "a little child" (v. 17). This fact is clearly brought out in the following story of the young ruler. In this short suggestive narrative we note—

I. An Important Question. "What shall I do to inherit eternal life?" (v. 18). There is no question more becoming a thoughtful young man than this. It is beautiful to see a man, while basking in the sunshine of worldly prosperity (v. 23), anxiously inquiring into the eternal sureties of the unseen. Why should the glory of earthly riches blind the eyes to the greater glory of the heavenly? This ruler came to the right person with this most momentous of all questions when he came to Jesus. He only has the words of eternal life. It was also a very *personal* question. "What shall *I* do." Salvation is a matter between Jesus Christ alone and our own individual souls.

II **A Searching Inquiry.** "Jesus said unto him, Why callest thou Me good?" (v. 19). Our Lord would have him understand that He deals not only with the language of the lip, but with the deeper motives of the heart. "There is none good but God" (v. 19). Do you believe that I am God? When we come to Jesus about the matter of "eternal life" we must come with full purpose of heart, believing that He is divine, and that He is the Way, the Truth, and the Life. Believest thou this?

III. **An Honest Confession.** "All these have I kept from my youth up" (v. 21). Doubtless this anxious ruler was perfectly sincere in saying this. He knew nothing against himself. There is a peace of conscience that is not the "peace of God." There is a justness of character in the sight of the law that does not justify in the sight of God, for the just shall live by *faith* (Gal. 3. 10, 11). "Without faith it is impossible to please Him" (Heb. 11. 6). The Pharisee who "went up to pray" had many good works, but he was destitute of faith in the atoning sacrifice (Luke 18. 11-14).

IV. **A Testing Command.** "Yet lackest thou one thing; sell all that thou hast, . . .and thou shalt have treasure in Heaven" (v. 22). Those who would have the "eternal life" that is in Christ must be prepared to let everything else go at His bidding. "Treasure in Heaven" is the coveted portion of all those whose heart is right with God. They look not at the things which are seen, but at the things which are unseen and *eternal*. We may possess many good things, and yet lack the *one thing* needful. One crack in the lantern will leave the pilgrim in darkness; one faulty link will make the chain worthless; one leak in the ship will sink it. If we offend in one point we are guilty of all. The one needful thing is a whole-hearted, unstaggering faith in the Lord Himself.

V. A Sorrowful Result. "When he heard this he was very sorrowful,...and Jesus saw that he was very sorrowful" (vv. 23, 24). To part with his all, even for the all of Christ was to him a sorrowful bargain, proving that he had more faith in his riches than in the Son of God. No man can serve two masters. Christ gave him the Word of life, but the deceitfulness of riches choked it (Matt. 13. 22). "He that trusteth in his riches shall fall" (Prov. 11. 28). One thing is needful, and Mary hath chosen that good part.

VI. A Forcible Application. "How hardly shall they that have riches enter into the Kingdom of God" (vv. 24-30). It is easier for a camel to get *unburdened* and to crawl through the narrow side gate into the city, and that was no light task. No camel, of itself, could untie the obstructive bundles from its back. No more can the rich free themselves from the burden and love of their riches, but "the things which are impossible with men are possible with God" (v. 27). To sacrifice self-interest for the interests of Christ is to "receive manifold more in this present time, and in the world to come life everlasting."

BARTIMEUS.
Luke 18. 31-43.

"I longed for light, but all the light I found was second-hand—
Reflected thought that had been tossed about for ages past."
—W. SMITH.

GOD, who made the heavens and the earth, through His Son, and who by Him divided the light from the darkness of old, is both able and willing now, through Christ, to open the blinded eyes and minds of men, and to illumine them with the glorious light of Heaven. "In Him was life, and the life was the light of men" (John 1. 3, 4). About this blind man, observe his—

I. Wretched Condition. He was "blind" and "begging"

(v. 35). His eyes were darkened, and his circumstances impoverished; he was utterly destitute. No fellow-mortals could restore to him the joy of saving *light*. What a picture of us all by nature, with our sin-blinded eyes and impoverished hearts! Satan hath blinded the minds of them that believe not.

II. Anxious Inquiry. "Hearing the multitude pass by he *asked* what it meant" (v. 36). Although he had lost his eyesight, he had his *hearing* and his *tongue* left, and he used them both. If we only put to a proper use the faculties we have, we would find ourselves, perhaps, richer than we imagined. All men have not faith in God, but all men have faith in some one or some thing. There are multitudes still following Christ, and who are willing and ready to lay down their lives for His sake. Have you ever seriously "asked what it means?"

III. Urgent Petition. "He cried, Jesus, Thou Son of David, have mercy on me" (v. 39). And when those in front of him sought to block his way, "he cried so much the more." The more he was rebuked the louder he cried. This is the holy logic of a man conscious of his need, and of a God-sent remedy within his reach. "Jesus of Nazareth passeth by." If the voice of his need doth not reach the ear of His mercy *now* it may never. To Bartimeus this was his "*accepted* time," and he took full advantage of it. They are un-Christlike followers of Christ who would seek to drown the voice of the prayer of the needy.

IV. Blessed Privilege. "Jesus asked him, What wilt thou that I shall do unto thee?" (vv. 40, 41). His importunity has prevailed. The Lord Himself invites him to his presence, and with these words, "What wilt thou?" He lays, as it were, all His divine treasures of wealth and power at the feet of this poor blind suppliant. He is now within the reach of all that his heart could wish. This is what every poor, destitute soul finds when they find the favour of the Lord Jesus Christ. "Seek, and ye shall find."

V. Definite Request. "Lord, that I may receive my sight" (v. 41). When we are as conscious of our sinfulness as this man was of his blindness we shall not fail to plead for the one thing needful. He was poor, but he did not plead for wealth; there is something which Christ can give us that is infinitely more precious than silver or gold, and that is *eyes* to see the Lord Himself as our own personal Saviour and Friend. This is what the blind man saw when his eyes were opened.

VI. Instant Cure. "Immediately he received his sight" (vv. 42, 43). The Son of God has but to speak and it is done. His word of power is always spoken in answer to *faith*. Jesus said, "Thy *faith* hath saved thee." Instant faith brings instant blessing. In *receiving* his sight, he received it, of course, from the Lord as the gift of His love and the evidence of His almighty power. "Believe, and thou shalt *see*." Worldly wisdom will never make the *blind* to see. Jesus is mighty to save.

VII. Practical Gratitude. "He followed Jesus, glorifying God" (v. 43). He did not go back to his miserable "begging." Having received his sight, he lost his right and title as a professional pauper, and become a *willing* disciple of his Saviour. How are others to believe that we have been healed by Christ if our lives are not glorifying God by following Him in the way? Those who have been delivered from the enemy of sin and blindness are to serve Him without fear, in holiness all the days of their life (Luke 1. 74, 75). Has your faith saved you?

ZACCHAEUS.
Luke 19. 1-10.

"Thou hast made us for THYSELF, and our hearts are disquieted until they can find rest in THEE."—ST. AUGUSTINE.

THERE is a striking contrast between the case of Bartimeus and that of Zacchaeus. While they were both near Jericho, yet they were found at the extreme ends of the city; the one was sitting on the lowly wayside, the other was perched on a tree; the one was poor, the other was rich; the one sought Jesus for *mercy*, the other sought to *see* Jesus; the one had to get up to be saved, the other had to get down. Jesus Christ is able to save to the uttermost heights of society, as well as to the uttermost depths of it. Let us look at his—

I. Social Position. "He was chief among the publicans, and he was rich" (v. 2). He was, perhaps, a contractor, with many tax-gatherers under him, and so had ample opportunity of enriching himself. These *Jewish* toll-keepers were severely hated by their brethren, because that through this business the Roman government, under whose galling yoke they groaned, being burdened, was strengthened and upheld.

II. Earnest Desire. "He sought to see Jesus, *who He was*" (v. 3). He not only wished to *see* Him, he evidently desired to *know* Him. He was undoubtedly moved by deeper feelings than mere curiosity. The Son of God never gratifies the professional sight-seer. Had there been no longing in his *heart* for a personal acquaintance with the Christ, the Lord would in all likelihood have passed him by. He who looketh upon the heart hath said, "Thou shalt find Me when thou shalt seek Me with all thine heart" (Deut. 4. 29).

III. Twofold Difficulty. "He could not for the press, because he was of little stature" (v. 3). A great crowd and a pair of short legs are really formidable obstacles in the way of *seeing*. The hindrance was both personal and circumstantial—in himself and in others. Who ever sought the Lord without being confronted with these two classes of difficulties? Our own *shortcomings* and the callous indifference of others to our spiritual interests are sure to test the sincerity of our desires after Christ.

IV. Fixed Determination. "He ran before, and climbed up into a tree to see Him" (v. 4). The chief of the tax-gathering clan running and climbing a tree like a schoolboy! Who would have thought of it? Ah, when there is *real anxiety* to know Jesus Christ and the power of His salvation there will be no concern about the "fear of man"—no feeling of *shame* in such a desperate search. Those who are ashamed to show any excitement over Christ and His cause are utterly unworthy of Him.

V. Unexpected Call. "Jesus looked up and saw him, and said, Make haste and come down, for to-day I must abide at thy house" (v. 5). Zacchaeus sought to see Jesus and to know Him, unaware of the fact that to see Jesus as He ought to be seen implies being seen and known by Him. "Make haste," the Lord is always ready to meet the need of an anxious soul. "To-day I *must* abide." Why this *must*? Does not the real heart anxiety of a sinner after Christ always lay a gracious necessity upon Him who came to seek and save that which was lost? (v. 10).

VI. Ready Obedience. "He made haste and came down, and received Him joyfully" (v. 6). His prompt response to the Master's call and his joyful reception of Him surely prove that the publican was both eager and honest in his new search. False professors have always an excuse to make when the personal call of Christ is pressed upon them (Luke 14. 18). A *hungry* man does not need much pressing to eat when suitable and savoury food is set before him. Those who are really anxious to be saved are never very far from the Kingdom.

VII. Instant Salvation. The whole crowd murmured when they saw that He had gone in as the guest of a publican. Perhaps it was to hush their murmurings and justify himself and also the Lord in coming into his house that Zacchaeus "stood up and said, Lord, the half of my goods I give to the poor," etc. (vv. 7, 8). But Jesus did not come into his house *because* "he gave to the poor," etc., but because he was an anxious sinner seeking fellowship with Himself—a lost one needing a Saviour. We are saved, not by our good works, but by the grace of God (Eph. 2. 8). The *day* that salvation came to his house was the day that Jesus Christ the Son of Man came. "He that hath the Son hath life." "There is none other Name given, whereby we can be saved." Salvation is certain to "as many as RECEIVE HIM" (John 1. 12).

THE PARABLE OF THE POUNDS.
Luke 19. 11-27.

LUKE has hung up the keys of this parable outside the door for us. He gives us two reasons why it was given—"because He was nigh Jerusalem, and because they thought that the Kingdom of God should immediately appear." So the parable has reference to the inhabitants of Jerusalem (Jews), and the coming of the King. We shall have a little word about—

I. The King. He is called here "a certain nobleman" (v. 12). This nobleman is the Lord Jesus Christ, and surely He is a *Noble-man*. He is of high birth, for He was born from above (Luke 1. 35). As the Son of Man He is indeed the noblest of men. Was it not David Livingstone who called him "a perfect gentleman?" All his words and works have the nobility of God about them.

II. The Journey. "He went into a far country to receive for Himself a kingdom" (v. 12). Jesus went into the far country when He ascended to the Father, and, as the Son of Man, He is now receiving "*for Himself*" a kingdom (Dan. 7. 13, 14). All who now believe in the Lord

Jesus Christ are being received by Him, and are being made unto Him a kingdom (Rev. 1. 6, R.V.).

III. **The Servants** (v. 13). These ten servants had delivered to them one pound each, and their commission was plain—"Occupy till I come." They were to occupy His place, and trade with His gift, till He would come again. This part of the parable found its perfect fulfilment in Pentecost, when His servants, gathered together in the upper room, had delivered to them the gift of the Holy Ghost by the Master Himself. This gift was not *divided* among them, for "it sat upon each of them" (Acts 2. 3, 4). Each one received his or her pound, with which they were to do business for Him till He came. It is impossible for us to *occupy* in Christ's Name unless we trade with Christ's gift, living and acting in the power of the Holy Spirit.

IV. **The Citizens**. "They hated Him, saying, We will not have this man to reign over us" (v. 14). They are called *"His* citizens" because that Jesus Christ was the rightful heir to the throne of David, established in Jerusalem. These citizens are typical of all those who hate Him without a cause, and who, through unbelief and pride of heart, will not submit to His rule, but cry, "Away with Him!"

V. **The Return**. "When He was returned…He commanded the servants to be called unto Him" (v. 15). The first thing our Lord will do, when He comes again, will be to call His servants together to give an account of how they have used or neglected His gift of the Holy Spirit. This is the judgment-seat before which all *we*, as His servants, must appear (2 Cor. 5. 10). Through grace we are accepted *in* Him, but we must labour in the power of the Spirit if we would be "accepted *of* Him."

VI. **The Reward of the Faithful**. Salvation is by faith, but the rewards of the coming King will be acccording to our works. There are three classes of servants represented here (vv. 16-24). They all had the same gift; the same possibilities were within the reach of each. The first had *great faith* in his pound, and gained with it other ten. The second had *little faith*, and gained but five. The third had *no faith* in it, and gained only the reproach of his Master. The application is plain and heart-searching. Every believer in Christ has the gift of the Holy Ghost brought within his reach, and in the strength and power of this divine money he is to do business for God in the place and Name of his Lord. He does not send us a warfare on *our own* charges. In this "pound" there was all-sufficient, whereby each receiver may accomplish all the will and work of their absent Master. Those who trade with their own gifts instead of this gift of God will certainly—like this man (v. 23)—be found fruitless at the coming of Christ. If we are working for Christ in our own strength and wisdom we are hiding our Lord's money, and can never be rewarded with His "Well done" (Matt. 25. 21).

VII. **The Doom of the Unbelieving.** Those who "would not that He should reign over them" were to be slain before Him (v. 27). All hatred and unbelief will be judged when He appears. Those who in their hearts and lives have said, "Not this Man," shall one day hear these awful words from the most merciful of lips, "Depart from Me, ye cursed." "For He *must reign* till He hath put all enemies under His feet" (1 Cor. 15. 25).

CHRIST WEEPING OVER JERUSALEM.
Luke 19. 28-48.

"The Son of God was seen
Most glorious: in HIM all His FATHER shone
Substantially expressed, and in His face
Divine compassion visibly appeared."—MILTON.

IN every single ray of white light we are told there are all the colours of the rainbow. In this portion we have a sevenfold revelation of the character of the Lord Jesus Christ.

I. His Wisdom. If the eyes of our Lord had not more light in them than that of ordinary mortals, how could He assure the disciples that they would find a young colt tied at a certain place named (v. 30)? Through faith He spake as one endued with Omniscience. Distance is as nothing in the eyes of God.

II. His Power. All the apology they were to offer on taking away the man's ass was, "The Lord hath need of him" (vv. 31-34). With this simple declaration there went forth such an influence from the presence of the absent Christ that no resistance could be offered. He will have a willing people in the day of His power. All who go forth, like these disciples, in His Name, to do His will, cannot fail to have the authority of their Master with them (Matt. 28. 18, 19).

III. His Humility. "They set Jesus thereon." The King of Glory sitting upon a borrowed ass, and with "*their* garments upon the colt" (vv. 35, 36). There was nothing too humiliating for the Son of God, if only the Scriptures might be fulfilled (Zech. 9. 9). He that so humbleth himself will surely be exalted (Phil. 2. 8, 9). The pride of man is for ever opposed to the revealed will of God.

IV. His Royal Dignity. "Blessed be the King that cometh in the Name of *Jehovah*" (Heb. 5. 38). Jesus was a King, although His face was more marred than any man's! He was bedless and penniless; yet His every word and act was stamped with the sovereign majesty of Heaven (v. 37). The glory of His kingly character manifested itself on the holy mount when it burst with overwhelming power through the concealing veil of His flesh, revealing "peace in Heaven, and glory in the highest."

V. His Compassion. "When He beheld the city He

wept over it" (v. 41). If we had the eyes and the compassion of Jesus Christ we would be constrained many a time to weep over what others are rejoicing in. Christ as the Son of God and the Redeemer of men can only look upon places and persons in their relationship to Himself. The temple stones may be large and beautiful, but what of that if there be no welcome for Him in His "Father's house" (v. 45). To Him the heart of the city was the heart of the citizen; if this was false and cruel, all else was desolation. "He wept over it." "Greater love hath no man than this." What about that city within our own hearts? What does the sympathetic Saviour see there?

VI. His Faithfulness. It must have been with a very heavy heart that our Lord uttered these solemn words recorded in verses 42-46, for He willeth not the death of any, but rather that they would come to Him and live. But even His tearful compassion does not hinder Him from speaking out these awful words of warning and of doom It is a fearful thing to fall, as an unbeliever, into the hands of the living God. Neither the city, the nation, nor the individual can finally prosper who reject the claims and resist the pleadings of the Lord Jesus Christ. "While ye have the light, believe in the light," for this same Jesus who wept and died shall yet judge the quick and the dead.

VII. His Influence. The chief priests...sought to *destroy Him*, for all the people were *attentive to hear Him*" (vv. 47, 48). To some He was a savour of death, to others of life. The sun which melts the wax will harden the clay. Everything depends on the attitude of our heart to Christ as to whether His influence will melt us unto salvation or harden us for judgment. The preaching of the Cross is either *foolishness* to us or it is *the wisdom of God* (1 Cor. 1. 23, 24).

PARABLE OF THE HUSBANDMEN.
Luke 20. 9-19.

"Dare I trust my heart and voice against the voice of the whole? Yet should the roar of the crowd ever drown the true voice of the soul?''—W. SMITH.

IT is not only Scotch-like, but it may at times be Christ-like, to answer one question by asking another. The chief priests and scribes asked, "Who gave Thee this authority?" Jesus answered by asking, "The baptism of John, was it from Heaven or of men?" They "could not tell," or rather, they *would not* say, lest they should commit themselves. Neither would He tell them. It is so still. Those who refuse to accept the testimony of His servants shall not know the secret of Christ's authority and power. There must be faith in His Word if we would have revelations of Himself. This parable, like that of the "pounds," has a decided dispensational character.

I. The Vineyard. "A certain man planted a vineyard" (v. 9). This nameless man is intended to represent Jehovah, the Eternal One; the *vineyard* is the whole house of Israel, whom He hath redeemed for Himself (Jer. 2. 21); the *planting* refers to their settlement in the land of promise, where they were carefully nurtured and guarded by the presence of God.

II. The Faithless Husbandmen. These were the proud rulers of the people, who "entreated shamefully" those sent by God to assert His claims upon them as His professing people. They persecuted and slew those servants of God who testified against them (Neh. 9. 26). Did not the Spirit-filled Stephen fling the same charge in their teeth when he said, "Which of the prophets have not your fathers persecuted?" These wicked husbandmen, like many in our own day, were willing to take all they could get from God that would enrich themselves, but refused to *give Him* anything in return.

III. The Divine Dilemma. "What shall I do?" (v. 13). His thankless people have transgressed and rebelled; His warnings and entreaties, through His servants, have been neglected and despised. "What shall I do?" Something *new* must be done if the Lord of the vineyard is to maintain His rights to the fruits thereof. Shall it be vengeance or mercy? Shall it be instant judgment or a further manifestation of His infinite grace? Shall it be the sacrifice of man for his sins, or a sacrifice from God for the sins of man? "Deliver from going down to the pit, for I have found a ransom."

IV. The Gracious Purpose. "I will send My beloved Son" (v. 13). It may be that when they see Him they will turn away their faces from shame, and confess their sins (v. 13). Instead of opening the flood-gates of wrath against those offenders, He opens the treasures of His heart, and sends forth His only Son. "Herein is love, not that we loved God, but that He loved us" (1 John 4. 10).

V. The Fond Expectation. "It may be they will reverence Him when they *see Him*" (v. 13). What did they see when they saw HIM? They saw the invisible yet frequently insulted God, manifest in mortal flesh, as a loving, sin-forgiving Saviour, the wisdom and the power of God. Surely when they behold such an exhibition of His condescension and forbearance they will feel rebuked for their pride and arrogance. It would seem as if the Lord of the vineyard hoped to kill their enmity with His kindness. The mission of the Son of the Highest was to save us from our sins, and to reconcile us to God. "He that honoureth the Son honoureth the Father." To refuse Him *reverence* is to dishonour the Father who sent Him.

VI. The Deliberate Refusal. "They cast Him out of the vineyard and killed Him" (v. 14, 15). They would not have this Man to reign over them. Although they knew him to be "the Heir," yet, in the pride of their hearts, they refused to submit to Him. What better are we than they, in acknowledging Christ to be the Son of God, if we have not yielded ourselves unto Him? Is our guilt not greater in that we are casting Him out of our hearts and homes; out of our businesses and pleasures daily. To cast Him out of our lives is to cast our lives into eternal bankruptcy and ruin (v. 18).

VII. **The Terrible Results.** The husbandmen shall be destroyed, and the vineyard given to others (v. 16). Neglected opportunities will bring corresponding judgments. The Word of God was *first* spoken to the Jews as His people, but they put it far from them, and now the vineyard is given to the Gentiles (Acts 12. 46). The blessed privileges offered us now will soon have gone to others. Are we laying hold of them for our eternal profit, or shall they pass, leaving us in the deeper condemnation through our pride and unbelief? "When they heard it they said, "God forbid." But all such "God forbids" from the lips of self-righteous rebels will never in any degree avert the just judgments of an insulted God.

CHRIST AND THE SCEPTICS.
Luke 20. 20-40.

"I have a life in Christ to live,
I have a death in Christ to die—
And must I wait till science give
All doubts a full reply?
Nay, rather while the sea of doubt
Is raging wildly round about,
Questioning of life and death and sin,
Let me but creep within
Thy fold, O Christ, and at Thy feet,
Take but the lowest seat."—SHARP.

THE man is a fool who would suffer himself to be lifted up or cast down according to the length of his own shadow;

but not more so than those who would set themselves, in the pride of their heart, against Christ, who is the wisdom of God. The chief priests and the scribes sought to lay hands on Him because He had spoken a parable against them. The light will always be against those who love the darkness (v. 19). We have here two different attempts to ensnare the Lord through His words; but in vain is the snare spread before Him. There is what we might call—

I. The Tribute Trap. Is it lawful to give tribute to Caesar or no? It was—

1. CUNNINGLY SET. All the craft of hypocrisy and wickedness was employed to catch Him in His *words*. Other men were easily caught in this fashion. These deceivers "feign themselves *just* men" that they might more easily accomplish their diabolical business. Notice their buttery words: "Master, we know...that Thou teachest the way of God truly" (v. 21). The truth was in their lips, but hypocrisy was in their hearts. As no honey was to be put in the meat-offering, so no flattery could move Him who is the Truth and the Life. They expected a "Yes" or "No" to their pressing question. If he said "Yes," then they would rouse the people against Him. If He said "No," then they would speedily report Him to the Roman officials. It was—

2. QUICKLY DETECTED. But He perceived their craftiness, and said, "Why tempt ye Me?" There is no mask thick enough to hide our motives from His all-searching eye. It is a fearful thing to fall as hypocrites into the hands of the Living God. "Show Me a penny," said the penniless Saviour, and as He turned it on His fingers He made that "image and superscription" to bring their wisdom to naught, and to humble their haughty pride. Learn how mighty little things become in His hands. Only a

penny, but used of Christ it becomes a witness for
Him that all the wisdom of men cannot gainsay.   We
sometimes say "a penny for your thought," but let
us give earnest heed to the thought connected with this
penny.   "Give to man the things that are man's,"
and "to God the things that are God's!" If ye are
Christ's, then ye are not your own.   Ye are bought
with a price, therefore give to God the things that are
His.   Then came—

II. The Resurrection Trap (vv. 27-40).   It was—

1. SET BY THE SADDUCEES. This sect denies that there
could be any resurrection, because to them it was contrary
to reason.   These Sadducees are the forefathers of our
modern rationalists, who would limit the workings of God
to the understanding of sin-blinded mortals.   In referring
to this woman who had been married seven times, they
were presenting their cause in the strongest possible
light, but their light was only the blackness of darkness
of ignorance.

2. BROKEN BY CHRIST. The truth of God will always
escape (like a bird) out of the snare of the fowler.   In the
world to come the children of God are equal to angels—
they don't need marriage to increase their happiness and
bliss; they never enter into one another's possessions
there, because they "die no more."   And as touching
the certainty of the resurrection, it is as sure as that
the Lord is the God of Abraham, of Isaac, and of
Jacob.   They are living now, for Jehovah is not the
God of the *dead*, but of the living? He who is our life
beyond the grave can easily lift our bodies from the
tomb and turn the corruptible into incorruption, and this
mortal into immortality.   "Thanks be unto God, who
giveth us the victory through our Lord Jesus Christ."
Have faith in God.

CHRIST'S LAST PASSOVER.
Luke 22. 1-23.

"With all His sufferings full in view,
And woes to us unknown,
Forth to the task His Spirit flew,
'Twas love that urged Him on.''—COWPER.

Lammenais says: "All that Christ asked of mankind, wherewith to save them, was a Cross whereon to die.'' He got it without a grudge.

THE word "passover" is derived from a verb meaning "to pass by," or "to spare." It was instituted in Egypt in the most solemn and suggestive circumstances (Exod. 12). Not a bone of the paschal lamb was to be broken. See how literally this was fulfilled in "Christ our passover" (John 19. 33). This *last* passover was the final fulfilment of the first. Associated with it here we see—

I. **Unreasonable Hate** (vv. 1, 2). In seeking how they might "kill Him," these chief priests and scribes manifested the diabolical enmity of their own hearts against the true character of Jehovah, whom they professed to worship. Little did they think that they were planning how to kill God's "passover Lamb." They hated Him without a cause.

II. **Cruel Betrayal** (vv. 3-6). Satan always finds a suitable instrument for his wicked work in a hypocritical professor. Satan entered Judas because the door of his heart stood open wide to every evil suggestion. The Devil's bait for him was money, because he knew that he loved it, and that at heart he was a thief.

III. **Special Provision** (vv. 7-13). The guest-chamber was appointed by Christ, "a large *upper room furnished*," to be noted for ever afterwards as a place connected with His death, resurrection, and with Pentecost. The place was there furnished for them, where Christ, God's paschal Lamb, was "made ready" as a sacrifice for the sin of the world.

IV. Sacred Fellowship (vv. 14-18).   There is intense longing in this desire of Christ to eat the passover with them before He would suffer. The awful shadow of the Cross, falling over His Spirit, seems but to intensify His love for His own. His love was stronger than death; many waters could not quench it. It was a hallowed time when He took the cup, saying, "Divide it among yourselves." The cup of salvation, and also of the "fellowship of His sufferings." Have we *taken it*?

V. Merciful Substitution (vv. 19, 20).   The language is infinitely tender and unmistakable, "My body *given for you.*" "My blood *shed for you.*" If God is to *pass over* us in judgment, it must be because the blood of Jesus Christ, His Son, cleanseth us from all sin.   "When I see the blood, I will *pass over* you" (Exod. 12. 13).   The atonement of Christ is the only covering for sin that can enable God righteously to "pass by," justifying the *believer* in Jesus.

VI. Infallible Prophecy (vv. 21-23).   "The Son of Man *goeth* as it was determined" (Luke 22. 22).   While with *wicked hands* they slew Him, yet His going was according to the determinate counsel and foreknowledge of God (Acts 2. 23).   In the purpose of God, Christ was the "Lamb slain from the foundation of the world" (Rev. 13. 8).   The unbelief and wickedness of men shall never make void the eternal counsel of Jehovah.   "Behold the Lamb of God who taketh away the sin of the world."

GETHSEMANE.
Luke 22. 39-54.

"So, as thou wert the seed and not the flower,
  Having no form or comeliness in chief,
  Sharing thy thought with thy acquaintance grief,
THOU wert despised, rejected in Thine hour
Of loneliness and God triumphant power.''—MACDONALD.

THERE is a deep, soul-moving pathos in these words: "He went, as He was wont, to the Mount of Olives." This was

Christ's prayer-closet, and this was His last, and for ever memorable visit. The saving interests of a dying world, and the eternal honour of His Holy Name are now to be cast into the crucible. The issues of this night's awful work will affect Heaven, earth, and hell, and stretch out to the uttermost ages of eternity. In a garden the first Adam fell through sin; in a garden the second Adam triumphed through suffering. Gethsemane was to Christ a place of—

I. Solemn Loneliness. "He was withdrawn from them about a stone's cast" (v. 41). Far enough to be beyond their reach of help. He trod the wine-press of atoning suffering alone. On the great day of atonement the High Priest *alone* had to do the work (Lev. 16. 29-30). "Jesus paid it all." "Nothing in my hand I bring."

II. Prayerful Resignation (v. 42). This woeful cup was enough to crush into nothing an ordinary mortal. Christ knew its terrible contents, for He well knew the holiness of God and the heinousness of sin. The only way this cup could pass from us was through the "nevertheless, not My will," of Jesus Christ.

III. Heavenly Succour. "There appeared an angel strengthening Him" (v. 43). This angel was highly honoured in having a hand in such needful and glorious work. Doubtless he would be remembered for it after the Ascension. Will we not feel like thanking Him when we go to Heaven for strengthening the Redeemer in His way to make atonement for our sins?

IV. Awful Suffering. The *agonising* prayer and the "drops of blood" tell of a tender, sensitive heart, crushed and bruised in the mortar of love by the weight of hated sin—not His own (2 Cor. 5. 21). But this prayer, with strong crying and tears, was heard (Heb. 5. 7). If sin *imputed* to Him brought such agony of soul, "How shall we escape if we neglect so great salvation?"

V. Cruel Betrayal (vv. 47, 48). The kiss of Judas was to the "Man of Sorrows" as the bite of a serpent. This was the first salutation Christ received from man after taking the cup of the curse on his behalf. "Man's inhumanity to man" is as nothing compared with his inhumanity to God. We but give Jesus the Judas kiss when we give Him the *lips* of profession and deny him a *heart* of love.

VI. Merciful Miracle (vv. 50-51). Even Christ's own unparalleled sufferings did not check His sympathy for the misfortunes of an enemy. "He touched his ear," undoing the revenge of Peter's sword. What self-forgetting love was His! The *power* that healed the ear could have hurled the whole band of mockers into perdition.

VII. Satanic Power. "This is your hour, and the power of darkness" (vv. 52, 53). All who oppose Jesus Christ are acting as the agents of the Devil. The triumph of the wicked is short (Job 20. 5). Creatures that live in the dark are usually fierce and furious. Walk in the light (John 3. 19-21).

PETER'S DENIAL.
Luke 22. 54-62.

> "Sirs, the significance of this your doubt
> Lies in the reason of it; ye do grudge
> That those, your lands, should have another Lord.
> Ye are not loyal, therefore ye would fain
> Your King should bide afar."—INGLELOW.

"To be forewarned is to be forearmed." But Peter did not seem to profit anything from the Lord's forewarning that "Satan desired to have him that he might sift him as wheat." It was more than Job got. Christ uses a *fan* to blow away the chaff, and cleanse the wheat; the Devil uses a *sieve* to save the chaff and cast out the wheat. Next to the power of Christ *dying* for us is the power of His *praying* for us. "I have prayed for thee" (v. 32; John **17**. 15). Let us note the steps in Peter's downfall.

I. Self Confidence. He said, "Lord, *I am ready* to go with Thee into prison *and to death*" (v. 33). Peter thought he was ready *now*, but the testing time had not yet come; he should have believed the Lord's Word, that *his prayer* for Him was greatly needed. Peter had not yet learned that "without Him he could do nothing" but faint and fail. "He that trusteth in his own heart is a fool" (Prov. 28. 26).

II. The Fear of Man. "Peter followed afar off" (v. 54). Now was Peter's time to "go with Him into prison," but his feet were caught in that snare that is always made by the "fear of man." Acts speak louder than words. Let us beware of imitating Peter's cowardly conduct by refusing to identify ourselves with Christ's cause when others are ruthlessly treating His Word and His work. "Following afar off" is nothing but a half-hearted denial.

III. Companying with the Scornful. "Peter sat down with them" (v. 55). Through the influence of John, Peter was allowed into the open court, but he joined the scoffers and warmed himself at the enemies' fire (John 18. 15-18). John doubtless followed Christ into the judgment hall. Following afar off will surely lead to mingling with the ungodly, and joining with them in their unholy mirth. After the prodigal went into the *far* country he was soon found joining himself to a citizen (Luke 15. 15).

IV. Denial. "He denied Him, saying, I know Him not" (vv. 56-60), and that three times over, as the Lord had said. The fruit of self-confidence is Christ-denial. Christ is always being condemned when pride sits in the throne of our heart. Let us take care that we don't throw stones at Peter for doing in one day what we ourselves may be doing every day we live—refusing to confess Christ our Lord. Then came his—

V. Repentance. "He *went out* and *wept bitterly*" (v. 62). The Lord Jesus Christ, while being led from the judgment hall across the open court to the guard-room, cast such a searching, pitiful, heart-melting look on Peter that wakened his sin-drugged memory, and filled his eyes with the bitter tears of sorrow and penitence. One look of Christ is enough to make the deep sea of the past to yield up its dead. "Peter *remembered.*" An awakened memory will be a blessing or curse, according to our relationship to the Lord Jesus Christ. "If we *confess* our sins. He is faithful and just to *forgive*" (1 John 1. 9).

PILATE AND CHRIST.
Luke 23. 1-25.

"Why should I quit my place and go and ask
　If other men are working at their task?
　And turn away from THEE, O THOU most Holy Light,
　To look if other orbs their orbits keep aright
　Around their proper sun,
　Deserting Thee, and being undone?''—CLOUGH.

CHRIST was accused of "perverting the nation, and forbidding to give tribute to Caesar." A double charge, which was a double-dyed lie (Matt. 22. 21). They are for ever found liars who would seek a cause for condemning the Christ. Let us note—

I. Pilate's Privilege. "They led Him unto Pilate" (v. 1). No man can ever be the same after being brought face to face with the saving Son of God. It is a high and merciful honour to have Jesus brought before us, but what will be the issues of our case?

II. Pilate's Question. "Art Thou the King of the Jews?" (v. 3). To this straight question Jesus gives a plain and emphatic answer that Pilate might, if he cared, feel the great responsibility of his present position. "To this end have I been born, and for this cause came I into the world," said the princely "Man of Sorrows" (John 18. 36). "What think ye of Christ?" Are we in any doubt as to His kingly character?

III. **Pilate's Confession.** "I find no fault in this Man" **(v. 4).** The challenge which Christ threw out in the early part of His ministry still stands unanswered in its holy defiance, "Which of you convinceth Me of sin?." (John 8. 46). No guile will ever be found in His mouth. There is no rock like our Rock, even enemies, like Pilate, themselves being witnesses. Infidels in every age have been compelled to make the same confession. Christ could not be an acceptable sacrifice for our sins if there had been any blemish in Him.

IV. **Pilate's Evasion.** "He sent Him to Herod" (vv. 5-12). He would have been glad if Herod could relieve him from giving a final decision on Jesus Christ; but no man was able to save him from this; so the Lord was brought back to him gorgeously robed in mockery! No more can we evade this great question: "What shall I do with Jesus?" He still stands before us as the "despised and rejected," waiting the decision of our hearts. No one can make this decision for us.

V. **Pilate's Proposal.** "I will chastise Him and release Him" (vv. 17-12). What a cowardly suggestion! He will chastise Him, as if He were guilty, to please the people, and release Him to accommodate his own conscience. Surely such conduct betrays "the contradiction of sinners!" Pilate was willing to substitute Jesus for Barabbas, but they would not have this; neither will they have it yet, for the world "loves its own." "Ye cannot serve God and Mammon" (Luke 16. 13).

VI. **Pilate's Decision.** "He gave sentence that it should be as they required: and delivered Jesus to *their will*" (vv. 23-25). They willed His death, although "God willeth not the death of any. " It were better for Pilate and for us that we had never been born than give such a sentence as this. Has not God, through the offer of His Gospel, delivered up Jesus to your will? What is your sentence? Is it that you will reject Him or receive Him? (John 1. 12).

CALVARY.
Luke 23. 24-48.

"From pain to pain, from woe to woe,
  With loving hearts and footsteps slow,
  To Calvary with CHRIST we go . . .
  Was ever grief like His? Was ever sin like ours?"
                                        —FABER.

WHO would not rather be Simon the Cyrenian, who was compelled to bear the Cross of Jesus, than the purple-robed Pilate, who, through fear, was compelled to deliver Jesus up to the will of the people? (vv. 24-26). But apart from Pilate's dastardly weakness, God has delivered up His Son to the will of the people. And every time we hear the Gospel of Christ we are in our hearts honouring Him or dishonouring Him (John 1. 12). The deep and solemn thoughts of this portion may be easily focused at *"the place which is called* CALVARY*"* (v. 33). It was a—

I. **Place of Guilt.** "There were two *malefactors* with Him" (v. 32). Christ was crucified *between* the thieves, as if He were the greater criminal. The passer-by counted the malefactors as one, two, three. Truly He was *"numbered* with the transgressors. " Yes; He bare the sins of many.

II. **Place of Compassion.** Jesus said, "Father, forgive them, for they know not what they do" (v. 34). What a prayer from a thorn-crowned sufferer! What a revelation of the love and mercy of God, welling up through the breaking heart of Christ, His Son, from the proud, guilty sons of men! He loved His enemies, and blessed them that cursed Him (Acts 7. 59).

III. **Place of Derision.** "The rulers derided Him,.... the soldiers mocked Him" (vv. 35-37). The fact that he did "save others" did not in any way lessen their enmity or modify their wrath, but rather intensified their diabolical rage. He could not "save Himself" because He came for the very purpose of *giving Himself* a ransom for many.

IV. **Place of Testimony.** "In Greek, Latin, and Hebrew" (v. 38) these words were written over Him, THIS IS THE KING OF THE JEWS. Although written and read in mockery and disdain, these words were absolutely true; although attributed to the irony of Pilate, they were in very truth the testimony of the Spirit of God. They had crucified their King, their Messiah, the Son of the Highest. Calvary reveals the natural enmity of the human heart against the image of God.

V. **Place of Salvation.** "To-day shalt thou be with Me in paradise" (vv. 40-43). This penitent thief was the first to enter paradise through the blood of the Lamb. The sum of Christ's redemption work is found in these two little words, "WITH ME." This dying malefactor was reconciled to God through the death of His Son. Those who are *with Him* now in Spirit and in life will be with Him hereafter in transforming power (1 John 3. 2).

VI. **Place of Miracle.** "The sun was darkened, and the veil of the temple was rent in the midst" (vv. 44, 45). The rending of the veil and the obscuring of the sun were outstanding symbols of the goodness and the severity of God as embodied in the Cross of Christ. The darkness declares His severity against sin, the torn veil indicates a God-made way, through the sufferings of Christ, into His own presence (Heb. 10. 20).

VII. **Place of Death.** "He gave up the ghost" (v. 46). He became obedient unto death, even the death of the Cross. A DEATH that has brought life and immortality to light; that has made peace with God, and that still makes sinful men "smite their breasts" in the beholding of it (v. 48); a death that puts our sins away, and is the death of death.

"Calvary! O Calvary! All Thy agony for me!"

RESURRECTION WONDERS.
Luke 24. 1-27.

"What is left for us, save in growth of soul to rise . . .
From the gift, looking to the Giver,
And from the cistern to the river,
And from the finite to the Infinity,
And from man's dust to God's Divinity."—BROWNING.

THE soldiers made His grave with the graves of the wicked who were crucified with Him, but He was "with the rich in His death," that the Scripture might be fulfilled (Isa. 53. 9), for Joseph, a rich counsellor, begged the body, and buried it in his own new tomb.   Christ offered Himself a sacrifice unto God, so His body was precious to Him, and like the *ashes* of the burnt-offering of old, must be "carried forth into a *clean* place" (Lev. 6. 11).   It is said that there are seven wonders in the world, but we have seven wonders in this chapter.   A—

I. **Wonderful Stone.**   "They found the stone rolled away" (v. 2).   This stone, which was sealed with Pilate's seal, and had Roman soldiers set apart to watch it, yet it is *rolled away* (Matt. 27. 27-66).   The great block-stones rolled in the way of Christ and His cause by the enemies of God are easily removed when the hands of the "Angel of the Lord" are laid upon them (Matt. 28. 2).   Who shall be able to stand when He appeareth?

II. **Wonderful Grave.**   "They found not the body of the Lord Jesus" (v. 3).   Here Jesus was buried; now the tomb is empty.   There lies the linen that wrapped Him, in the same place and in the same form as when the body was within it; but He is gone. It was quite clear from the *position* of the clothes that no one had *stolen* Him away. "O grave, where is thy victory?"

III. **Wonderful Vision.** "Behold two men stood by them in shining garments" (v. 4). In following Jesus *into* the tomb, they were privileged to *see* the glorified ones. Every place, even the dark and lonesome grave, is hallowed and illumined when Jesus has been there. The glory of the resurrection life is first seen in the grave of Jesus. To be buried with Christ is to be raised with Him in newness of life (Rom. 6. 4).

IV. **Wonderful Message.** "He is not here; He is risen" (vv. 5-8). "He is not here"—all the powers of earth and hell have failed to keep Him. "He is risen"— all the authority of Heaven has been given Him. These angels *remembered* the words that Jesus had spoken, while the disciples had forgotten them (v. 6). It is easy to forget what we do not *believe.*

V. **Wonderful Incredulity.** "They believed them not" (vv. 10, 11). The Lord Jesus Himself had told them that He would be *raised again* on the *third* day (Matt. 17.23). Now the two women declare to them that the grave was empty, yet they "believed not." The truth about the resurrection of Christ is soul-resurrecting truth; men are always slow to believe it.

VI. **Wonderful Conversation.** "They talked together" (vv. 13-17). As they "communed, Jesus Himself drew near," for the Lord delights to hearken and hear when they that fear the Lord speak one to another (Mal. 3. 16). No scientists were ever more interested in any discovery than these two men were in the report that "Jesus is risen." How could it be otherwise, when, so to speak, the whole of their capital for time and eternity was sunk in this business.

VII. **Wonderful Stranger.** "Art Thou only a Stranger?" (vv. 15-27). "Only a Stranger!" How suggestive these words must have been to Him who had been "wounded in the house of His friends," but how comforting to hear Himself spoken of as "a prophet mighty in deed and word before God and all the people." Yet this "Stranger" rebuked them for their foolishness in not believing "all that the prophets had spoken;" and *beginning at Moses*—where the "higher critics" make shipwreck—He expounded unto them *in all* the Scriptures the things *concerning Himself*. He who was the TRUTH could never sanction a falsehood. He delights to reveal *Himself* to the seeking ones. "Seek, and ye shall find."

WONDERS OF GRACE.
Galatians 2. 20.

THERE are seven spiritual wonders in this marvellous text.

1. That the Son of God should **love** a persecutor like Saul. "Who loved me."

2. That the Son of God should be **crucified.** "Crucified with Christ."

3. That Christ should **give Himself** for sinners. "Who gave Himself for me."

4. That a man should **be crucified** in the Christ. "I am crucified with Christ."

5. That a crucified man should **still be alive.** "Nevertheless I live."

6. That Christ, who was crucified, should be found **living in a crucified man.** "Yet not I, but Christ liveth in me."

7. That a man can live this new life by **faith on the Son of God.** "The life which I now live in the flesh I live by the faith of the Son of God."

BIBLE READINGS.

JOSHUA.

I.—CALLED AND EQUIPPED.

'Yet the cloud of witness solemnly advances,
  Widening as each clarion voice is hushed in death below;
Yet the heavenly vision gleams on raptured glances,
  Prompt through changing vesture, their changeless Lord to know."

As soon as Moses was dead, the divine call came to Joshua, "Now, therefore, Arise" (Josh. 1. 2). God may bury His workman, but He still carries on His work. The Greek form of the name Joshua is Jesus. As a servant of God, there are many precious lessons that we might learn from his most wonderful life and work. We see him as—

I. An Inquirer. "But Joshua, a young man, departed not out of the tabernacle" (Exod. 33. 11). In verse seven we read, "Every one which *sought the Lord* went into the tabernacle which was without the camp." We infer that the choice of this young man to *abide* in the tabernacle of the LORD proved his love for His fellowship and desire to know more fully His mind and will. Souls who are really anxious do not wait for stated hours to learn the way of life. When the heart is truly seeking God, His house and His Word will have a new fascination. The "broken cisterns" will be forsaken for the fountain of living water.

II. A Changed One. "And Moses called Oshea the son of Nun Jehoshua" (Num. 13. 16). This change of name was surely the indication of a change of nature. The old name, *Hosea*, implied that *salvation* was in himself; the new name, Jehoshua, taught that the "LORD *is salvation.*" It is the old story of a conversion, when self-confidence is turned into faith in God, when the old supplanting nature is transformed into the princely and the divine, having power with God and with men, and prevailing (Gen. 32. 28). He waited on the Lord, and now his strength is exchanged. "Not I, but Christ."

III. **A Witness.** "Joshua said, The land which we passed through to search, it is an exceeding good land" (Num. 14. 6-9). At the time of murmuring, fear and dissention, he with Caleb, boldly took his stand upon the Word of God. He testified that the land *was* all that God had said it was. It wàs quite evident that *he* was on the Lord's side. We are not following cunningly devised fables when we make known the power and faithfulness of our Lord Jesus Christ. What need there is to-day for a fearless standing by the statements of God's Word, in the face of all the murmurings of those unbelieving spies, who are now known as "higher critics." The cry of all rationalists is not "back to Christ," but "back to Egypt." "But the Lord is with us: fear them not" (v. 9).

IV. **One Called to Honour.** "Take thee Joshua, and lay thine hand upon him,...and thou shalt put of thine honour upon him" (Num. 27. 18-20). Having taken his stand for God, he is now filled with the spirit of wisdom and power (Deut. 34. 9). He has sought the honour that comes from God only, and now he is abundantly rewarded with promotion in the service of the Lord. This is the anointing which they that believe should receive (John 7. 29). The spirit of Moses rested on Joshua as the spirit of Elijah afterwards rested on Elisha, and as the Spirit of Christ should now rest upon us.

V. **One Taught of God.** In the book of Joshua, chapter 1, and verses 1 to 9, we have the Lord Himself giving Joshua his marching orders. He received his great commission directly from God. This portion is worthy of the careful attention of all the Lord's servants, as it reveals the spirit and manner in which He would have the work done.

1. EVERY STEP must be taken in *faith* (v. 3).

2. The great PURPOSE OF GOD must be kept ever in view (v. 4).

3. There must be the CONFIDENCE OF VICTORY (v. 5).

4. There must be COURAGE and FAITHFULNESS in adhering closely to the Word of God (vv. 6-8).

5. His abiding presence must be continually RECKONED ON (v. 9).

Truly the servant of God has a meat to eat that others know not of.

VI. **One Seeking the Glory of God.** "Joshua said unto the *people*, Sanctify yourselves; and to the *priests*, Take up the Ark of the Covenant, and pass over *before the people.*" He would have God FIRST, and a *sanctified* people following. In such circumstances well may they expect the Lord to do "wonders among them." Before the Lord can be glorified before all the people, He must be sanctified *in His own* (see Lev. 3. 10). But notice the result of this God-honouring action on the part of Joshua. *"That day the Lord began to magnify him* in the sight of all Israel" (v. 7). They who put God first will always have a first place of honour in His service. "Him that honoureth Me, I will honour" (Phil. 2. 9).

VII. **One Entirely Consecrated to the Will of God.** When he suddenly met the "Captain of the host of the Lord . . . he fell on his face to the earth, . . . saying, What saith my lord unto His servant" (Josh. 5. 13-15). Joshua would be perfectly satisfied just to know that *His will* was being done. This to him was a holy place; it is always such where HIS PRESENCE is. The shoes of our self-willed service must be taken off if we would stand accepted on the "holy ground" of His abiding presence. "Yield yourselves unto God. "

VIII. **One Victorious in the Cause of God.** "The Lord said unto Joshua, See, I have given into thine hand Jericho" (Josh. 6. 2). "By *faith* the walls of Jericho fell down" (Heb. 11. 30). "This is the victory that overcometh the world, even our faith." They that honour their God shall be strong and do exploits (Dan. 11. 32). It is in the weakness of our child-like faith that His strength is perfected (2 Cor. 12. 9). Success in the work of God is absolutely certain, when all the conditions are perfectly fulfilled. "Only be thou strong and very courageous; turn not to the right or to the left,...then shalt thou have good success" (Josh. 1. 7-9). The apostle said, "This *one thing* I do. "

JOSHUA.

II.—TRIED AND TRIUMPHANT.

ALTHOUGH the Christian experience ought to be a going from strength to strength, and from glory to glory, yet between each successive and higher attainment there may lie deep valleys of trial and temptation that casts the very shadows of death over the pathway of the heaven-bound pilgrim. In this respect the noble life of Paul and that of the true-hearted Joshua are in many ways akin.

I. **He was Severely Tested.** "Joshua rent his clothes and fell to the earth upon his face before the Ark of the Lord" when he heard that his "three thousand men had fled before the men of Ai" (Josh. 7. 4-9). What a victory they had at great Jericho, what a shameful defeat at little Ai! The bloom of their new life has been suddenly blasted and withered. The enemy is rejoicing, and the name of God has been dishonoured. What is the cause? "Israel hath *sinned*" (v. 11). The Lord cannot permit His conquering power to rest upon those who are not in their hearts right with Himself.   But let no young Christian be discouraged, although at the beginning of their life of testimony for Christ there should be shameful defeats, but let this rather lead to deeper humility and heart searching. It is God's purpose to give us the victory over all our enemies, but He can only do this in a way that will bring glory to His own Name (Heb. 10. 38).

II. **He Makes no Compromise with Known Sin.** "Joshua rose up early in the morning, . . . and Achan was taken, . . . and stoned with stones" (chap. 7. 16-26). This solemn business was not only his, but God's; so for His sake he must not allow human reason nor feelings to stand in the way of a complete expulsion of the whole concern.   What a lesson for us to beware of that covetousness which is idolatry, "for which things' sake the wrath of God cometh upon the children of disobedience" (Col. 3. 5, 6).

III. **He Gives Great Prominence to the Word of God.** "Then Joshua built an altar unto the Lord God of Israel,...and wrote there upon the stones a copy of the law of Moses... the blessings and the cursings" (chap. 8. 30-35). He knew the power of it in his own experience, and in faithfulness he fearlessly declares "the whole counsel of God keeping back nothing." Preach the Word. Let the blessings for the obedient and the cursings for the disobedient have both their rightful place in your testimony. What God has joined together let no man put asunder.

IV. **He was not Infallible.**   The Gibeonites, with their false pretensions, "did work so wilily" that he was prevailed upon to "make a league with them," contrary to the command of God.   After all, he was a man of "like passions as we are," so that his mistake is a source of encouragement for us.   If God could so mightily use a man capable of making such a great blunder, surely there is good hope for us!   Yes, this is the sort of material that the grace of God

has to deal with.   We see how truly human this stalwart
servant of God was.   Nevertheless, we should give earnest
heed that while we take counsel we forget not the Lord
(Isa. 30. 1).

V. **He showed Prodigious Faith.**   "Joshua said in the
sight of all Israel, Sun, stand thou still upon Gibeon"
(chap. 10. 12-14).   His failure in no way hindered him
from asking and expecting great things from God as soon as
the need arose.   This was altogether a unique exhibition of
the possibilities of faith.   The faith that could make such a
demand from God was surely fit for anything.   He took
full advantage of the promise of His grace, "Command ye
Me."   This record of faith has never been broken, but how
very far short we do come of what lies within the reach of
every servant of God who really seeks the glory of His
Name.   All things that will bring glory to God are possible
to them that believe (1 John 3. 22).

VI. **He Claimed the whole Land of Promise.**   "So
Joshua took the whole land, according to all that the Lord
said unto Moses" (chap. 11. 23).   He claimed it by faith,
although the people were slow to take possession of it
(chap. 13. 1).   He did not think it presumption to accept
all that God had promised.   What is our faith doing for us
if it is not laying hold of that which God hath promised
us in Christ Jesus? (1 Cor. 1. 30).   It is honouring to Him
that we should receive those things freely given us by Him.
"He that believeth not God hath made Him a liar."

VII. **He Encourages Others to Enlarge their
Possessions.**   When the children of Joseph complained
about the smallness of their lot, he said, "Get thee up, and
cut down for thyself;...drive out the Canaanites;...thou
hast great power" (chap. 17. 14-18).   It is easy to get
dissatisfied with our Christian life when we are more taken
up with its narrowness and shallowness than with the all-

sufficient promise of God. The effectual cure for such grumbling is to "get up" and "drive out" the doubts and fears, and lay hold of the unsearchable riches of Christ, for "thou hast great power" if thou hast faith in God. There are not a few who, like the tribe of Joseph, have just got about as much of the "land of promise" as make them miserable, always crying out about their leanness and poverty when the cause of it is sheer spiritual laziness. O ye of little faith, how long will ye be slack to go in and possess the land? (chap. 18. 3).

VIII. **He Testifies to the Faithfulness of God.** "Ye know *in your hearts* that not one thing hath failed of all the good things which the Lord spake concerning you; all are come to pass" (chap. 23. 14). All that God hath promised He is prepared to give. Many know this *in their hearts*, like the Israelites, but they have not the courage, like Joshua, to put it to the test, and to say so. Although we believe in our hearts that "it is easier for Heaven and earth to pass than one tittle of the law to fail," yet how slow we are to claim the promises of God with the feet of faith (chap. 1. 3). If there is any shame in Heaven it will surely be that we expected so little from our exalted and glorified Redeemer and Lord.

IX. **He Exhorts to Whole-hearted Service.** "Now, therefore, fear the Lord, and serve Him in sincerity and truth" (chap. 24. 14, 15). In considering "how great things He had done for them," and promised to them, surely this was but *reasonable* that they should serve Him. Does not the great apostle beseech us by the *mercies of God* that we present *our bodies* as our reasonable *service*? (Rom. 12. 1). "Know ye not that *to whom* ye yield yourselves servants to obey, his servants ye are," whether that be to sin or righteousness, self or Christ (Rom. 6. 16).

X. **His Posthumous Influence.** "Israel served the

Lord all the days of Joshua, and all the days of the elders that overlived Joshua" (chap. 24. 31). The powerful life of this Prince with God kept speaking through those with whom he had been associated after he was gone. The life of faith always dies hard, while the memory of the wicked soon rots. The garments of a consecrated life, even when laid aside, are like the smell of Lebanon, recognised a long way off (Cant. 4. 11). "Blessed are the dead which *die* in the Lord to all self-interest, they do rest, and their works follow them."

CONSECRATION; or, Hands Filled.

THIS word, in its various cognate forms, occurs in the Bible forty-two times. In the sense of "to separate" it is used three times; "to set apart," seven times; to "denote" and "dedicate," once each; but "to *fill*," or "being *filled*," twenty-nine times. Only once is it used in the sense of "to perfect," and that in connection with the eternal and only begotten Son (Heb. 7. 28). Let us view this subject in the above fourfold aspect. It means—

I. **To be Separated from the Unclean.** The law of the Nazarite clearly taught this (Num. 6. 1-13). To *touch* the unclean was to bring instant defilement and to mar his holy relationship. Separation is no new doctrine. It began with Adam; it appears in Abel. It is seen in Enoch and Noah. It is taught in the *calling out* of Abraham, in the lives of the patriarchs, in the God-raised Judges, the prophets, and the apostles. The Church itself is the *out-called* of the grace of God. The very name *saint* tells us that we are *separated ones*. Ye are not of the world, says our Lord, but I have chosen you *out of* the world (John 15. 19). "Wherefore come ye out from among them, and be ye separate, saith the Lord, and touch not the unclean" (2 Cor. 6. 14-17).

II. **To be Set Apart for God.** Separation does not mean isolation. The Lord hath set apart him that is godly *for Himself* (Psa. 4. 6). The word godly here has reference more directly to the *gracious* state of the soul. All the subjects of His saving grace are marked out as His own. By the holy anointing Aaron and his sons were consecrated (set apart) that they might minister unto the Lord (Exod. 30. 30). So with all the vessels of the Tabernacle, which were set apart for the service of God, by being anointed. These vessels, although they were a "new creation" for the work and worship of God, yet they were unfit for use until they had received the baptism of the holy oil (Lev. 8. 10, 11). They were *sanctified* and made meet for Jehovah's use as soon as they occupied their true place, and were set apart by the special anointing. In this sense, that *sanctification* which fits for service is not a growth, it is a *gift*. We grow in *grace*, but we are made meet for the Master's use by the anointing of the Holy Ghost. We cannot grow into the promise of the Spirit. We receive it by faith (Gal. 3. 13, 14). Who then is willing to set himself apart, that he might receive the unction from the Holy One?

III. **To be Devoted to God.** It was said of Jericho that "the city shall be *devoted*, and all that is therein, to the Lord" (Josh. 6. 17, R.V.). Achan took of the "devoted thing" and brought trouble upon the camp and condemnation upon himself. Surely this is a solemn warning to us never to appropriate for our own selfish use what has been devoted to God! "Ye are not your own, ye are bought with a price" (1 Cor. 6. 20). Samuel was devoted to the Lord "as long as he liveth." Every offering laid upon the altar was devoted to God. It would have been sacrilege to have taken it back. The servant with the bored ear became for ever devoted to his master (Exod. 21. 5). Who then is willing to devote himself unto the Lord?

IV. **To have the Hands Filled for the Service of God.**
As we have already noticed, the word "consecrate" is used
twenty-nine times in the sense of "filling the hands." So
that the most prominent thought in connection with consecration is not giving, but taking; not yielding, but
receiving. The marginal reading of that well-known text,
1 Chronicles 29. 5, is, "Who then offereth willingly to *fill
his hands* this day unto the Lord" (R.V.). The Lord would
not have us to serve Him with empty hands. What have we
worth offering, either to Him or to perishing men, that we
have not *received*? Our Lord Jesus Christ did not send
the hungry multitude away because the disciples had not
enough to satisfy them. He *filled their hands* with the
heaven-sent bread, and so equipped them for the carrying
out of His gracious will. Are our hands so filled with
Christ, the "Bread of God," that hungry souls are being
satisfied. We cannot bless the people with *empty* hands.
And what shall it profit if our hands are full of other things
than those which God Himself puts into them. Our hands
will hang down in emptiness and feebleness until they are
"given unto the Lord," and filled with the gift of His Son
(2 Chron. 30. 8, *margin*). Empty hands mean powerless
and fruitless service for God. As the priest's hands were
only filled after he was cleansed and anointed, so must we
be saved and sanctified ere our hands can be filled with
acceptable service in His sight. And what a filling He
gives when Jesus Christ, in all the unsearchable riches of
His grace, is made ours in reality by the revelation of the
Holy Spirit (John 16. 14).

THE CHRISTIAN'S THREEFOLD RELATIONSHIP.

John 15.

THIS chapter will always be a fathomless deep of spiritual
instruction, because the twenty "I's" that are in it are each

a tree of life as big as God, laden with the fruits of grace. All the words of Jesus Christ are everlastingly fresh and seasonable. The breath of eternal life has been breathed into them, so they are destined to live on for ever. The whole chapter might be divided into three parts, each showing a distinct relationship of the believer.

I. **Our Relationship to Christ** (vv. 1-11). Here we are taught that it is one of—

1. LIFE. "I am the Vine, ye are the branches" (v. 5). The connection is a vital one. Each branch is made a partaker of the life that is in the vine. So, by His grace we are made "partakers of the divine nature," planted into *Him*, who is the life of men and the fullness of the Godhead bodily (1 John 5. 11).

2. ENTIRE DEPENDENCE. "The branch cannot bear fruit of itself; no more can ye" (v. 4). The chief purpose of the branch is not merely to draw as much life from the vine as maintain its own existence, but to bring forth fruit. For this, unbroken fellowship with the vine is absolutely necessary. To be fruitful unto God (the Husbandman) we must moment by moment abide in Christ, so that His Spirit and Word may continually abide in us.

3. CO-OPERATION. "Without ME ye can do nothing" (v. 5). The vine and the branches labour together in fruit-bearing. Jesus, as the true Vine, desires that the Father should be glorified in the fruitfulness of those who, as branches, are united to Him by a loving faith, and being made the recipients of His grace and Spirit. If the "good pleasure" of God is to be wrought out in our lives, it will be because of *His* working in us both to will and to do (Phil. 2. 13). A barren branch is a dishonour to the vine; the fruitful bring glory to its name.

4. GREAT POSSIBILITIES. "If ye abide in Me, . . . ye shall ask what ye will, and it shall be done unto you"

(v. 7).   Who has ever yet proved all the spiritual poten-
tialities that lie hidden in these few simple words, "I
IN YOU" (v. 4).   Our union with Christ brings the things
which are impossible with men within easy reach.   Paul
knew the power of it when he said, "I can do all things
through Christ which strengtheneth me."   Have faith
in God.

II. **Our Relationship to One Another** (vv. 12-17).
"That they all may be one" was the prayer of our Lord for
His followers (John 17. 21).   As believers, we are closely
related to one another.   There is a—

1. ONENESS OF LIFE.   Each branch is possessed by the
same sap (Spirit), and dependent on the same source.
One spiritual life, governed by the one Head, animates the
whole body of Christ.   "Christ our life."   All are born
of the same Spirit, and members of the same family.

2. ONENESS OF LOVE.   "Love one another, as I have
loved you" (v. 12).   To love one another as *Christ loved us*
is to love with the *love of God* shed abroad in our hearts
His love was unmerited, unselfish, and abiding.   We
love Him because He *first* loved us, so if His love is in
us we will not wait till we are loved before we love others.
We will go on loving *first*, because it is Christ's love in us.
He who loveth God will love his brother also (1 John 4. 21).
Love one to another is the universal mark of discipleship
(John 13. 35).

3. ONENESS OF FRIENDSHIP.   "I have called you
friends, for all things I have heard of My Father I have
made known unto you" (v. 15).   The *doing of His will*
constitutes this holy friendship (v. 14).   "Whosoever shall
do the will of My Father, the same is my brother" (Matt.
12. 50).   In our obedience to the will of God we are brought
together into this divine brotherhood, where the "secret of
the Lord" becomes common property (Psa. 25. 14).   Was

it not because of Abraham's faithfulness to the will of God that He said, "Shall I hide from Abraham that thing which I do?" (Gen. 18. 17).

4. ONENESS OF WORK. "I have *chosen you* and ordained you, that ye should go and bring forth fruit" (v. 16). Our unity of life and privilege leads to unity of service. We have been *unitedly* chosen and ordained to go and bring forth the fruits of Christ's character in our lives for the glory of the Father, not for the glory as the individual branch. Where this truth is known experimentally there is no room for jealousy or envy. If one branch is more successful than another there will be mutual joy that the heart of the husbandman has been made glad. The source of all fruitfulness is not in the branch, but in the vine. "From ME is thy fruit found" (Hosea 14. 8).

III. **Our Relationship to the World** (vv. 18-27). This may be stated under the following three words—

1. SEPARATION. "Ye are not of the world" (v. 19). The whole world lieth in the wicked one, but ye have been chosen *out of the world*. Chosen to be a special people unto Himself, not because ye were better or mightier than others, but because the Lord loved you (Deut. 7. 6-8). Called by His grace, cleansed by His Blood, and made meet for His fellowship by the indwelling of His Spirit.

2. OPPOSITION. "Because ye are not of the world, therefore the world hateth you" (v. 19). As soon as we became sons of God the world "knew us not and despised us as strangers and foreigners" (1 John 3. 1). The true disciple cannot expect to fare better than his Master (Matt. 10. 22). The "contradiction of sinners" must be expected by all who would follow in Christ's steps (Heb. 12. 2-4). "Blessed are ye when men shall revile you, . . . for great is your reward in Heaven" (Matt. 5. 11).

3. WITNESSING. "Ye shall bear witness, because ye
have been *with Me.*" (v. 27). We have been separated by
Him, to be witnesses for Him, in the midst of a crooked and
perverse generation. In any ordinary court the witnesses
are *separate* persons; they are there not to see and be seen,
but to give their evidence. Our business in the great open
court of this world, where Christ is still being judged and
condemned, is as witnesses for Him. The more intimately
we know HIM—His Word, His work, and His will—the
more powerful and convincing will our evidence be (Luke
24. 28). We are His witnesses of these things. What
things? We are witnesses to His death, because we have
been crucified with Him; to His resurrection, because we
have been raised from the dead; to His ascension, because
we are seated together with Him in the heavenlies. "Let
your light so shine" (Matt. 5. 16).

THE ABILITY OF GOD IN AND THROUGH
HIS PEOPLE.

"The exceeding greatness of *His power to us-ward* who believe,
according to the working of His mighty power, which He wrought *in
Christ*, when He *raised Him* from the dead, and *set Him* at His own
right hand in the heavenly places, *far above all*'' (Eph. 1. 19-21).

"I also labour, striving according to *His working*, which worketh
in me mightily'' (Col. 1. 29).

"When I am weak, then am I strong'' (2 Cor. 12. 10).

THIS is a great thought, the invisible and Almighty God
working in us—His believing people—and through us,
accomplishing all the good purposes of His will. It is God
who worketh in us, both to will and to do of His good
pleasure (Phil. 2. 13).

I. **What God is able to do for us.** He is—

1. ABLE TO SAVE US (Heb. 7. 25). For this He came,
for this was His Name called Jesus, for this He died and

rose again. He saves from wrath, from sin, from the world, from self, from the Devil, and from death and the grave.

2. ABLE TO DELIVER US (Dan. 3. 17). He delivers by shutting the mouths of our enemies and quenching the violence of their fiery passions (Heb. 11. 33, 34).

3. ABLE TO MAKE US STAND (Phil. 3. 21). This is a great comfort in these slippery days, when men will not endure sound doctrine. We will be able to stand if we are able so say, like Elijah, "The Lord God of Israel, *before whom I stand*" (1 Kings 17. 1).

4. ABLE TO KEEP US (Jude 24). He can even keep from stumbling. In Christ, we are kept in the Father's hand, where no thief can steal. "Kept by the power of God through faith" (1 Peter 1. 5).

5. ABLE TO SATISFY US (2 Cor. 9. 8). What a treasure is here! "All grace abounding toward *you*, that you always may have all-sufficiency in all things." Is it so with you? Why not? God is able—able to do exceeding abundantly.

6. ABLE TO RAISE US (Heb. 11. 19). He is able to keep that which we have committed unto Him—spirit, soul, and *body*. Joyful anticipation—this mortal shall put on immortality. What a change—a body like unto His own glorious body.

7. ABLE TO PRESENT US FAULTLESS (Jude 24). What a joy to Jesus! What a consolation to the Father! What a prospect and privilege for the Christian!

II. **What God is able to do in us.** He is—

1. ABLE TO DWELL IN US (Eph. 3. 17-20). Know ye not that your body is the temple of God, and that God dwelleth in you? Christ dwelling in us by His Spirit in the inner man is to be the power that worketh in us, as the sap worketh in the branch.

2. ABLE TO SUBDUE (Phil. 3. 21). If Christ reigns within, the enemies within will be subdued. He will subdue the lusts of the flesh, the fiery temper, and the hasty tongue.

3. ABLE TO SUCCOUR (Heb. 2. 18). Temptations are common. If we are in fellowship with Christ we shall be succoured with His sympathy in the hour of trial. "He knows what sore temptations are."

4. ABLE TO STRENGTHEN (2 Tim. 4. 17). Abiding in us by His Spirit, we are conscious of Him standing by us. A sense of His presence inspires with freshness and vigour.

5. ABLE TO BUILD UP (Acts 22. 32). The inner life and character need building up—the new man—whose builder and maker is God. He builds up the believer by revealing the truth through the Holy Spirit, which is able to build us up into the image of His Son (Col. 2. 7).

6. ABLE TO FILL (Col. 1. 9). What a precious portion is ours, "Filled with the knowledge of His will" (Col. 1. 9); and again, "Be filled with the Spirit" (Eph. 5. 18). God has reserved to Himself the right to *fill* a human soul.

7. ABLE TO WORK (Heb. 13. 21). Sweet thought, that amidst all the stubborn material within He is able to work in us that which is pleasing in His sight. Yield all, and all will be well (1 John 4. 4).

III. **What God is Able to Do Through Us.** He is—

1. ABLE TO REVEAL (Gal. 1. 16). If His Son has been revealed in us, it is that He might be revealed through us. If the light hath shined in our hearts, it is that others might see it and glorify God (1 Cor. 4. 6). The treasure is put in the earthen vessel that the power may be of God.

2. ABLE TO RECONCILE (2 Cor. 5. 18-20). What a responsibility that God should commit unto us the word of reconciliation! What a privilege that God should, through our feeble ministry, reconcile sinners to Himself!

3. ABLE TO MINISTER (2 Cor. 3. 16). Able to serve others through His consecrated servants. May He give us the tongue of the wise to know how to speak a word to the weary!

4. ABLE TO OVERCOME (Eph. 6. 11). Our defeat is His dishonour. When we, clothed with the armour of God, get the victory over the wiles of the Devil, it is Christ conquering through us.

5. ABLE TO BEAR FRUIT (Col. 1. 10). Walking worthy of the Lord, He will make us fruitful in every good work. The vine needs the branches to bear its fruit, so Christ needs His people to show forth the riches of His grace (John 15. 5).

6. ABLE TO DO HIS OWN PLEASURE (Phil. 2. 13). God worketh in you both to *will* and to *do* of His good pleasure. He is shut out from the hearts of the ungodly, but may His will be done in us as it is done in Heaven. We are "workers together with Him" (2 Cor. 6. 1). We "dwell with the King for His Work" (1 Chron. 4. 23).

> "Oh, to be filled with life divine;
> Oh, to be clothed with might;
> Oh, to reflect my Lord, and shine
> As shine the saints in light!"

GOD'S QUESTIONS.

IT would appear that from the very beginning it was the manner of Jehovah to impress the thoughts of His heart upon the minds of men by asking them questions. Almost at every great crisis in the history of His ancient people some definite interrogation falls from His lips. What method is better calculated to make people think? It was also the manner of Jesus Christ—God manifest in the flesh. He began in the temple by "asking questions," and all through His ministry they were continually falling like coals of fire upon the heads of His unbelieving followers, and often with startling effect upon His own beloved disciples. Every question asked by God is intended to arrest the attention and direct the thoughts of the human mind to some definite purpose of His heart. So that behind every question there seems to be a revelation. The following questions, asked by God Himself, have been put into three sections, under different topics, and may be used as so many different readings.

I.—GOD'S QUESTIONS IN RELATION TO SIN.

I. **"Adam, where art thou?"** (Gen. 3. 9). An interrogation calculated to make him "consider his ways." Why was he now troubled at the presence of God? (Job 23. 15). Why does his heart condemn him? (1 John 3. 20).

II. **"Who told thee that thou wast naked?"** (Gen. 3. 11). How is it that your innocency as a "garment of glory and beauty" has suddenly dropped off and left you clothed only in your own shame? The hand of *sin* strips the soul naked of all comeliness in the sight of God.

III. **"What is this that thou hast done?"** (Gen. 3. 13). Something awful has been done, and *thou* hast done it. What is it? Think it all over again in the very presence of the Holy One, of Him who hath blessed you with every needful blessing. What a humbling experience this *should be*; but she attempts an excuse. "Be not deceived; God is not mocked."

IV. **"Why art thou wroth?"** (Gen. 4. 6). Is God unjust and partial in His dealings with men that you should be at enmity with Him in your heart? Why do you let your "countenance fall" instead of coming and reasoning together with the Lord? (Isa. 1. 18). He is no respecter of persons (Rom. 2. 11).

V. **"How long wilt thou refuse to Humble thyself before Me?"** (Exod. 10. 3). Dost thou not know that "before *destruction* the heart of man is haughty" (Prov. 18. 12). Refusing to humble thyself is to declare war with the Almighty.

VI. **"How long will it be ere they believe Me?"** (Num. 14. 11). As long as ye *believe* HIM *not*, ye are companying with those who shall have their part in the lake of fire with all liars. In believing Him not ye make Him a liar. He has sworn that "them that believe not" shall not enter into His rest (Heb. 3. 18).

VII. **"Who would set the briers and thorns against ME in battle?"** (Isa. 27. 4). Your reasons and excuses for not believing His Word and obeying His will are just so many briers and thorns set up to oppose the progress of an unquenchable fire. "I would go through them," saith the Lord. "Who can stand before His indignation?" (Nah. 1. 6)

VIII. **"Can any hide himself that I shall not see him?"** (Jer. 23. 24). If I make my bed in Hell, Thou art there. The "thick clouds" that hide Him from thee cannot hide thee from Him (Job 22. 13, 14). "The eyes of the Lord are in every place, beholding the evil and the good" (Prov. 15. 3). All things are naked and bare before the "high and lofty One that inhabiteth Eternity."

IX. **"Wilt thou condemn ME, that thou mayest be righteous?"** (Job. 40. 8). We are condemning Him when we say that we have not sinned, and seek to establish our own righteousness. We treat Him as a liar when we believe not His Word. The life that is built on God-dishonouring principles is built on sand and doomed to sudden destruction (Matt. 7. 24-27).

II.—GOD'S QUESTIONS IN RELATION TO SALVATION.

I. **"What aileth thee?"** (Gen. 21. 17). How ready the Lord is to hear the voice of the needy, and to be touched with compassion at the cry of a desolate, penitent heart. What *aileth* thee? is the language of this Great Physician, who can well heal all the *ailments* of the human soul.

II. "To whom will ye liken ME?" (Isa. 40. 25). You cannot *liken* the HOLY ONE to any created thing. O man, with all the multitude of your ailments, liken not God, the Fountain of Life, to the broken cisterns of earth, or His way to the deceitfulness of your own heart! Where will you get His *like* for mercifulness, mightiness, and readiness to save?

III. "To what purpose is your sacrifices unto Me?" (Isa. 1. 11). Your gifts and your religious works are to no *purpose* as long as the *heart* is at enmity with God. The sacrifices of God are a broken spirit (Psa. 51. 16, 17). To obey the voice of His Word is better than sacrifice. A hearing ear is better to Him than the fat of rams (1 Sam. 15. 22).

IV. "Wherefore do ye spend your money for that which is not bread?" (Isa. 55. 2). Why go on with religious forms which bring no strength or satisfaction into the heart and life? Why do ye set your affections on those things which are perishing, and leave your own imperishable soul to face an eternal famine? Why do you labour to establish *your own* righteousness, when after you have done your very best you have gained nothing but "filthy rags?" (Isa. 64. 6).

V. "How shall I pardon thee for this?" (Jer. 5. 7). It is not possible for man to give any cogent reason why God should pardon sin apart from the "Blood of Christ." When God does pardon He has always a good reason for it, but that reason is never found in our own worthiness, but in the worthiness of Him who died for us.

VI. "How shall I put thee among the children?" (Jer. 3. 19). How can God put the "children of disobedience" among His own sons? Only by *redeeming* them from all iniquity and sending forth the spirit of His Son into their hearts so that they may truthfully cry, "Abba, Father" (Gal. 4. 4-6). The constraining motive on God's part is love (1 John 3. 1).

VII. **"Wilt thou not cry unto me, My Father?"** (Jer. 3. 4). If He has loved you so much as to give His Son up to the death for you, that you might have the right to take your place among His children, wilt thou not cry, "My Father" (John 1. 12). Wilt thou not own Him as your Father? We are the children of God *by faith* (Gal. 3. 26).

VIII. **"Is there anything too hard for ME?** (Jer. 32. 27). Has He not power over all flesh, that He might give eternal life to as many as believe? (John 17. 2). Is He not "able to save to the very uttermost" all that come. Is there anything in your heart, your life, or your circumstances that is *too hard* for HIM? Things too hard for you are easy for God (Matt. 19. 26).

IX. **"How shall I give thee up?"** (Hosea 11. 8). Surely this is good proof of the willingness of God to keep a hold of His own. Are you afraid that you may not be able to hold on. Listen. "How shall I give thee up?" Your safety lies in *His power* to keep. "He is able to keep that which we have committed unto Him. " This is a question that might melt the heart of any backslider.

III.—GOD'S QUESTIONS IN RELATION TO SERVICE.

I. **"What seest thou?"** (Jer. 1. 13). There are those who *see* no beauty in Jesus, no attractiveness in His Word. Dost thou see those things which are set before thee in the vision of the Gospel? Then thine eyes have been anointed with the holy eye-salve (Rev. 3. 18). "Set thine heart upon all that I shall show thee" (Ezek. 40. 4).

II. "**Where is thy brother?**" (Gen. 4. 9). Andrew found his brother, and brought him to Jesus (John 1. 41, 42). Those who have seen the Lamb of God and believed on Him should seek, that others may see Him also. Are you so taken up with *yourself* that you forget that you have a brother?

III. "**Who will go?**" (Isa. 6. 8). Jesus Christ went forth to the place of shame and death, that God's message of salvation might come to us *through* Him. Who will go *for* Him? There is no compulsion in the service of God but the compulsion of *love*. "Here am I, send me," for the love of Christ constraineth me.

IV. "**Wherefore liest thou thus upon thy face?**" (Joshua 7. 10). There is a time to pray, and to humble thyself before God, but there is also a time to be up and doing (Exod. 14. 15). Sin must not only be confessed in ourselves, but must also be rebuked in others. We may lie on our face until we become a grief to our Lord and Master.

V. "**What is that in thine hand?**" (Exod. 4. 2). It is a good thing to have something *in hand* that may bring glory to God. The thing itself may seem small and useless for this great end; but HE *can* make it mighty to the pulling down of the strongholds of Satan. Every lawful thing that's in your hand may become a conquering weapon for God.

VI. "**Cannot I do with you as this potter?**" (Jer. 18. 6). "Woe unto him that striveth with his Maker" (Isa. 45. 9). If the potter can work wonders in a piece of clay, can not the Lord Almighty work in you both to will and to do of His good pleasure? Ye are bought with a price, therefore it is surely lawful for Him to do what He will with His own (Matt. 20. 15). *Yield* yourselves unto God, lest ye become as marred vessels unto Him.

VII. **"Is not My Word as a fire?"** (Jer. 23. 29). Does it not make the *heart to burn* when it comes from the lips of love? (Luke 24. 32). It is a divine light that needs but the oxygen of human faith to make it a burning flame in the soul. The Word of God is no carnal weapon; it is a tongue of fire unquenchable. The words of men are as thorns and briars in the presence of this holy flame (John 6. 63).

VIII. **"Can these bones live?"** (Ezek. 37. 3). Can God raise up out of these dead, dry, and severed bones, living, moving, mighty men? (Rom. 4. 17). How are the dead raised up? It is the Spirit that quickeneth. Faith prophesies, but God causes the breath to enter. "In Him was life" (John 1. 4).

IX. **"Who is blind . . . and deaf, as my messenger?"** (Isa. 42. 19). As Saul was blinded by the "brightness of that light,'" so has all the Lord's true servants been blinded to the perishing things of earth by the revelation of the glory of the things of Heaven. This one thing they do— they "glory in the Cross of the Lord Jesus Christ," and are blind to the glory and deaf to the voices of this world that had nothing for Him but a crown of thorns. "Ye cannot serve God and Mammon." As the messengers of God, we must have the blindness and the deafness of those who *don't want* to see or hear anything that would distract us in our soul-saving mission.

ENCOURAGEMENT TO PRAYER.
Psalm 50. 15.

1. The Time,	.. ..	"Day of trouble."
2. The Counsel,	.. ..	"Call upon Me."
3. The Promise,	.. ..	"I will deliver."
4. The Result,	.. ..	"Thou shalt glorify Me."

GOSPEL OUTLINES.

THE WAY OF CAIN.

"Woe unto them, for they have gone in the way of Cain" (Jude 11).

GRACE does not run in the blood, so the *way* of Cain is spoken of as opposed to the way of God. The broad and the narrow way may still be distinguished as the way of Cain or the way of Christ. "My way is not your way, saith the Lord. " The way of Cain is—

I. **The Way of Mere Human Opinion.** He offered the firstfruits, the best that he had, as an atonement for his soul. Well, says the modern Cainite, if a man does the best he can, what more can he do? The best way we can do is to take God's way. Cain refused to come to God as a *sinner*. By *faith* Abel offered unto God a more acceptable sacrifice.

II. **The Way of Wilful Ignorance.** Cain must have known, from the fact that he was born *outside* Eden, and from the example of his father and mother, that he was a sinner in the sight of God. The very coats of *skin* given them by God revealed the need of an atonement to cover. But this he, like many to-day, was "willingly ignorant of. " God cannot accept our thankoffering as long as we refuse to acknowledge His sin-offering (John 1. 29).

III. **The Way of Utter Rejection?** "Unto *Cain* and his *offering* God had not respect" (Gen. 4. 5). The *spirit* of Cain was unacceptable, as well as his offering. The offering, and the offerer, must always stand or fall together. *We* are accepted *in* the beloved. By one offering He hath perfected them that are set apart. Jesus says, "I am the Way, no man can come unto the Father but *by Me*. "

IV. **The Way of Unyielding Pride.** "And Cain was very wroth, and his countenance fell" (Gen. 4. 5). Although he knew that the *way* he came to God was of his own choosing, and displeasing to Him, there is no desire for repentance, no willingness to confess his sin and forsake his way. Abel had found his sin-offering at his door among the flock. A sin-offering also lay at the door of Cain, waiting his reception and ready for his use, but he would not. The preaching of Christ, and Him crucified, is the laying of the God-appointed sin-offering at the door of every sinner who hears the Gospel. If thou doest *not well*, this *sin*-offering is for thee (Gen. 4. 7).

V. **The Way of Manifest Hatred.** "Cain talked with his brother Abel, and slew him," because his own works were evil and his brother's righteous (1 John 3. 12). Sin, when it is finished, bringeth forth death. The quarrel between good and evil is an old one. To reject Christ the sin-offering is to take the place of a murderer. He that hateth his brother is a murderer. The first murder was committed by a man who denied the doctrine of substitution and the need of atonement.

VI. **The Way of Divine Condemnation.** *"Now* art thou cursed" (Gen. 4. 11). "He that believeth not is condemned already." Where can the man hide who has fled from the only refuge under Heaven for a sinner—the sin-offering? The Lamb of God. The guilt of the unforgiven cries unto God like the blood of Abel. Sin always cries unto God for vengeance, but Christ our sin-offering answered this terrible cry by the sacrifice of Himself (1 Peter 2. 24).

VII. **The Way of Hopeless Despair.** Cain said, "Mine iniquity is greater than that it may be forgiven" (Gen. 4. 13, *margin*). "He *went out* from the presence of the Lord" (v. 16). All who reject the sin-offering are doomed to go out for ever from the presence of the Lord **and** from the glory of His power (2 Cor. 1. 9). Cain's guilt began by taking his own way, and it was aggravated by refusing to repent after light and guidance had been given. He is now confirmed in his unbelief and sealed in his doom. "Woe unto them, for they have gone in the way of Cain" (Isa. 1. 18).

WHAT HAVE I DONE?
Jeremiah 8. 6.

THE divine complaint is, that no one seems so sensible of sin and guilt in His sight as to say, What have I done? All are so full of self-confidence that they feel no need of repentance. Is there not an urgent need of pressing this question now?

I. **What have I Done with God?** Is He not the Author and Preserver of my life? Have I been mindful of His goodness and thankful for His mercies? What place have I given Him in my thoughts?

II. **What have I Done with Christ?** He has been offered me as the gift of God. What have I done with Him? Have I accepted Him or rejected Him? Have I crowned Him with thorns or with honour and glory? Is His blood sprinkled on my heart or is it under my feet?

III. **What have I Done with the Holy Spirit?** Have I grieved Him by my unbelief? Have I turned a deaf ear to His entreaty, and hardened my heart against the melting influences of His presence? Have I received Him in all His fullness, or am I still doing despite to the Spirit of grace.

IV. **What have I Done with the Warnings of Providence?** In the day of adversity have I been led to *"consider?"* Have all my afflictions been sanctified? Has the loss of loved ones on earth drawn my affections more intently after the things that are above?

V. What have I Done with my Bible? Have I been reading it as God's written message to my soul? Have I been using it as a lamp from Heaven to guide my footsteps thither? Have I made it the "Man of my counsel," and is its message hid in my heart? Have I openly confessed its truth, or am I ashamed of it?

VI. What have I Done with my Talents? My brain, my money, my time, and my tongue, have they been used for the glory of self, or for the glory of God? Have they been buried in the napkin of self-preservation, instead of used for the advancement of the kingdom of the Lord Jesus Christ?

VII. What have I Done with my Opportunities? Have I taken advantage of my many God-given privileges, to hear His Word, to speak in His Name, to reprove, to rebuke, to exhort? Have I been more anxious to *kill* the time than to *redeem* it?

VIII. What have I Done with my Neighbours? Have I sought to take advantage of them, rather than be a blessing to them? Have I loved them as myself, or have I treated them as inferior creatures? Have I received of the saving grace of God, and have I treated those beside me as if I owed them nothing?

IX. What have I Done with the Inner Cry of my Own Need? Have I been conscious of the need of God's forgiveness and deliverance from the power of sin, and yet have sought to stifle the voice? What have I done with my sense of weakness, powerlessness, and fruitlessness in living the Christian life? Have I sought comfort instead of confession, the pity of my fellow-believers instead of the power of the Holy Ghost? Are you among those of whom the Lord complains, that they do not repent saying, "What have I done?"

FREE SALVATION.
Isaiah 55. 1.

I. The Articles for Sale.   "Wine and milk."

1. MILK, emblematic of that which contains *all the essentials of life.* The Gospel of Christ meets man's every need.

2. WINE, emblematic of that which cheers and inspires. The Gospel not only saves, but satisfies and inspires the soul with new and higher motives.

II. The Price to be Paid.   "Buy *without* money and without price."   "Nothing in my hand I bring."   Any price, in the form of works, prayers, emotions, or doctrines, offered to God for eternal salvation is an insult to His GRACE. The condition is *without money*, with absolutely nothing but your need and emptiness, that his "lovingkindness" may be known.

III. The Customers Invited.   The—

1. THIRSTY.   "Ho, every one that thirsteth!"   If this invitation was found over some publican's door there would likely be a good many applicants.   Soul thirst is your qualification for the "waters of life."   "If any man *thirst*, let him come (John 7. 37)."

2. BANKRUPT.   "He that hath no money."   Already "sold under sin."   Debtors, having nothing wherewithal to meet a merciless creditor.   It was when the prodigal began to be in *want* that he said, "I will arise and go to my father."   "Come, for all things are now ready."   "By grace are ye saved through faith, and that *not of yourselves*, it is the *gift of God.*"

ALIENATED FROM THE LIFE OF GOD.
Ephesians 4. 18.

I. What is Meant by "the Life of God?"   Jesus Christ was the perfect exhibition of this life.   In Him this life was manifested as a life of—

1. HOLINESS. He was the image of God, although in the likeness of sinful flesh. A life lived in the fellowship and favour of God.

2. SELF-SACRIFICE. He pleased not Himself. He loved us and gave Himself for us. Always pleasing unto God (Matt. 17. 5).

3. INWARD JOY AND PEACE. He could say, "*My peace* I give unto you," and that "*My joy* may remain in you." The life of God is a life in perfect harmony, with a perfect environment.

4. POWER AND VICTORY. Power over all His enemies, and victory over death and the grave.

II. What is Meant by being "Alienated" from this life? It is to have—

1. NO LIKENESS TO GOD. No kinship of nature. Separated by sin, and living at enmity with Him (Rom. 8. 7).

2. NO FELLOWSHIP WITH GOD. As soon as Adam sinned he fell out of communion with God. Those in fellowship with the powers of darkness cannot walk in this light (Acts 26. 18).

3. NO HOPE IN GOD. Where there is no faith in Jesus Christ there is no hope, and those without this hope are without God in the world (Eph. 2. 12).

4. NO FITNESS FOR GOD. The carnal mind cannot please Him, and without holiness no man shall see the Lord. "Except a man be born again he cannot see the Kingdom of God."

III. What is the Cause of this Alienation? It is threefold—

1. IGNORANCE. "Alienated through the ignorance that is in them." This is wilful ignorance, for Jesus said, "If ye had known Me, ye would have known My Father also." "Ye will not come to Me."

2. BLINDNESS. "Because of the blindness of their *heart.*" Those who prefer the darkness to the light will surely be smitten with heart-blindness. Spiritual ignorance is the most favourable condition for a "deceitful heart."

3. DARKNESS. "The understanding darkened." Spiritual things become foolishness to them. These are the fetters with which the god of this world binds the enemies of God (2 Cor. 4. 3, 4).

IV. What is the Cure for Alienation? We may instantly escape from this awful condition by—

1. CONFESSION. If we confess our sins, He is faithful and *just* to forgive us, because God's Lamb has been slain (John 1. 29). *Propitiation* has been made (1 John 2. 2).

2. RECEPTION. "As many as receive Him, to them gives He the right to become the *sons of God*" (John 1. 12). The prodigal was no longer alienated after he "came to his father " "No man can come to the Father but by ME."

3. SUBMISSION. To abide in His fellowship there must be a continual surrender of the will to God. "If ye keep My commandments, ye shall abide in My love" (John 15. 10).

REGENERATION.
John 3. 3, 6, 7.

IT is John, the apostle of love, who speaks most directly on the doctrine of the "new birth." It is referred to seven times in his first epistle. To be regenerated is to be "born from above" (*margin*), "born of God" (John 1. 13). For the sake of clearness, think of—

I. What this Change is Not. It is not—

1. A NATURAL BIRTH. "Ye must be *born again*—born from above." That which is born of the flesh is flesh, and flesh and blood cannot inherit the Kingdom of God.

2. A SYSTEM OF DOCTRINE. Nicodemus *knew* that Jesus was a teacher come from God, and was acquainted with much of His teaching, yet Jesus said to him, "Ye must be born again."

3. OUTWARD REFORMATION. No adorning of the external character can change the heart, and make a man a new creation. It may be possible to keep the hands of a clock right at times, but that does not make *it* right when the main spring is wrong.

4. MAKING A PROFESSION. Merely professing to be saved does not save. A sow in a sheepskin does not make the sow any better. Not he that *saith*, but he that *doeth* the will of the Father.

II. What this Change Really Is. It is—

1. A DIVINE CHANGE. It is the Spirit that quickeneth. To be "born from above" implies the forth-putting of the creative power of God. If God is to be our Father, then we must be *born* of God.

2. A COMPLETE CHANGE. If any man be in Christ he is a *new creation*. Old things have passed away. The winter of darkness and death is gone, and the time of singing the new song has come. The transformation of character is still as radical as it was in the case of Saul of Tarsus (Acts 9).

3. A CONSCIOUS CHANGE. No one can be brought out of such a horrible pit of ignorance and sin without being sweetly sensible of it (Psa. 40. 1-3). "One thing I know, whereas I was blind, now I see." We know that we have passed from death unto life.

III. Why this Change is Needed.

1. THE CHARACTER OF MAN DEMANDS IT. "Except a man be born from above, he *cannot see* the Kingdom of God." Man's way is to educate and legislate, but God's way is to *regenerate*. There is no other remedy for that carnal mind which is enmity against God.

2. THE CHARACTER OF GOD DEMANDS IT. How can two walk together except they be agreed? God is holy, so without holiness no man shall see the Lord. The Kingdom of God is not meat and drink, but righteousness and peace, and joy *in the Holy Ghost.*

3. THE WORK OF CHRIST DEMANDS IT. He came and suffered and died that we might have life through His Name. The voice of His Blood cries for a thorough change in man before he can come with acceptance to the Father (John 14. 6).

4. THE WORK OF THE SPIRIT DEMANDS IT. It is the Spirit that quickens, the flesh profiteth nothing. If it were possible for an unrenewed soul to enter Heaven it would be an eternal insult to the Son and to the Holy Ghost.

5. THE WORD OF GOD DEMANDS IT (v. 3). This Word, which is settled in Heaven, cannot be broken. "The words that I speak unto you, they are Spirit and life." Incorruptible.

IV. How this Change is Effected.

1. THE AGENT IS THE SPIRIT. "Not by might nor by power, but by My Spirit, saith the Lord. "He is the Holy Breath that breathes upon the slain, that they may live (Ezek. 37. 9).

2. THE INSTRUMENT IS THE WORD. "Born again by the Word of God" (1 Peter 1. 23). It is not man's thoughts that the Holy Spirit uses in regenerating any soul, but God's.

3. THE CONDITION IS FAITH. "Whosoever *believeth* that Jesus is the Christ is born of God" (1 John 5. 1). "Whosoever *believeth in Him* should not perish, but have everlasting life." This is our Lord's own answer to the great question of Nicodemus, "How can a man be born when he is old?" (John 3. 14-16).

REMEMBER LOT'S WIFE.
Luke 17. 32.

THERE are very solemn reasons why *we* should remember Lot's wife, in the near approach of the coming of the Son of Man (v. 30). To be unfit for His appearing will be to be overtaken with that vengeance which shall come upon those who have not "obeyed the Gospel" (2 Thess. 1. 6-10). Some things about her that should be *remembered*—

I. **She Perished, although she was the Wife of a Righteous Man.** Lot was not all that he might have been, but he was a "righteous man who vexed his soul" (2 Peter 2. 8) with the filthy conversation of the Sodomites. She was also related to Abraham, the man of faith.

II. **She Perished, although she was Warned of her Danger.** A special message had come from Heaven, warning them to "escape for their life." Have we not also had a special warning from God through His own Son? (John 3. 36).

III. **She Perished, although she Made an Effort to be Saved.** She heard the warning, partly believed it, and ran for a while, but stopped short of salvation. She did not "forget the *things that were behind.*" Like Simon the sorcerer, her *heart* was not right with God (Acts 8. 21). "Doing the best you can," apart from a steadfast faith in Christ, is to perish by the way.

IV. **She Perished, although Separated from the Sodomites.** Her body was outside the city, but her affections were in it. She was not so bad as the wicked citizens of the plain, but still fatally fettered by the love of the world. She could thank God, like the Pharisee, that she "was not like others," but she was unsaved (Heb. 10. 38, 39).

V. **She Perished, although she Committed but**

One Sin. That one awful sin was the sin of unbelief, which manifested itself in a disobedient *look*. The command was, "Escape for thy life: look not behind thee" (Gen. 19. 17). Sinners perish, not because of the *number* of their sins, but because of the *nature of sin*. By one man sin entered into the world, and *death* by *sin*, not *sins*. To offend the law of God in *one point* is to be guilty of all. She would never have *looked back* if she had kept her eye on the mountain set before her (Heb. 12. 2).

THE RICH FOOL.
Luke 12. 16-21.

"A MAN's life consisteth not in the *abundance* of the things which he possesseth" (v. 15). An abundance of straw will not supply the place of wheat: neither will the abundance of a man's rags adorn him. Life consists not in *abundance*, but in having that which is truly meet. Man's covetous eyes looks for quantity, although it should rot like the kept up "manna." "Consider the ravens" (v. 24). "Consider the lilies" (v. 27). "Your Father knoweth that ye have *need of these things*"(v.30). A man's life is not in *things* at all, but in God, just as there is no life in the chaff, so there is no true life in the things of the world. The Laodiceans had abundance, but it was a miserable portion (Rev. 3. 18-20). Life means peace, faith, hope. The things of the world cannot give them.

I. **A Plentiful Portion.** "The ground brought forth plentifully" (v. 16). Unprecedented success has attended his effort. The sun and shower has favoured him, the horn of plenty has been poured into his lap, and with this plentiful harvest comes also a plentiful opportunity of doing good by making the hearts of the poor sing for joy. In the Lord Jesus Christ God has given us a very plentiful portion. They are infinitely rich who possess Him. And as a consequence greatly responsible.

II. A Perplexing Thought. "What shall I do" (v. 17). Give thanks unto the Giver of every good gift of course. "But no, not a word about God, *my* fruits, *my* goods" (v. 18). Alas, this is but the influence of the abundance of the things of this life, to increase the perplexity of the possessor. The more corn, the more care. The more pounds, the less pleasure if *God is forgotten*. The young ruler went away sorrowfully for he was very rich. A child will be happy with *one* apple in its hand and miserable with three, because it has more than it can hold. How different with spiritual blessings. Christ, "the blessing of the Lord maketh rich and addeth no sorrow" (Prov. 10. 22). Here are riches that satisfy, and cure all perplexity. Pilate said, "What shall I do with Jesus (which is called Christ)." This precious gift of God is worthy of a new and bigger heart.

III. A Reasonable Conclusion. "This will I do, I will pull down my barns and build greater" (v. 18). There is nothing foolish in this. It is wise to make large provision for God's larger gift. It would be good for some Christians to have their old barns pulled down and to build greater, to make more room for Christ the Gift of God in their hearts, the "exceeding riches of Christ" are often crowded out of hearts because they are too contracted. The *fullness of the blessing* cannot be contained in the old barns, there must be a *pulling down* and an enlargement, or else there will be a suffering of loss. The windows of Heaven *are* opened, but we cannot say we have not room enough, because faith is small.

IV. A Selfish Consideration. "I will say to my soul, Take thine *ease, eat, drink, be merry*" (v. 19). God's great gift in providence has been received, but how is it to be used? All for the *ease* and gratification of self. "My soul, eat, drink, etc." Self only is in his reckoning, and here is his folly. It is a *foolish* thing then to be *selfish* and to seek abiding happiness where it can never be found in material things. Having got abundance, he would now rest in idleness and ease. Are there not many who, having received abundant salvation for themselves, revel in spiritual luxuries and forget the poor and the needy outside the Kingdom of God. It is foolish, selfish, and sinful to *"take thine ease,* and eat,*"* etc., while others are perishing.

V. A Solemn Message. "This night thy soul shall be required of thee" (v. 20). This is an awakening word to those who are seeking their happiness only in the things which satisfieth not. Death, to the rich worldling, is their bill of bankruptcy, while dreaming of peace and plenty sudden destruction and spiritual poverty, cometh upon them. With regard to *their enjoyments,* "death ends all." In all his planning there is no "if the Lord will." Those who have been occupied only with *their own good* can never receive the Master's "Well done." "Inasmuch as ye did it not to one of the least of these, ye did it not to Me." It is blessed to receive, but it is more blessed to give.

VI. A Remorseful Question. *"Then* whose shall those things be?" (v. 20). *Then* what a thrust at the heart this is, by the sword of the Spirit "whose," they will not be his at anyrate. His expectation of "many years" is suddenly cut off, and the foolishness of his conduct is clearly seen. Oh, that men were wise, especially *rich* men, to consider their latter end! But there is a thought here still for the selfish Christian: "Whose shall these *privileges* be?" With every blessing there is privilege, and with the privilege corresponding responsibility. See that others get a share of the legacy of your own experience, otherwise "whose shall they be?"

VII. A Pointed Application. "So is he that layeth up

treasure for *himself*, and is not rich toward *God*" (v. 21). Whether he is a worldling or a Christian he acts the fool, if he lays up for self instead of God. Men lay up for themselves by *gathering*, and for God by *giving*. Self cries, Give, give, like the greedy sea. Grace says, Give give, like the generous sun. "Lay up treasure in Heaven." Self is a bag that will wax old (v. 33). The woman that cast her farthing into the treasury was laying up treasure in Heaven. The Samaritan who paid the two pence for the wounded did the same. So did the woman that poured her ointment on the Master's head. The world cannot see the true Christians' riches, they are in God's bank. Is your heart right with God? Where is it? Just where your treasure is (v. 34).

PRAYER, A NECESSITY AND PRIVILEGE.

"He spoke unto them, saying, that men ought always to pray, and not to faint'' (Luke 18. 1).

OUR Lord first gives the precept, then follows the example. There are five examples of prayer in this chapter: (1) A praying *widow* (v. 3), (2) a praying *Pharisee* (v. 10), (3) a praying *publican* (v. 13), (4) a praying *ruler* (v. 18), (5) a praying *beggar* (v. 38). All men ought to pray.

I. **MEN ought to Pray.** It has been said that man is the only animal that can look up. Alas! that so many should play the man with the muck-rake described in Bunyan's *Pilgrim's Progress.* Man, made in the image of the God of Heaven, should look up. When Nebuchadnezzar looked up his understanding returned (Dan. 4. 34).

II. **Men OUGHT to Pray.** Some sneer at the efficacy of prayer, and talk about the *unchangeableness* of God. As if the unchangeable God could not ordain the means as well as the end. Man *ought*; this allows for the free action of his will. He ought; but he may not or *will* not, yet his responsibility remains.

III. Men ought ALWAYS to Pray. To pray about everything, and to be thankful for anything (Phil. 4. 6). "In everything by prayer and supplication," etc. Regard the things which would distract as the bark of a dog, for they are sure to be the howlings of the flesh. This reaches to every extremity and detail of our daily and humdrum life. We need God's counsel and strength, even when we don't think it, or are at least unconscious of our need.

IV. Men Ought always to PRAY. The Greek word is *"wish* for." Men ought always to *desire* and ask. Praying without desiring is mockery. To be always *wishing* does not mean always begging, but a speaking to God, as a Father, and as one who delights in His fellowship. It is a life of walking and talking with God. It is not a task to those who have the Spirit of prayer. It is their very breath of life.

V. Men Ought always to Pray and NOT TO FAINT. These are the words of Him who will avenge His elect who cry day and night unto Him. He knows that *importunity* will not go unrewarded. Abraham fainted when he ceased pleading for Sodom. Joash also stopped too soon, and fell short of the full blessing (2 Kings 13. 19). Paul's importunity prevailed, although the thorn was not taken away. The causes of fainting are usually doubt and delay. In this chapter there are great *encouragements* to prayer. Pray on. If you cannot pull God nearer you, you will pull yourself nearer to Him.

VI. Why Men do not Pray.

1. BECAUSE OF UNBELIEF. They do not believe God, and show by their practical infidelity that Jesus Christ has no place in their lives.

2. BECAUSE OF SELF-CONFIDENCE. They have such great thoughts about their own character and abilities that

they feel not their need of seeking the help and guidance of the Lord.

3. BECAUSE OF THE LOVE OF SIN. Some are so conscious that their lives are opposed to the will of God that they dare not pray unless they are prepared to make confession.

"BELIEVE, AND THOU SHALT SEE."
John 11. 40.

THE happy home at Bethany had been suddenly overshadowed with sorrow, Lazarus was sick. The loving sisters hasten to breathe their trouble into Jesus' ear. When He heard, He said, "This sickness is for the glory of God." What? *Sickness* for the glory of God. How slow we are to believe this (Rom. 8. 28). Jesus Loved Martha and her sister and Lazarus, and abode two days still in the same place where He was. How strange that His absence from them should be a proof of His love for them. In refusing *their* request He desires to give them far above what they asked (v. 15). They had "prayed," now He asks their "trust." Having declared Himself to be the "Resurrection and the Life," He said, "Believest thou this?" Such faith needs to be tested before it can be rewarded. We notice then the—

I. **Test of Faith.** "Take ye away the stone" (v. 39). If you believe that your brother will rise again, and that "*I am* the Resurrection, then roll away this stone." Faith without works is dead. James says, "I will show you my faith *by* my works." If we expect great things from God, then we will attempt great things for God. But here we see—

II. **Language of Doubt.** "Lord by this time he stinketh" (v. 39). Corruption will be doing its loathsome work. Just so, Martha. You are looking at the difficulty more than at the promise. Your eyes are still on the dead more than on the Life-giving One. Is not this the reason why many of us fail to see the glory of the Lord's power? We are looking more at the giants in the land than at the arm of Omnipotence. We see our friends lying in spiritual death, and we mourn their sad condition as hopeless, because our eyes are not fixed on Him who *is* the Resurrection and the Life. Then came—

III. **Rebuke of Love.** "Said I not unto thee that, if thou wouldest believe, thou shouldest see the glory of God" (v. 40). Doubtless these tender, burning words fell with melting power as tears upon the face of Martha's heart. Doubting is not an infirmity, but a sin; a denial of the Word of Him who cannot lie. Oh, how often our unbelief hinders the manifestation of His power (Matt. 13. 58). How often do we pray, "Lord, if thou hadst been here?" while He is saying to us, "If thou wouldest believe." Now comes—

IV. **Obedience of Faith.** "Then they took away the stone" (v. 41). The stone of unbelief—the unbelief of God's people—often lies in the way of the dead in sin being raised. "Believe, and thou shalt see." There are other stones that lie in the way, such as the *fear of man*, the *love of the world*, and selfish *indifference*. This last is a sort of morbid Calvinism or fatalism that says, "If they are going to be saved they will be saved." But what saith the Lord? "Said I not unto thee that, if *thou* wouldest believe, *thou* shouldest see the glory of God?" After obedience came the—

V. **Glory of God.** How was His glory seen? In giving *life* to the dead and *liberty* to the living (v. 44). Lazarus was restored to their home and their hearts. All their desires and longings were fully met. They believed, and saw His glory, and were satisfied. Have you beheld the glory of His life-giving power in answer to your obedient trust, or are you still mourning *hopelessly* over the dead, forgetting Him who hath said, "Believe, and thou shalt see?" This prescription, "Believe, and thou shalt see," given by the Great Physician to those troubled sisters, might be taken as a word in season to the—

1. QUESTIONING UNBELIEVER. How am I to know that the Bible is the Word of God? How am I to know that the Blood of Jesus cleanseth from all sin? How am I to know that eternal life is in Jesus Christ? *"Believe, and thou shalt see."*

2. ANXIOUS SEEKER. I do not see how I can be justified by simply believing. No, but *"Believe, and thou shalt see."* "All that *believe* are justified from all things" (Acts 13. 39).

3. SUFFERING BELIEVER. No affliction for the present seemeth joyous, but rather grievous, *nevertheless afterwards* it yieldeth the peaceable fruits of righteousness to them who are exercised thereby. "Believe, and thou shalt see."

4. DISCOURAGED WORKER. "We have toiled all night and taken nothing: launch out into the deep." "At Thy word we will let down the net." "Believe, and thou shalt see." The Sunday school teacher says, "I long to see my scholars brought to Christ." *"Believe, and thou shalt see."*

5. DYING CHRISTIAN. The tide of life is ebbing, the things of this world fast fading from the vision, the eyes fast closing to the light of day; but Jesus is near with His sure Word of promise. "BELIEVE, AND THOU SHALT SEE THE GLORY OF GOD."

THE POWERLESS STAFF.

"Gehazi laid the staff upon the face of the child; but there was neither voice nor hearing" (2 Kings 4. 31).

THE staff belonged to Elisha the prophet, and was doubtless a good staff, quite fit to do all the work of a *staff*, but it was useless in bringing life to the dead.   There are many things good enough in their own way as *helps*, but which are utterly powerless to save the soul from sin and death. There is, for instance—

I. The Staff of Religious Upbringing.   This is a beautiful staff, and quite prophetic in a way.   It is a great advantage to be trained from youth to honour and respect everything religious.   But to trust in this as fitness for the Kingdom of God is to lean on a rotten stick.   "The child is *not awaked.*"

II. The Staff of Regular Praying.   This is another staff, good in itself, that is often trusted to bring life to the dead.   "I have said my prayers from my youth up."   Very good, but dead prayers cannot bring to life any more than a dead staff.   We are not saved because *we pray*, but we use prayer as a staff to help us to the God of salvation.

III. The Staff of Good Works.   Good works are always good, but those who lean on them to help them to Heaven are always found glorying in *themselves*, because they don't feel indebted to any other for the hope that is in them. They are limping on with these two crutches what they *have* done and what they have *not* done.   They are leaning on the arm of flesh and refuse the arm of God.

IV. The Staff of Godly Parentage.   To be *well connected* in a religious sense is much to be thankful for, but remember that *Judas* was also well connected, and that the rich man who "lifted up his eyes in hell" (Luke 16. 23) was a son of Abraham.   Lot's wife was very well connected, yet she perished.   If you are trusting to this staff you are depending on a rope of sand.

V. The Staff of Church Membership.   Those who trust this crutch to save them generally lean hard on it. They make a point of hearing the Word preached at least once a week, and never miss a communion if they are well. They seem to think that every attendance at a communion gains for them a mark of favour in the Book of Life. To use the *means* of grace is good, as you would use the cup hanging at a fountain; but to *trust them* is to remain in your sins.

VI. **The Staff of Scriptural Knowledge.** This staff is perhaps the most ornamental of all; at least it is well varnished. Those who lean on this for salvation seem very wise. You can tell them nothing new; they have known it all from their youth. Yet are they utter strangers to that new life begotten by the Spirit of God. They say, "We know," and then ask, "How can a man be born when he is old" (John **3.** 4). Life is not found in *searching* the Scriptures, but in Christ.

VII. **The Staff of Historical Belief.** This staff appears to be both long and strong, so there be many who hope for life through it. They believe in the Bible, the Creed, and the Confession of Faith; they believe in Heaven and in Hell, in Christ and the Devil, in demons and in angels, and in everything that is in the Bible, just as they believe everything that is in the History of Scotland, and with the very same result. They are dead while they live.

BARABBAS OR JESUS.
Matthew 27. 17.

IT was a solemn day when Jesus stood in silence before Pilate and the people, a day heavily laden with far-reaching consequences. It is always such a day when a soul is called upon to make its final decision for God or the world. Observe—

I. **Who they are.** Barabbas and Jesus.

1. BARABBAS. One who also bears the name of Jesus. A law-breaker, a robber, and a murderer. An enemy to God and to all the best interests of society.

2. JESUS. The Son of God and the Friend of man. One who went about continually doing good. A sufferer for the salvation of others.

II. What they are. They are *representatives* of two different kingdoms—of two different rulers that are opposed to each other.

1. THE BARABBAS KINGDOM. The kingdom of this present evil world—the kingdom of darkness governed by the prince of darkness. Their great business is to rob men of their time, of their affections, their wills, and their souls. They seek to rob both God and man.

2. THE JESUS KINGDOM. Jesus represents the *Kingdom of God*. He stands for the sacrifice for sin, the eternal life which is the gift of God. He is the light and life of men, the substitute Redeemer.

III. Where they are. They stand *together* before the people (v. 21), waiting for their individual choice. In one way or other they have been standing together before each generation ever since that day   All to whom Christ is preached must make their choice.

1. YOU CANNOT HAVE BOTH. Barabbas and Christ are opposites, as diametrical as darkness and light. "Ye *cannot* serve God and Mammon. " Ye cannot love the world and love God also. Whosoever is the friend of the world is the enemy of God. There is no alternative, you must choose the one or the other.

2. YOUR ETERNAL DESTINY HANGS ON YOUR CHOICE. They said, "Barabbas, " and what followed? His blood is on them till this day. What do you say? In Christ there is *life*; in the Barabbas of this world there is *death*. Both life and death is *set before you*. "Choose life" (Deut. 30. 15).

"My heart is fixed, eternal God—fixed on Thee;
And my immortal choice is made—Christ for me."

HOW TO BE BLESSED.
Psalm 40. 1-4.

THIS is the testimony of a man who knew by experience
the blessedness or happiness here spoken of. There are two
conditions referred to—*in* the pit, and *on* the rock; the
position of the unsaved and the position of the saved.
Look at—

I. **The Position of the Unsaved.** In a "horrible pit."

1. Its DEPTH is horrible, for those in it are "afar off"
from God and beyond the reach of the help of man.

2. Its DARKNESS is horrible. The darkness is so dense
that those in this pit cannot see themselves or their own
lamentable state. They are often stone blind to the light
of God's grace or the beauty of His Son.

3. Its NOISE is horrible (*margin*). There are many
noises, but no soul-soothing music. The noise of strife and
the clamour of many tongues—the tongue of business, the
tongue of pleasure, the tongues of greed, of riot, and of
blasphemy—noises that are so loud that the still small
voice of the Spirit of grace is often unheard.

II. **The Position of the Saved.** "Upon a rock." The
place of safety. And instead of the horrible noise there is
a new song in the mouth.

1. Upon the rock of His INFALLIBLE WORK. The
work finished on Calvary's Cross is a sure foundation
for the feet of faith.

"On Christ the solid Rock I stand,
All other ground is sinking sand."

2. Upon the rock of His INFALLIBLE WORD. He hath
promised, and He cannot lie. His "hath" is as sure as His
throne (John 3. 36). "Thy Word is settled in Heaven."
All the efforts and arguments of ungodly men will never
unsettle it.

3. Upon the rock, SINGING A NEW SONG. This singing implies gladness and perfect *satisfaction*. The noise of the pit has given place to the music of Heaven. The agony arising out of self-interest has been exchanged for "Praise unto our God."

III. **The Power of the Saviour.** "He brought me out." HE only could go deep enough down to lift us out of such miry clay. No human arm was long enough or strong enough for such a great deliverance. All who ever get out of this pit of sin will have to praise HIM for it. Make the Lord your trust, and this blessedness will be yours (v. 4). "Look unto Me, and be ye saved."

THE BARTERED BIRTHRIGHT.
Genesis 25. 27-34; Hebrews 12. 17.

ESAU, like Cain, stands out in the Word of God as a beacon of warning—like the mast of some sunken ship still seen above the overwhelming tide. Observe here a—

I. **Privilege Inherited.** Esau was the *first*-born, and so by birth he had the opportunity of becoming heir. Although it is true that natural birth will not bring *us into* the heirship of God's promises, yet it does bring *us* into a marvellous place of opportunity compared with those who, through no fault of their own, have been born in the darkness of cannibalism. All born in Bible lands are heirs of a priceless privilege.

II. **Privilege Despised.** Esau said, "What profit is this birthright to me?" (v. 32). It could be no profit to him when he esteemed other sensual things of more importance. The pottage to him was the chief thing at that moment. He allowed his *appetite* to overrule the higher instincts of his nature. Men constantly make this mistake when they suffer temporal things to take the place of spiritual. Things of *first* importance should always be put first. Seek *first* the Kingdom of God and His righteousness, and these things for which so many hunger after shall be *added.* To despise Gospel privileges is to despise your birthright.

III. Privilege Lost. "He *sold* his birthright" (v. 33). He deliberately parted with it as a thing of no value. An opportunity not accepted is an opportunity lost. There are always plenty of the Jacob sort about, who are ready, at any cost to others, to make personal gain out of their spiritual stupidity. Moses looked at his birthright with a very different eye when he chose rather to suffer affliction with the people of God than enjoy the pleasures of sin for a season (Heb. 11. 25, 26). The heart is never more deceitful than when it covets the things which are seen and *temporal*, and lets slip those things which are eternal. It is a bad bargain to sell the spiritual for the natural.

IV. Privilege Lamented. "Afterward, when he would have inherited the blessing, he was rejected, . . . though he sought with tears" (Heb. 12. 17). The sin of unbelief is sure to be followed with a terrible *"afterwards."* His dying father brought conviction home to his heart and conscience; but his tears, though many and bitter, did not avail to bring him into the hitherto despised blessing. "Son, remember that thou in thy lifetime received good things," was a stinging "afterward" to the rich man spoken of in Luke 16. How shall we escape the sorrowful afterward "if we neglect the great present salvation?" (Heb. 2. 3).

SEVEN FOOLS.

A FOOL is a man whose stupidity is proven by his actions or words. The—

I. Atheistical Fool. He says in his heart, "There is no God" (Psa. 14. 1). He *wishes* there was none, and so ventures to think and say there is no God. He is a fool

for saying so, but he does not know   He has not searched
every corner of the universe to see.

II. Rationalistic Fool (1 Cor. 15. 35, 36).   He doubts
the resurrection and denies all miracles, because he knows
not the Scriptures nor the *power of God*.   An American
sceptic was overcome and conquered by these two woods,
"*Thou fool*, that which thou sowest is not quickened except
it die." The weakness of man's *reason* to grasp cannot
make the Word of God of none effect.

III. Shameless Fool.   This fool "makes a mock at
sin" (Prov. 14. 9).   A miner in Tasmania lately had his
eyes blown out of his head by an explosion.   He was a
thoughtless and profane man.   A very common expression
of his was, "God curse my *eyes*." Sin is the abominable
thing which God hates, and for which Christ shed His
Blood.   Yet fools make a mock at it.

IV. Thoughtless Fool (Matt. 7. 26).   He goes on
building the house of all his hopes for the future on *the
sand*.   So foolish is he that he expects to save himself by
his own works, apart from that only foundation laid by
God, the rock Christ Jesus.

V. Industrious Fool (Luke 12. 20).   This man is not
a sceptic; he does not make a mock at sin.   He is a thoughtful, active, and careful business man.   But earthly goods
are all that he is concerned about.   He did well for himself, and men would praise him, but he was a fool in the
sight of God, who weighs human lives in the balance of
eternity.   To trust in the abundance of riches and make not
God your strength is supreme folly.   What is your present
life?   It is but a vapour, therefore lay up treasure in
Heaven.   "Seek first the kingdom of God and His righteousness, and all these things shall be added unto you."

VI. Self-Confident Fool (Rom. 1. 21, 22).   This man

knows there is a God, but glorifies him not as God. Neither is he thankful, but becomes vain in his imaginations, and professing himself to be wise he becomes a fool. Oh, the folly of believing in God and honouring Him not as God! Following the vain thoughts of his own foolish heart instead of the thoughts of God, substituting his own imaginations for the revealed will of God, he sees the light but loves the darkness better.

VII. **Christian Fool** (1 Cor. 4. 10). "We are fools for Christ's sake." It is infinitely better to be a fool in the eyes of Christless men, and be wise in the sight of God, than be a fool in the sight of God and wise in the eyes of sin-blinded men. The wisdom of Christ is as far above the highest wisdom of men as the folly of a fool is below it. So to be wise in Christ is to be as a fool in the eyes of the worldly wise. After the learned Saul was converted he was called a "babbler." Festus called him "mad." The natural man receiveth not the things of the Spirit of God, for they are foolishness unto him. For the Christian fool there is prepared a great and blessed asylum (John 14. 2).

THE DIVINE CALL TO AWAKE.
Isaiah 52. 1-3.

IT is a great mercy that God does call; for the Jew, the Gentile, and the Church of God are all alike prone to become insensible to their spiritual privileges. He that hath ears to hear let him hear. Note—

I. **What this Call Implies.** "Awake! awake!" Surely this denotes—

1. A STATE OF SLEEP. They were utterly unconscious of the *nearness* of God, and of His willingness at once to help them. God is at hand, but eyes sealed in the sleep of selfish ease see Him not and hear Him not till the awakening takes place.

2. A STATE OF DEGRADATION. Zion was to "shake her-self from the dust." The dust of worldliness and sin will quickly gather on the garments of those who become spiritually drowsy. Bunyan's "Man with the Muck Rake" is an illustration of this grovelling spirit that is wilfully blind to the better riches.

3. A STATE OF CAPTIVITY. "Loose thyself from the bands of thy neck." Zion is here represented as being *self*-bound. "Loose thyself." The bands that bind many are self-made. What are some of them? Love of ease and of pleasure, the fear of man and the fear of women, pride of heart and desire for praise. Awake! awake! and loose thyself! Step out into the liberty of God's children.

II. **What this Call was to.** It was a call to *awake*, to *shake off*, and then to *put on*, that the shame of her naked-ness may not appear.

1. PUT ON THY STRENGTH. Thy strength is not in thyself, but in Him who is thy God. Put it on, because thou art a weak child without this. Paul had put on strength when he said, "I can do all things through Christ who strengtheneth me." Put on, therefore, the Lord Jesus Christ, and His strength will be made a perfect fit for thy weakness.

2. PUT ON THY BEAUTIFUL GARMENTS. Awake! awake! and put off thy *night*-dress, and put on those garments for glory and beauty which are offered thee in Him. Put on thy beautiful garments of holiness and praise, for the Bridegroom is at hand and the marriage day is near. Put them on, that the world may see that you belong to Him and that you are looking for His appearing. Put them on, lest you may be found among the speechless at the coming of the King (Matt. 22. 12).

WHY GOD SENT HIS SON.
John 3. 17, 18.

THERE is something that has been more expensive than war—that is SIN. What pardoned *sin* has cost no one can fully reckon up. The wealth of Christ's sufferings and death, to us-ward and to God, is to a finite mind unsearchable. What *un*pardoned sin will cost the sinner is a terrible and far-reaching question. No sinner can *ever* be able to pay the price that the holy and eternal Son of God hath paid. In this portion there is—

I. **A Great Fact.** "God sent His Son" (v. 16). These are the words of the sent One Himself. He surely knew from whence He came. That mother in Kentucky who, in the time of the war, said to her only son, "Go, my son, I give you freely," was exhibiting a faint picture of the self-sacrificing love of God to a perishing world. She could not see all that was before her son, and doubtless hoped he might return unscathed; but God saw the awful depths of sorrow and suffering into which He willingly gave His Son. Herein is love.

II. **A Great Purpose.** "Not to condemn the world, but that the world through Him might be saved" (v. 17). The world *deserved* condemnation, and Christ was *able* to condemn it, but with respect to its condemnation "He opened not His mouth." He came to SAVE. He Himself was God's great and unspeakable donation to this poor and needy world (John 3. 16). All that man can contribute to the salvation of the world, apart from the gift of God, is but a few paltry coppers that can never redeem a soul from sin and death. The work of the Socialist and the Philanthropist, like a copper coin, is good so far as it goes; but without Christ it does not go far enough by a long way. CHRIST came to save the world. Nothing else will be a substitute for HIM.

III. **A Great Responsibility.** "He that believeth *on*
Him is not condemned, but he that believeth not is condemned already" (v. 18). It is one thing to believe in
religion; it is another thing to believe in Him. The promises of God are all made to us in Him. *Believing* will
avail nothing unless it is in the personal Christ, who gave
His life a ransom for all. Not to believe on Him is to be
"condemned already," because He is the *"Only* begotten
Son of God," the only Name under Heaven given among
men whereby we can be saved. "As many as are in the
works of the law are *under the curse"* (Gal. 3. 10); but
as many as *receive Him,* to them gives He power to
become the children of God. There is no condemnation
to them which are in Christ Jesus. "Dost *thou* believe
on the Son of God?" (John 9. 35).

"NOT I, BUT CHRIST."
Galatians 2. 20.

I. **Think of those Two Personalities.** "I," "Christ."
There is a mystery in each of them. The mystery of evil
is connected with the first, and the mystery of godliness
with the second. Each is the medium through which
another great Personality works. "The prince of the power
of the air; the Spirit that now worketh in the children of
disobedience" (Eph. 2. 2) operates in and through the
one, while the Almighty Father of all manifests Himself
through the other. The one is the instrument of Satan,
the other is the servant of God. This unregenerate *"I,"*
in his ignorance, selfishness, pride, and unbelief, is a fit
subject for the prince of darkness. The Heaven-anointed
Christ, in his unselfish devotion to the will of God, is perfectly fitted for the accomplishment of His purposes.

II. **Think of their Relationship One to the Other.**
What is there in common between this "I" and the

"Christ?" between the servant of Satan and the servant of God? What communion hath light with darkness? What fellowship hath righteousness with unrighteousness? What concord hath Christ with Belial? What part hath he that believeth with an infidel? (2 Cor. 6. 14-16). Each is animated and controlled by a different and opposing spirit. The principles of the *flesh* and of the *Spirit* are contrary, the one to the other. That which is born of the flesh is flesh, and belongs to the kingdom of this world; that which is born of the Spirit is spirit, and belongs to the Kingdom of God. Corruption cannot inherit incorruption (1 Cor. 16. 20). Self is carnal, Christ is spiritual. "To be carnally minded is death; to be spiritually minded is life and peace" (Rom. 8. 6). This *I*, the natural man, receiveth not the things of the Spirit of God, and so can have no fellowship with Christ. It is not subject to the law of God, neither indeed can be.

III. Think of the Meaning of this New Relationship. "Not I, but Christ." These words imply a putting off of the old man, and a putting on of Christ. The sinful, self-seeking "I" has surrendered and given place to the life and rule of the Holy One. It used to be, "I, not Christ," but now it is, "Not I, but Christ."

1. In the matter of SALVATION. The works of the law and of the flesh have given place to *faith* in the Lord Jesus Christ. The sandy foundation has been exchanged for the infallible Rock. His own righteousness has been cast aside for the righteousness of God. It is also, "Not I, but Christ."

2. In the matter of SANCTIFICATION. "Christ liveth in me." The usurper within has been dethroned, and the Lord of life and glory has been crowned. Holiness has come, not by working, but by admitting the Holy One and giving Him His true place in the heart as Lord. The old

"I" has been crucified with Christ, and a new Spirit-formed "I" has come into being which delights to say, "Not I, but Christ."

3. In the matter of SERVICE. "To me to live is Christ." "Whose I am, and whom I serve." He seeks now not his own will but the will of Him who saved him and sent him. "If I *yet* pleased myself I would not be the servant of Christ." "I can do all things through Christ which strengtheneth me" (Phil. 4. 13). "If any man be in Christ he is a new creation."

CHRIST, THE TRUE MANNA.
John 6. 47-51.

THERE can be no question as to the manna being typical of the character and mission of Christ, for we have the Lord's own authority for believing it to be so. A beautiful type it is. Like Christ—

I. **It was Needed.** The children of Israel were ready to perish for lack of bread. There was no help for them in the wilderness. It was so with this world before Christ came. There was a great hunger in the hearts of men for the *true* bread. The world needed Christ.

II. **It was the Gift of God.** The manna was not, and could not be, grown or manufactured on earth. The Saviour that man needed could not be man-made. All that the world could give the Christ was a cross. God loved the world and *gave* His Son. The manna, like Christ, was not *deserved*, but was the gift of infinite mercy to grumbling, discontented souls.

III. **It was Satisfying.** The manna was exactly suited to meet all the cravings of hunger. It was prepared by God for this very purpose. So Christ's character and work, as appointed by God, meets all the needs of a destitute soul.

Bread is not more suitable for the hungry than the Saviour is to the sinner. The one is the divinely-appointed remedy for the other.

IV. **It was Within the Reach of All.** The manna did not fall on the tree-tops, but on the ground, and so was quite within the grasp of every soul in the camp. No price was put upon it. It was free to all. Christ, the Bread of Life, is also within the reach of all who hear the Gospel. We don't need to climb to Heaven to bring Christ down. The Word of salvation is nigh thee, even in thine heart. Whosoever will may take.

V. **It had to be Personally Received.** No one could eat the manna to save his brother. It had to be taken into each individual life. So with Jesus Christ, the gift of God. "As many as *received Him*, to them gives He power to become the sons of God" (John 1. 12). As every man must breathe for himself if he is to live, so must he believe for himself if he is to be saved.

VI. **It was the only Means of Saving their Lives.** Not to appropriate this Heaven-sent gift was to die of starvation. There was no alternative but to eat or die. "If ye believe not that I am He," says Jesus Christ, "ye shall die in your sins" (John 8. 24). There is no alternative but to accept Christ or perish. "There is none other name under Heaven given among men whereby we must be saved." "He that eateth this bread shall live for ever" (John 6. 58).

NOAH, A TYPE OF CHRIST.

Genesis 6.

I. **He Came as a Blesser.** His Name means "comforter" or rest (Gen. 5. 29). God sent His Son to bless you (Acts 3. 26).

II. He Found Grace in the Eyes of the Lord (v. 8).
So was it with Christ. "This is My beloved Son, hear
Him" (Luke 9. 35).

III. He was Just and Perfect (v. 9). Christ delighted
to do the will of God. He was holy, harmless, separate
from sinners.

IV. He Walked with God (v. 9). Jesus could say, "I
and My Father are one." Thou in Me, and I in Thee (John
17. 21). One with the Father in all His desires and
purposes.

V. He had the Will of God revealed to Him (vv.
13-15). The Ark, and the fashion of it, was a revelation
from God. It was His way of salvation made known
through Noah. Was it not so also with Christ? He came
to manifest His Name (John 17. 6). He spoke not His own
words, but the words of God the Father (v. 8).

VI. He Prepared the Way of Salvation (v. 14). He
made the Ark. Christ has made for us a new and living
way (Heb. 10. 20). "The gift of God is eternal life, *through*
Jesus Christ our Lord" (Rom. 6. 23).

VII. He Finished the Work Given Him to Do.
"Thus did Noah, according to all that God commanded
him" (v. 22). He left nothing undone. So also the anti-
type—"I have finished the work Thou gavest Me to do"
(John 17. 4). His last words on the Cross were, "It is
finished."

VIII. His Salvation was Effectual (chap. 7. 1). It
was sufficient—

1. FOR HIMSELF. "Noah entered in." The great work
of Christ has been the means of bringing new honour and
glories to Him.

2. FOR HIS HOUSE. "Come thou and all thy house into
the Ark." "All that the Father hath given Me shall come

to Me. " He will bring many sons unto glory. The whole household of faith shall be saved (Eph. 3. 15; 5. 27).

3. FOR ALL THINGS. All in the Ark passed over the flood into a new and purged world. All things shall yet be put under Christ, who is not only head of the Church, but of angels and of all. All under the sweep of His redemption shall be cleansed and renewed (Acts 8. 19-22).

IX. He was Remembered by God. "And God remembered Noah, and all that was *with him*" (chap. 8. 1). God will never forget His Son and all that are with Him in the Ark of His saving grace. They shall be held in His everlasting remembrance. He who numbered the stars and the sparrows shall not be unmindful of His sons, purchased by His blood and born of His Spirit. "I will remember My covenant" (Gen. 9. 15).

CHRIST TRANSFIGURED ON THE MOUNT.
Luke 9. 28-36.

WE have before us here the most rapturous picture that the eyes of mortal ever gazed upon—a moving picture, a transformation scene. A despised and rejected Man, radiant and luminous with the ineffable glory of God. Notice the—

I. Appointed Time. "About eight days after" (v. 28). We are always inclined to associate the *eighth* day with resurrection glory. It was eight days after He had told them that some were standing here that should not taste of death till they had seen the *Kingdom of God* (v. 27). The transfiguration was at least a manifestation of the glory of God's appointed King.

II. Favoured Company. "He took Peter, and John, and James" (v. 28). He might have left them behind, but in His love and pity He took them *with Him*. Little

did they know what was in store for them while they
followed Him up the mount. Do we realise now, as we
follow our Lord up the hill of life, what a vision awaits us?
It is still His desire that we should be *with Him* where He
is, and *behold His glory* (John 17. 24).

III. **Special Purpose.** "He went up to pray." He
could have prayed at the foot of the hill as well as at the
top, but He would teach us the necessity of going alone
purposely to meet and speak with God. Many pray before,
or after, they go to bed, but how few go into the quiet
room or lonely hill-side *purposely* to pray. We should go
as definitely into our closet for prayer as we go into the
kitchen or dining-room for our meals.

IV. **Glorious Change.** It was while He prayed that
"the fashion of His countenance was altered," and the
hidden glory of His nature burst forth, as the sun through
the rifted clouds (Matt. 17. 2). No one has ever yet
proved to the full the possibilities of secret prayer. It
was while Moses communed with God that the skin of his
face shone. The perfect fellowship of Heaven means perfect
conformity to *His likeness* (Rev. 1. 16; 1 John 3. 2). Prayer
is a mighty antidote for an evil temper, and every other
uncharitable feature of our character; instead of wrath
there will come forth glory.

V. **Heavenly Visitants.** "Behold, there talked with
Him two men, which were Moses and Elias" (v. 30).
Moses and Elias had both experienced what it was to
"depart and be with Christ, which is far better." The
company of Jesus Christ is such a privilege and blessing
that even the glorified delight to come to earth to share it.
How much more ought we to prize it now! In His presence
is fullness of joy.

VI. **Wonderful Theme.** "They spake of His decease"
(v. 31). What a subject for such an occasion! What a

terrible prospect for such a glorious One! What a value we ought to set on such a death! It was probably the greatest event that has ever been heard of in Heaven. What place has it in our conversation? What power has it over our hearts and lives? He died for our sins.

VII. **Foolish Proposal.** Peter, who had just awaked out of sleep and saw His glory, asked of Him permission "to make *three* tabernacles" (vv. 32, 33). What were they going to do with *tabernacles*, when Moses and Elias were going back to Heaven, and Jesus to a Cross? Those who *sleep* when they should be awake are sure to talk foolishly. Did he think that *this glory* could be shut up in temples made with hands? (1 Cor. 2. 13, 14).

VIII. **Assuring Voice.** "There came a voice out of the cloud saying, This is My beloved Son; hear Him" (vv. 35, 36). Peter afterwards declared that this voice they heard when they were with Him on the mount (2 Peter 1. 17, 18). The divinity of Christ is here attested by the invisible Father. Let us give earnest heed lest we should let this assuring Word of Christ's power to redeem us by His death slip away from us. Hear Him. "Hear, and your soul shall life" (Isa. 55. ·3).

SHUT OUT THROUGH UNBELIEF.

"So we see that they could not enter in because of unbelief"
(Heb. 3. 19).

THE children of Israel were overthrown in the wilderness because they *believed not* His Word and hearkened not unto the voice of the Lord (Psa. 106. 24-26). As unbelief hinders the sinner from entering into the salvation of God which is in Christ Jesus, so does it hinder many of God's own people from entering into the fullness of the blessing— a life satisfied in God and victorious in His Name. They could not enter in *because of unbelief.*

I. **It was not Because they did not Know God's Will.** They knew that it was the will of God that they should go in and possess the land, yet they perished outside. He is not willing that any should perish. Although many know this, yet they remain outside the promise of life that is in Christ Jesus. They know that Christ died for all, yet they tarry and murmur in the wilderness of unbelief.

II. **It was not for Want of Evidences of God's Power.** They had been eye-witnesses of many wonders that He wrought—the plagues of Egypt, the Red Sea, the manna from Heaven, etc. Surely in the heavens above, and in the earth beneath, and within the domain of the human soul and the Divine Book there are abundant proofs of the presence and power of God to fulfil all the promises He hath made. The *invisible* things may be understood, or rendered intelligible, by the things which are visible, so that they are without excuse (Rom. 1. 20).

III. **It was not for Want of Seeing the Fruits of the Land.** The grapes and pomegranates of the good land were shown them (Num. 13. 26). Fruits that could never grow in the wilderness were laid before their eyes. Yet they failed because of unbelief. Unbelievers to-day are not without the same powerful evidence. The fruits of the Canaan-life—*love* to enemies, *joy* in the Holy Ghost, *peace* with God, and the peace of God—these are fruits that cannot grow on nature's barren soil. The fruit of the Spirit in the Christian's life is a revelation to those outside "the good and pleasant land" of its reality and richness. These fruits can be seen almost anywhere, and as they are not the products of the natural life, they are evidences of Christ's power to save, sanctify, and satisfy.

IV. **It was not for Want of a Desire for Something Better.** They were not satisfied with their present wilderness lot; they felt deeply their need of a better and more enduring portion; they longed intensely for something more than they had. Yet they entered not in because of unbelief. Their name is legion who are in the same condition spiritually. Conscious of their need for a better and more satisfying life, yet refusing to believe God's Word concerning His Son. This "good land" of promise is offered them, yet they cannot enter in because of unbelief. The evil heart of unbelief always seeks its good in *departing* from the living God (v. 12). The heart's need can only be fully met by a faith that enters into the promise of God and rests there. "Believe, and thou shalt see."

ARE YOU READY?

"How wilt thou do in the swelling of Jordan?" (Jer. 12. 5).

JORDAN may be looked on here as symbolic of death. The act of crossing over from this world into the next—from time into eternity—must always be a solemn one. How wilt thou do? Are you ready for the river? This question is—

I. A Practical One. "How wilt thou DO?" Something must be done. Can we be prepared to do when dying that which we are not prepared to do while living? It is not what we feel, or think, or say, so much as what we *are* that will determine what we shall do at that trying hour. Those who trust in Jesus Christ now will have no difficulty in trusting Him then.

II. A Personal One. "How wilt THOU do?" No one can do the dying for you. It is your own feet that must go down through the river, your own soul that must meet God. Although, like Queen Elizabeth, you may offer "a million or money for a moment of time," it will profit you nothing. It is not how will your companion or neighbour do? but, how wilt *thou* do? The answer, the fitness or unfitness, is to be found in yourself.

III. A Testing One. "The swelling of Jordan." A swollen river suggests danger and difficulty. Will your own strength be sufficient to carry you through the flood? or have you the promise of Him who conquered death to support you? "The river is deep or shallow according to your faith," says Bunyan in his "Pilgrim's Progress."

IV. An Urgent One. "How wilt thou do?" Time is short, life is uncertain, and you may be nearer the brink than you think. Some time ago a Glasgow minister went to see a dying woman, but she said to him, "It's too late." Her feet were already in the swelling of Jordan. How wilt thou do? What is your answer? Will you trust to your Church membership or good works of charity then? These will not allay the swellings of Jordan. The sparks of your own kindling will never be able to exist in the midst of this flood. Will you trust to the craft of your own opinions? This swift-rolling stream will make terrible havoc of that. Such frail things will be swept away as refuges of lies. The only wise and safe thing to do is to yield yourself to Jesus Christ now, and then, "When thou passest through the waters, He will be with thee; and through the rivers, they shall not overflow thee" (Isa. 43. 2). "I will fear no evil, for Thou are with me."

IMPLICIT TRUST BRINGS INFALLIBLE GUIDANCE.
Proverbs 3. 5, 6.

1. The OBJECT, ... "The Lord."
2. The METHOD, ... "Trust in the Lord."
3. The MEASURE,   .. "With all thine heart."
4. The WARNING, ... "Lean not on thine own understanding."
5. The OCCASION, ... "In all thy ways."
6. The PROMISE, ... "He shall direct thy paths."

SEED THOUGHTS.

THE POWER OF HIS PRESENCE.

THE *presence* of Christ means *power*, whether we are conscious of it or not. When He gave His last commission to His disciples, saying, "All power is given unto Me . . . Go ye therefore. . . . Lo, I am *with you* alway." He was pledging His presence as the guarantee of every needful thing for the fulfilment of His will through them. His presence—

1. Gives SECURITY to the perplexed (Gen. 28. 15).
2. Gives ENCOURAGEMENT to witness-bearing (Exod. 3. 12; Heb. 13. 5, 6).
3. Gives STRENGTH to the warrior (Josh. 1. 5).
4. Gives COMFORT to the timid (Jer. 1. 8).
5. Gives VICTORY to the tempted (Gen. 39. 2-21).
6. Gives CONFIDENCE to the servant (Matt. 28. 20; Phil. 4. 13).
7. Gives REST to the pilgrim (Exod. 33. 14).

SALVATION.

"In whom we have redemption through His blood, the forgiveness of sins, according to the riches of His grace" (Eph. 1. 7).

1. The SUBSTANCE. (1) It is a *purchase*; "Redemption through His blood." (2) It is a *pardon*; "Forgiveness of sins."
2. The MEASURE. "According to the riches of His grace."
3. The CONDITION. "In Whom."
4. The EXPERIENCE. "We have."

THE LORD WILL PROVIDE.
Genesis 21. 14 (*margin*).

I. **The Provider.** The Lord.

1. In Him is infinite WISDOM to know our need.
2. In Him are infinite RICHES to meet all our need.
3. In Him is infinite GRACE to give us all we need.

II. **The Provision.** "The Lord will provide." He has provided—

1. REDEMPTION in His Son.
2. SANCTIFICATION in His Spirit.
3. SUSTENTATION in His Word.

THE HOPE THAT MAKETH NOT ASHAMED.
Romans 5. 5.

I. **What this Hope Is.**

1. It is hope in the Lord.
2. It is a hope begotten through His Word.
3. It is a hope inspired by the love of God.
4. It is a hope upheld by faith in God.

II. **What this Hope Does.**   "It maketh not ashamed."

1. Of the Master (2 Tim. 1. 12).
2. Of the Gospel (Rom. 1. 16).
3. Of the Scriptures (Mark 8. 38).
4. Of the Lord's people (2 Tim. 1. 8).
5. Of his own confidence (Heb. 6. 17-20).

CHRIST NEAR BUT OUTSIDE.
Revelation 3. 20.

1. A Present Saviour,   "At the door."
2. A Waiting Saviour,   "Behold I *stand*.
3. A Seeking Saviour.   "And knock."
4. A Pleading Saviour,   "If any man open the door."
5. A Promising Saviour.   "I will come in.
6. A Providing Saviour.   "And sup with him, *and he with Me.*"

A WONDERFUL PEOPLE.

2 Samuel 7. 23.

1. SOUGHT, ... "God went for them."
2. REDEEMED, .. "Whom God went to redeem."
3. CLAIMED, ... "A people to Himself."
4. USED, ... "To make Him a Name."
5. HONOURED, .. "Do for you great things" (Deut. 33. 29).

GOD'S PROMISE TO INQUIRERS.

"Thus saith the Lord God: I will yet for this be inquired of by the house of Israel, to do it for them" (Ezek. 36. 37).

THE promises of God are not intended to stifle *inquiry*. Learn from this—

I. That God Longs to be Inquired Of. "Ye have not, because ye ask not" (James 4. 2). The prodigal got much by inquiry.

II. That any Man can be an Inquirer. "Men ought always to pray" (Luke 18. 1). This door is ever open, and man may do business at any time.

III. That a Man may Inquire about Anything. "In everything by prayer," etc. (Phil. 4. 6).

IV. That Inquirers must come in the Right Way. "Ask in *My Name*" (John 16. 26). Israel must approach God through the High Priest. There is but one Mediator.

V. That Inquirers must be Honest in their Inquiry. Questions of mere curiosity are left unanswered. Saul was an anxious inquirer (Acts 9. 6).

VI. That Honest Inquirers will be Fully Satisfied. "Ask, and ye shall receive. Knock, and it shall be opened unto you" (Matt. 7. 7. 8). As Solomon satisfied the Queen of Sheba, so will the Lord grant the desire of your heart (Psa. 81. 10).

HOW TO BE TAUGHT OF GOD.
Psalm 25. 12.

I. The Man Spoken Of. "The man that feareth the Lord. "

1. This is not the fear of ALARM.
2. This is the fear of LOVE.

II. The Promise Given. "Him shall He teach. "

1. The Teacher (Psa. 32. 8-11).
2. The Teaching (1 John 2. 27).

III. The Condition Mentioned. "In the way that He shall choose. "

1. The way of His CHOICE (Isa. 30. 21).
2. He teaches those IN THIS WAY (John 7. 17).

A PRIVILEGED PEOPLE.
Deuteronomy 33. 3.

1. LOVED,   .. "Yea, He loved the people. "
2. KEPT,   .. "All His saints are *in Thy hand.* "
3. RESTED,   .. "They sat down. "
4. TAUGHT,   .. "Every one shall *receive of Thy words.* "

A WARNING TO BOASTERS.

"Boast not thyself of to-morrow, for thou knowest not what a day may bring forth'' (Prov. 27. 1).

The boaster is—

1. **A foolish** man. He *knows not* what a day may bring forth.
2. **A presumptuous** man. "To-morrow" is not his.
3. **A blind** man (Luke 17. 29).
4. **A thankless** man (Matt. 24. 48-51).
5. **A self-deceived** man (Luke 12. 19-21).

LOVE AS THE FRUIT OF THE SPIRIT.
Galatians 5. 22.

I. The Author of It. "The Spirit."
1. He begets it by revealing the work of Christ.
2. He sustains it by applying the Word of Christ.

II. The Character of It. "Love."
1. It is of the nature of God (1 John 4. 8).
2. It is to dwell in us (1 John 4. 16).

III. The Outcome of It. "Fruit."
1 Fruit is the evidence of life (1 John 4. 19).
'2. Fruit is the proof of a healthy condition (2 Cor. 5. 14)

ATTITUDE TOWARD CHRIST AND HIS CAUSE.

1. FREEZING, ... Philippians 3. 18, 19.
2. COLD, ... Revelation 2. 4.
3. LUKEWARM, ... Revelation 3. 15, 16.
4. BURNING, ... John 5. 35.

FRUITFUL IN AFFLICTION.
"God hath caused me to be fruitful in the land of my affliction"
(Gen. 41. 52).

I. The Condition. Affliction. This is a condition—
1. Alarming to the ungodly.
2. Rejoiced in by the believing (Rom. 5. 3).

II. The Blessing. Fruitfulness.
1. A comfort to the afflicted (1 Cor. 1. 5).
2. A means of satisfaction to the Saviour (John 15. 2).

III. The Source. "God hath caused me."
1. By His abounding grace (2 Cor. 9. 8) including His overruling providence.
2. By His indwelling Spirit (John 15. 4).

THE PRAYER OF A MAN OF GOD.
Psalm 90. 12-17.

1. For **Teaching** (v. 12). Job 28. 28; Eph. 5. 15-17.
2. For **Fellowship** (v. 13). Matthew 5. 4.
3. For **Satisfaction** (v. 14). Psalm 85. 6.
4. For **Gladness** (v. 15). Psalm 126. 5, 6; Isaiah 61. 2, 3.
5. For **Reviving** (v. 16). Habakkuk 3. 2.
6. For **Adorning** (v. 17). Isaiah 52. 1.
7. For **Success** (v. 17). Psalm 16. 3; Philippians 2. 12, 13; 1 Corinthians 3. 7.

BEHOLD HE COMETH.
Matthew 25. 13.

I. **The Fact**. "The Son of Man cometh. "
II. **An Uncertainty**. "Ye know neither the day nor the hour. "
III. **An Exhortation**. "Watch, therefore" (Rev. 21. 15).

ASKING, SEEKING, KNOCKING.
Matthew 7. 7, 8.

I. **A Threefold Condition.**
   1. Knocking at the door.
   2. Seeking for the Master.
   3. Asking what ye will.

II. **A Threefold Promise.**
   1. He that knocketh shall have the door opened.
   2. He that seeketh shall find.
   3. He that asketh shall receive.

JESUS AS KING.

1. The vision of the King and His kingdom (Dan. **7**. 13-14).
2. Appointed by God as Son and King (Psa. **2**. 6-8).
3. The manner of His coming, and character (Isa. **9**. 6, 7).
4. The promise before His birth referred to royalty (Luke 1. 31-33).
5. The search for the King (Matt. 2. 1, 2).
6. The attempt to crown Him as King (John 6. 14, **15**).
7. Publicly acknowledged as King (Luke 19. 37-40).
8. Charged with making Himself a King (Luke 23. **1-3**).
9. Confessed Himself a King (John 18. 33-37).
10. Mocked as a King (John 19. 1-5).
11. Crucified as a King (John 19. 14, 15, 19).
12. Preached as a King (Acts 17. 7).
13. Coming as King (Matt. 16. 28; 17. 5).
14. Reigning as King (Rev. 11-15).

HEART DIRECTION.

"The Lord direct your heart into the love of God, and into the patient waiting for Christ" (2 Thess. 3. 5).

1. **Our hearts need directing,** because they **are** wayward and deceitful.

2. Our privilege is to have them **directed into the love of God;** here to find peace, rest, and satisfaction.

3. Our hearts, directed into ·the love of God, will then be made **partakers of the patience of Christ** (R.V.).

(1). Into His patience in SUFFERING.

(2). Into His patience in SERVICE.

4. Our heart director is **the Lord Himself.** "He knoweth what is in man, and, like Boaz, he speaks to the heart" (Ruth 2. 13, *margin*).

GREAT SALVATION.
Hebrews 2. 3.

1. The Needed Blessing—"Salvation."
2. The Character of It—"So great."
3. The Common Danger—"Neglect."
4. The Unanswerable Question—"How shall we escape if we neglect?"

———

THE PRAYER OF JABEZ.
1 Chronicles 4. 9, 10.

1. It was a prayer TO GOD.
2. It was the prayer of an HONOURABLE MAN.
3. It was an EARNEST prayer. "Oh, that thou wouldest!"
4. It was a prayer for DEFINITE BLESSING. "Bless me *indeed.*"
5. It was a prayer for ENLARGED POSSESSIONS. "Enlarge my coast."
6. It was a prayer for POWER AND GUIDANCE. "That thine hand might be with me."
7. It was a prayer for PROTECTION FROM EVIL. "Keep me from evil, that it may not grieve me."
8. It was a prayer that was ANSWERED. "God granted him that which he requested."

———

LOVE SUPERLATIVE.
1 John 4. 10.

1. A Woeful Possession. "Our sins."
2. A Shameless Confession. "Not that we loved God."
3. A Blessed Revelation. "He loved us."
4. A Wonderful Condescension. "Sent His Son."
5. A Gracious Provision. "Propitiation for our sins."
6. A Joyful Acclamation. "Herein is love."

WHOLESOME FEAR.
Hebrews 4. 1.

1. The Blessing, .. "His rest."
2. The Offer, ... "Promise being *left us.*"
3. The Possibility, .. "To 'Come short of it.'"
4. The Warning, .. "Let us therefore fear."

GOD OUR SAVIOUR.
Titus 2. 10.

I. **A Great Salvation.** "God our Saviour." What a blessing that—
   1. There is a SAVIOUR.
   2. That this Saviour is GOD.

II. **A Wonderful Revelation.** "The *doctrine of God* our Saviour."
   1. Revealed in His Word.
   2. Embodied in His Son.

III. **A Beautiful Occupation.** "That they may *adorn* the doctrine."
   1. By believing it (Phil. 4. 8).
   2. By living it (Phil. 1. 27).

THE GOSPEL OF JEHOVAH.
Exodus 6. 6-8.

THIS old Gospel is ever new. It implies—
   1. **Deliverance.** "I will rid you out of *bondage.*"
   2. **Liberty.** "I will bring *you out.*"
   3. **Redemption.** "I will *redeem you.*"
   4. **Acceptance.** "I will *take you to Me.*"
   5. **Rest.** "I will bring you from *under the burdens.*"
   6. **Knowledge.** "Ye shall *know.*"
   7. **Inheritance.** "I will bring you *unto the land*" (v. 8).

UNSELFISH BLESSING.
Psalm 103. 2.

It is not bless *me*, but Bless *the Lord*, O my soul.
1. The Reason for it.   "All His benefits."
2. The Way to do it.   "Bless the Lord."
3. The Danger of Neglecting it.   "Forget not."

THE VICTORY.
Romans 8. 37.

1. What?   ..   "More than conquerors."
2. Who?   ..   "We are."
3. When?   ..   "In all these things."
4. How?   ..   "Through Him that loved us."

A SERVANT'S REQUIREMENTS.
1 Corinthians 15. 58.

1. Be Active.   ..   "Work."
2. Be Devoted.   ..   "Work of the Lord."
3. Be Steadfast.   ..   "Unmovable."
4. Be Liberal.   ..   "Always Abounding."
5. Be Hopeful.   ..   "Forasmuch as ye know that your labour is not in vain in the Lord."

THE MANIFOLD MERCIES OF THE LIVING GOD.

"Trusting in the living God, who giveth us richly all things to enjoy" (1 Tim. 6. 17).

1. **An Unfailing Source**   "The living God."
2. **A Bountiful Supply.**   "All things."
3. **A Gracious Offer.**   "Who *giveth* us."
4. **A Happy Experience.**   "All things richly to enjoy."
5. **A Simple Condition.**   "Trusting."

SONSHIP.
1 John 3. 2.

1. A Wonderful Privilege. "Sons of God."
2. A Comforting Negative. "Not yet appear what we shall be."
3. A Blessed Certainty. "We know."
4. A Glorious Hope. "We shall see Him as He is."

THE THRONE OF GRACE.
Hebrews 4. 16.

1. The Place of Blessing. "The Throne of Grace."
2. The Manner of Approach. "Come boldly."
3. The Certainty of Supply. "Obtain mercy and find grace to help."

SALVATION NOW.
2 Corinthians 6. 2.

1. A Great Blessing, ... "Salvation."
2. A Gracious Offer, ... "Accepted time."
3. A Present Necessity,   .. "Now, now."
4. A Pressing Call, ... "Behold! behold!"

RESIST THE DEVIL.
James 4. 7.

I. **The Enemy.** The Devil.
  1. Personal (Matt. 4. 10).
  2. Mighty (1 Peter 5. 8; 2 Cor. 2. 11).
II. **Our Attitude Towards the Devil.** "Resist."
  1. Resist, don't argue (Eph. 6. 10, 11).
  2. Resist, don't compromise (Matt. 4. 10, 11).
III. **The Promise.** "He will flee from you." The victory will be—
  1. Sudden. "He will *flee.*'
  2. Complete. "He will flee *from you.*"

HELPUL ILLUSTRATIONS.

A CURSE CURED BY A CURSE.

THERE is an old legend that during a plague an angel showed to Charlemagne the root of the carline thistle as a cure for the plague. Thistles are a fruit of the curse. We do not much believe the legend that the root of that which represents a curse should cure the curse of a plague, but we do know and believe that the Christ who was ''made a curse for us" is an infallible remedy for the curse of sin (Gal. 3. 13).

CARPET CHRISTIANS.

A CARPET knight is one who has been dubbed a knight, not because of his military exploits, but on account of mere court favour. He bears the name but lacks the nature of a true knight. Many in like manner are dubbed with the name Christian because of their kindly, genial character, but who know nothing at all experimentally of the fight of faith or "overcoming by the blood of the Lamb" (Rev. 12. 11).

TEMPER.

A MAN is said to be ''nettled'' when he has got into a hot temper. Does that mean that the man has been seized with a moral *nettle-rash*, and that his whole being bristles with sharp, stingy things, so that no matter where you touch him you are sure to smart for it? Temper is the madness of selfishness. A bad temper is a great curse to a man, although he may have as many fine points as a hedgehog.

EVANGELISTIC STEAM.

It is very suggestive that the word ''breath'' literally means *''steam,''* something gentle, yet most powerful, from a warm and glowing *source*. ''Come, O breath, and breathe'' (Ezek. 37. 9). The Holy Ghost is the *breath* of God, the gentle, glowing all-powerful *steam* of the Almighty. A preacher filled with the Holy Ghost has always the steam up. It is easy driving when you have plenty of steam on, but oh, how stiff when this heavenly motor is absent! The way to keep the steam up is to have a heart set on fire of love to God, and to have it fed constantly with the coals of divine promises.

DISCIPLINE.

WITHOUT the hard and arduous process of ''breaking-in,'' a horse is not fit for steady and profitable labour. Much of our bitter trials and heart-bruising hardships come upon us by way of *breaking-in*. They chasten the spirit, and make us more ready and willing to do the will of God. ''No affliction for the present seems joyous, but rather grievous, nevertheless *afterwards* it yieldeth the peaceable fruits of righteousness'' (Heb. 12. 11)

JIB CHRISTIANS.

IT is not wise or safe to be turning about with every wind, like the weathercock. The *jib-sail* in front of the foremast shifts itself to *catch* the wind, the ship is thereby helped on its course. Old forms, like the windmill, may be beautiful, but they are useless when the power is gone. It will be often necessary for us, like the jib-sail, to *turn ourselves* if we would catch the breath of Heaven and be *filled* with the Holy Spirit.

THE NEW BIRTH.

THE law of limitation is everywhere visible in nature. Many attempts have been made to preserve the white bear, the Esquimaux dog, and the reindeer in this country, but without success. If such are to live in this kingdom either the climate must be changed or their natures must be transformed. The character of the kingdom of God cannot be changed to suit the sinful nature of man, so man must be transformed if they would dwell in the kingdom of God. "Except a man be born again he cannot see the kingdom of God" (John 3. 7).

THE BEAUTIFUL INCARNATION.

WE are all familiar with the beauty of the *carnation* flower, which takes its name from its *flesh-coloured* appearance. It is said that no other flower presents such scenes of wonder and beauty under the microscope. What an emblem of Him who was made in the likeness of sinful *flesh*! What hidden wonders there are in the great incarnation, only to be seen through the Christ-magnifying power of the Holy Spirit.

PROVISION FOR THE FLESH.

JUST before Lent the Roman Catholics have what they call the time of carnival, which literally means the *solace of the flesh*. If they must fast during Lent the flesh must have special license beforehand. Solacing the flesh is not confined to Romanists. We are warned to make no provision for the flesh. If we live in the flesh the flesh will make provision for itself; if we live in the Spirit the lusts of the flesh will be crucified.

RELIGIOUS BOGGLES.

A BOGGLER means a *doubter*, or one who has turned aside from the right path. We have all seen the potato boggle, and know that the object of it is to frighten the crows out of the field. Beware of those sceptics and doubters who have turned aside from the truth of God, and who attempt to frighten timid souls out of the field of the infallible Scriptures—Satan's boggles. You know that a boggle succeeds only by putting on an *appearance*.